Date Due

FE18'89		
March 10-89"		

PAT
ROBERTSON

The Authorized
Biography

PAT ROBERTSON

The Authorized Biography

JOHN B. DONOVAN

MACMILLAN PUBLISHING COMPANY
New York

COLLIER MACMILLAN PUBLISHERS
London

For my wife, Nancy

Macmillan Publishing Company
866 Third Avenue, New York, NY 10022
Collier Macmillan Canada, Inc.

Photographs are property of and appear through the courtesy
of Americans for Robertson and the Pat Robertson family.

Library of Congress Cataloging-in-Publication Data
Donovan, John B.
  Pat Robertson: the authorized biography/John B.
Donovan.
     p. cm.
  Includes index.
  ISBN 0-02-532120-X
  1. Robertson, Pat. 2. Evangelists—United States—
Biography.
3. Statesmen—United States—Biography. 4. United States—
Politics
and government—1981– I. Title.
BV3785.R595D66 1988
973.927'092'4—dc19
[B]   87-31767
                                                                        CIP

Macmillan books are available at special discounts for bulk purchases for sales promotions, premiums, fund-raising, or educational use. For details, contact:
                Special Sales Director
            Macmillan Publishing Company
                866 Third Avenue
                New York, NY 10022

                10 9 8 7 6 5 4 3

        Printed in the United States of America

Contents

	PREFACE	vii
ONE	Lexington	1
TWO	Searching	18
THREE	On the Air	45
FOUR	On the Brink	61
FIVE	On the Move	77
SIX	Reaching the World	99
SEVEN	Mind and Spirit	123
EIGHT	Beyond Church Walls	156
NINE	The Body Politic	175
	INDEX	209

Contents

Preface

The Robertson phenomenon occurs at a moment of national schizophrenia. On the one hand, the cry for "family values" has become so loud that most politicians feel compelled to make vigorous references to that theme. On the other hand, movies and songs, especially those aimed at teenage audiences, become just slightly more laden with sexual innuendo each year, and our newspapers chronicle the amazing frequency of immorality on Capitol Hill, Wall Street, and other arenas.

Into this cultural milieu has come a voice from one of the most notorious of those controversial areas of life—daytime television—a voice offering an unapologetic exposition of traditional faith as it relates to everyday personal and public life. The voice is soft rather than strident, intellectual rather than simplistic, and in many other respects the opposite of what many expect.

In Pat Robertson we encounter a man in a quest far more ambitious than promulgating a few points of religious or political philosophy. In him we see the representative of the vast cultural underclass that seeks to overthrow the hegemony of an entrenched elite. The family values movement, which may be the most powerful social trend of this century, makes no secret of its aims to usurp leadership from those whose values they have weighed and found wanting.

The nearest antecedent to this broad-scale cultural revolution took place in the sixties. Then, as now, an "establishment" was identified—the seemingly complacent generation that had emerged out of World War II and into prosperity. Their bored offspring in many instances sought escape in pacifistic and socialistic values that were guaranteed to outrage their elders. While the banner of love was held aloft, the slogan "Do your own thing!" became the prevailing ethos, and the surviving influence of that ethos is now the target of the family values movement.

A confusing countertrend has been the understandable outcry against mixing church and state. Yet it is curious that political candidates automatically invalidate their aspirations if any hint of personal immorality appears. Why exactly is that? Is it only that people mistrust their judgment? Is it only that they wouldn't be able to trust them to be honest in other matters? I think it goes deeper than that: it goes to that place within many people that affirms an inescapable connection between personal faith and public leadership. This differs from a connection between church and state, since almost everyone agrees that there should be a separation between government and the institutional church and between particular beliefs and the policies that might affect those who don't share those beliefs. Still, if national leaders show no evidence of reliance on a higher wisdom than their own, how much confidence can we repose in their capacity for sound decisions? How much firmness and selfless energy can we expect of their followers? From this point forward in American politics, it may not be required of candidates only to have a clean reputation but also to show evidence of leadership in propagating God-and-family values.

As a New Yorker of Roman Catholic background who almost never watches television, it was not clear to me at first that Robertson was a figure of much interest. But after reading about him here and there, his skill as an all-round thinker and communicator loomed larger in my mind, and I wrote him a quick proposal about doing a book like this one.

I found that he had a signal ability to relate the perspective of traditional faith to the problems facing ordinary people as well as those facing sophisticated observers of international affairs. He has organized a television show that involves constant interaction with the general public (the din of ringing telephones forms an ever-present background noise); this has forced him to keep his finger on the pulse of American life. I didn't receive a favorable response to my proposal until a year later, when my friend, the author David Aikman, mentioned such a project to him, together with my name, without even knowing about my prior proposal.

By any reckoning, Pat Robertson is an anomaly. Steeped in fervent religious convictions, he is a business buccaneer with a penchant for risk-taking and the administrator of what could be justly termed a corporate conglomerate. As one long acquainted with corporate chief executives as a financial and policy writer, it is clear to me that Robertson is among the most literate and informed of that breed. Yet upon meeting him and delving into the story of how he built his broadcasting empire, he impressed me as very much a man of negotiations and transactions—every inch the no-nonsense, all-business type of person in his demeanor. He was responsive to all my probings and yet made no demand for control over the project.

Looking for keys to understanding the managerial side of Robertson, I first sought to interview Dr. Homer Figler, a former management consultant who now heads the business school at the Christian Broadcasting Network University. Figler is a thirty-year veteran of advising chief executives on organization and management matters and was tapped by Robertson to advise him on improving CBN as an organization being managed as a business.

Upon arriving at CBN several years ago, Figler drew up a list of points that criticized the management of several CBN departments—a no-holds-barred report that he assumed would go no further than Robertson himself. Robertson called him one day, however, and said, "We're having a board meeting tomorrow. Is your report ready?"

"Yes. But I'd suggest I just give it to you personally."

"No," he replied. "I want the board to hear it."

Figler said he would offer the board a modified version, since the report implied that Robertson himself had neglected to attend to certain deficiencies.

"No, give it to them straight," Robertson said. "Don't hold anything back."

Figler said it was the first time in his career as a management consultant that a manager urged him to give his board a unexpurgated report that didn't cast the manager himself in an overwhelmingly favorable light. Although I was admittedly not seeking a muckraking account, I hope this book has a touch of that same open spirit.

It has been my privilege to have the editorial assistance of three extremely talented and dedicated professional writers as I struggled with a very tight deadline: Professor Gerald Gee, Angela Hunt, and especially David Sampugnaro. They each brought a distinctive and valuable perspective to the project, and I look forward to future efforts with them. I'd like to extend my thanks also for the assistance and advice given to me by Jack Grazier and Eric Evans.

JOHN B. DONOVAN
Larchmont, New York

CHAPTER ONE

Lexington

In a close-in suburb of New York called Mount Vernon stands the stately Historic First Dutch Reformed Church, whose walls contain some of the finest examples of period stained glass in the New York area. "We loved that old stone church," recalls Pat Robertson, who was its assistant pastor in the late fifties. "With its flying buttresses, graceful arches, and jewel-like windows, it was a bit of Holland in a suburban America setting."

Population trends, however, were rapidly decimating the ranks of church members. Mount Vernon was one of the first places to show the changes that have become common to border suburbs since World War II. Says Harald Bredesen, the pastor, "Mount Vernon experienced the fastest white flight of any of the suburbs of the five states, including New York. The historic churches were then high and dry and sold off to the invasion. Our people loved the church so much that they were going to move it farther up the line."

Though the church had only about seventy people and an annual income of about $13,000, Bredesen decided to hire a student assistant from the Biblical Seminary in New York City, and his choice was a Southerner called Marion Gordon Robertson, who went by the name of Pat. The newcomer, right from the first, displayed a keen interest in breathing new life into the dry bones of the Historic First, and the first item on the agenda was to restore the building.

"This church has to be restored to its first-time glory," he said to Bredesen. "Anybody visiting here would think God was dead."

"The money just isn't there," Bredesen replied. "We're $1,600 in the red as it is."

Soon, out of the blue, a total stranger left $27,000 to the church, just about the figure needed to restore the stained glass and the ceiling, from which plaster was falling on the worshipers.

The second item on the agenda was to enlarge the congregation. Robertson's wife, Dede, suggested that he start "pounding the pavement for customers." In particular, no one had ever invited any blacks to the church and, as a result, there was not a single black face in the congregation on Sunday morning.

Concluding that some special days of preaching might be the answer, Robertson rounded up a large group of fellow seminarians and brought them to Mount Vernon to hand out flyers. "He really took command," Bredesen recalls. "Here we were a tiny church, and to cover the town of 60,000 people with 60,000 flyers took leadership and organization. He was a real Tom Sawyer. He sparked enthusiasm, and he gave a vision for us to throw our shoulders to the wheel." Within a short time a number of blacks had become members of the church and a black man was named as a deacon.

Others at Historic First were less favorably impressed. Said one member of the Old Guard, "Pastor, I love your sermons, but I find it difficult to concentrate on them because, in order to see you, I have to look past so many black faces." While some expressed similar annoyance about Robertson's zeal in evangelizing blacks, others expressed amusement.

Bredesen himself was not entirely pleased; his displeasure had nothing to do with the new influx of blacks but with the popularity of the Bible studies being held by his assistant when compared to his own. Rather than focusing on the obscure depths of Scripture, Robertson tried linking its truths to the everyday situations of people. Says Bredesen, "He was able to meet men where they were. Pat was really always the leader. He didn't try to assert himself as a leader, but he was recognized as one. People loved him. He was like a young Jack Kennedy, and they were a little awed by him."

The initial culture shock among those who had never known blacks in the church didn't linger, according to Bredesen. "Actually, that had an amazingly short life. The blacks were so nice. They just won the hearts of our people and they just loved our people too. We were all so grateful that God had sent in black people. One became a church soloist and another one became one of the most successful men in the church. Pat Robertson, more than any other person, was responsible for our church integrating and staying an integrated church."

This proved to be the first of the predictable patterns that this white Southerner named Pat Robertson was to shatter during the ensuing twenty-five years.

No town in America has quite the same combination of natural beauty and historical charm as Lexington, Virginia, where Pat Robertson was born and raised. Mountains form a soft green amphitheater that encloses rolling cattle farms, and the views from many points are spectacular. Nearby are the headwaters of the James River, which flows into the Atlantic at the point where the first English settlers landed in America in 1607.

The traveler visiting Lexington, Virginia, finds a small graveyard just off the main street known as the Stonewall Jackson Memorial Cemetery. In the center of this cemetery, mounted on a pedestal, is a statue of the Civil War general, with one hand on his field glasses and the other on his sword. Just a few yards from the statue is the gravestone of former Virginia Senator A. Willis Robertson, the father of Marion G. "Pat" Robertson.

From that point can be seen the prominent dome of the Memorial Baptist Church, which the Robertsons attended, and if a visitor walked out to the main street, he could look down main street lined with the pleasant road of nineteenth-century buildings toward Virginia Military Institute at the far end. Prominent also are the steeples of Presbyterian churches, which reflect the Scotch-Irish heritage of the Shenandoah Valley. This, in microcosm, is the religious and military environment in which Pat Robertson was reared.

The ghost of Stonewall Jackson fairly hangs over the town. His house is still there, preserved in its original state, and his earthly remains are respectfully enshrined in the city's cemetery. Jackson's embodiment of military discipline and Southern chivalry are embodied best in the graduating exercises of Virginia Military Institute, which everyone in town attends annually.

On May 15 in 1864 the cadets of Virginia Military Institute marched three days north to New Market to bolster the sagging Confederate Army because the Yankees were sweeping through Virginia. Some twenty cadets lost their lives in the battle, and the event is still celebrated on May 15 in Lexington. The New Market parade and the sham battle that takes place down on the parade ground is a part of every Lexington boy's memory. Guns fire, artillery sprays blanks in every direction, and war games continue through the day. When the "battle" is done the smaller boys come out and scour the parade grounds for souvenir shells, trinkets, and an occasional Rebel cap.

The scavenging boys gather their troops on VMI graduation day as well. When the cadets throw their caps the town's small boys rush after the flying caps like squirrels going for winter nuts. These caps will be worn proudly until they are ruined in rough play. Young men who manage to snatch an officer's cap are assured of respect at least until the next year's graduation exercises.

Compared to many villages in rural America, Lexington appears today much as it did in that simpler era, and one gains the strong impression of children living an idyll of the kind portrayed by Norman Rockwell. At the base of the hill, behind the high school, sits a pond where Robertson and other children went ice-skating while other children were sledding down a neighboring hill.

The son of forty-three-year-old Congressman A. Willis Robertson, Marion G. (Pat) Robertson was born on March 22, 1930. Though the winters can sometimes be snowy in that part of Virginia, that spring came early and bright with japonica, forsythia, and redbud. The Robertson house, a large beige stucco manor house with a green roof, was no exception to the general rule of houses in that neighborhood, surrounded by crocuses and snow-drops.

Pat was the second and last child. The first, A. Willis, Jr., was called Taddy and was two and a half at the time of Pat's birth.

Robertson's mother, Gladys Churchill Robertson, was born into a well-educated family in a town in Florida called Switzer-land-on-the-St. Johns, and she grew up in Alabama. Her father was a lawyer who later became a minister—foreshadowing some-what the pattern of her son's life—and her grandfather had been a professor at Judson College, which had been founded by an-other relative.

Well known for her beauty, both in Lexington and in Washing-ton, where they spent the winters while Congress was in session, Gladys Robertson was a proud woman, with an almost worshipful delight in her distinguished lineage and with high ambitions that her sons would perpetuate it.

"My mother was especially proud of her heritage," Robertson recalls, "and she went to great lengths to involve herself in genealogy and to trace the family tree." On her side of the family tree were the Harrisons, the Virginia family that produced two presidents. America's ninth president, William Henry Harrison, was the son of a signer of the Declaration of Independence. He was best known as the victorious general at the battle of Tippe-canoe, the opening skirmish of the War of 1812. Inaugurated in 1841, he died just one month later. His son served in the House of Representatives, and his grandson, Benjamin Harrison, be-came the nation's twenty-third president. Born in Ohio, Benja-min was an ardent believer in the anti-slavery cause and became a brigadier general on the Union side during the Civil War. He was a lawyer known for his thoroughness, and his term brought about a significant number of international agreements regarding matters ranging from territorial to commercial disputes.

Also on Robertson's mother's side was a line of Churchills, from the same English family that included Winston Churchill, and a John Armistead, who, like the Churchill ancestor, had been a member of the Virginia House of Burgesses in the days when Williamsburg was the capital of the American colony.

"My mother would not only tell me about them," Robertson

says, "but she would always be talking to me about such-and-such nobleman or king who was part of my ancestry. Her whole approach was to convince me that I was born for leadership, that she had great expectations for me, and that she would be disappointed with anything less.

"It has been said that Nancy Hanks, Abraham Lincoln's mother, was distantly related to some prominent political figure of her day," says Robertson. "She supposedly did with Abraham Lincoln what my mother did with me—she constantly talked about setting higher than average goals and standards."

Robertson's contemporaries from Lexington report that Gladys Robertson doted on her sons and didn't allow their hair to be cut until they were several years old. The early Pat Robertson, being slightly rotund in appearance, therefore had the further distinction of being the Little Lord Fauntleroy of Lexington, who received adoring looks from women and pestering pinches from other children.

Dr. Rupert Latture, a neighbor of the Robertsons, now in his nineties, recalls receiving a telephone call from Mrs. Robertson: "She complained that my son was abusing Pat and she wanted to put a stop to that," he recalls.

Belying his angelic mien, however, was his reputation as a mischief-maker. While his older brother was reserved to the point of being dour, the overactive Pat had already established a lasting penchant for seeking new diversions. In one of his earliest recollections, Pat seized a knife from the kitchen and, instead of putting it down as his mother had told him to do, went racing through the yard and fell on it, jabbing himself just under the eye. As in other instances, his mother maintained her serenity, expressing only her "disappointment" with his antics, but his father, who would brook no foolishness, lost his temper.

Diversions of a more sociable nature included battles with the mock oranges that fell from the trees in the neighborhood near the high school. The mock oranges in Woods Creek Park were hard and dangerous when they were green, but heavy and mellow after they had ripened. When a boy was struck by an overripe mock orange, the resulting splash brought howls of delight from the other boys. The mock-orange battles were intensely serious:

the boys would duck behind trees and try to isolate one particular boy for a messy ambush. Some kids devised sling shots; others planned extensive strategies.

The town was divided into unofficial districts, with kids growing up in the Houston Street crowd, the Monroe Park gang, or as part of the East Lexington bunch. The black kids all lived in Diamond Hill and attended their own school. But when by chance the black kids and the white kids met in a pickup ball game, no one thought of "us" and "them." Everyone was simply "just one of the kids."

"The kids" seemed all to be equal and no one was better than anyone else. Ball games were played with old balls found along the railroad tracks, where the grown-ups hadn't bothered to look. Every boy learned how to wrap those old baseballs in tape so they would be as good as new. Baseball bats, too, were salvaged from the grown-ups' playing field and repaired with a few penny nails and the ubiquitous roll of tape.

Boys like Pat Robertson usually spent summer mornings in the city pool, afternoons playing baseball, and evenings at the State Theater and the State Drug Store. When none of those activities would do, Lexington boys just sat on the bank steps on Main Street and watched people walk up and down. They peered at girls, inspected new cars, and on Saturdays they could watch the farmers bring their produce to town and create a new and lively stir on Main Street.

Lexington didn't offer organized sports like Little League, but the kids were always playing. "We played king of the hill, we went fishing, and we visited in each others' houses. It was a very closely knit community in Lexington when I was growing up," Robertson recalls.

As "going out to play" can sometimes be deadly serious for children, so it was on occasion for Robertson. "You'd wrestle out in the yard, and most of the time it was friendly, but when I was in the eighth grade, there was a bunch of boys in the neighborhood who were older that I was, and there would be fights. That wasn't sociable at all; that part was a bit of a struggle.

"Even as a little boy I knew I had a tendency to be mischievous and 'bad,'" Pat says. "I think it was in the sixth grade that I first knew that God had called me, as he does everyone else. My life was not in conformity to Him, and I'd pray even though I knew my life wasn't what it should be. We lived mostly as little children, reacting to sensations rather than taking control of our environments, bringing some rational order out of it. I was the total center of my world, and I was terribly aware of my limits. I knew that somehow God had something better. Even in those days, when I was hardly doing anything, I still felt that I was far short of God's standards."

From his mother's viewpoint, her sons were the scions of a kingly heritage. Her genealogical research extended back to the Norman conquest of England and uncovered a number of kings and other nobles. "She wasn't one to lecture," recalls Robertson, "but she maintained this quiet and continuous holding of standards. They stemmed from who we were and from accepting the Lord, and the standard implied a level of achievement. It wasn't her approach to criticize, but rather to compliment us. She was so delighted any time I did well that sometimes it got to be embarrassing. That was the worst thing for me. It was too much praise. I couldn't accept that because I never believed that I was what she felt I was."

For all his rambunctiousness, Robertson developed a meditative side that caused him to delight in nothing more than taking books home on Friday night and reading them eagerly. In those early years he nourished his intellectual appetites with a steady diet of science fiction, and he notes that many of the subsequent accomplishments of technology were little surprise to him, having been described in great detail in the space adventures he devoured on weekends in the early forties.

By all accounts, including that of Robertson himself, Gladys Robertson was a kindly woman who was continually looking for ways of being helpful to others. Her method of influencing Pat apparently included all the advantages of the carrot with none of the consequences of the stick. In his words:

"My mother was always saying to me, over and over again when I was young, 'You're a leader, you're a born leader.' I didn't really know what she was talking about, but she continued to instill this into my mind. She would be disappointed because it wasn't that they were forcing me to do something I wasn't able to do, they were just saying, 'You have extraordinary ability, a good mind, with the mind and ability you have, anything short of the "A" route is underperforming.' Had I been a 'B' or a 'C' student, they would have been happy. They just wanted me to live up to the potential. If you use what you've got, it grows.

"In those days I didn't understand those things at all. I only knew that if I didn't keep pace with what they considered extraordinary ability, my mother would be disappointed and her feelings would be hurt. She never became angry, although my father certainly could, but she could be very hurt.

"At the same time, I was able to get away with anything I wanted to do. It was a dual thing. My mother constantly held up high ideals. She was a wonderful teacher because she expected the very highest. If I came home with 'B's,' my father would want to know what in the world was wrong. I guess they both realized I had some potential, and they did not settle for a second-best effort."

The Robertsons' neighbors from Lexington report that Gladys Robertson was "probably one of the most beautiful women you ever saw. She had great influence over Pat."

Her husband, A. Willis Robertson, had grown up under more straitened circumstances, a descendant of one of the many Scottish immigrants to that region. Willis Robertson was also a minister's child, but his father lived the hardscrabble life of a missionary to the hills of West Virginia. Eventually Willis's family moved to a poor rural congregation in a town not far from Lexington that didn't even have a high school until his mother raised the money to build one.

A star athlete at the University of Richmond, he graduated from college in 1908, began practicing law that same year, and involved himself in politics shortly thereafter. By the outbreak of World War I, he was elected to the Virginia State Senate.

Willis Robertson was everything a politician should be. He was vibrant, knowledgeable, warm, charismatic, and gregarious. When he walked into a crowded room, every eye sooner or later turned in his direction. Tall, elegantly dressed, and possessed of a majestic no-nonsense air, Willis Robertson knew how to carry himself.

Dominating the outlook of the senator, as Robertson recalls, was the ancient concept of noblesse oblige, which unites the concept of excellence and of attending to the well-being of others. "We were on earth to serve and to excel. We had standards given to us because of who we were. That was his concept all the way through. He was a public servant and we were all servants in some way. You did well because that was your duty in life—to do the best you can do. The second best was just not acceptable. If you want to use the phrase 'To whom much is given, much will be required,' that was his belief. We are privileged. Out of that privilege is expected a performance. Well, in those days I didn't understand those things at all. But not doing well or not achieving just didn't enter into my frame of reference."

Robertson often jokes that his first two words were "Mama" and "Daddy"; his third word was "constituent." Born as he was into a political family, it wasn't long before he was campaigning himself. In the seventh grade he formed a Robertson for Congress committee simply to "get into the fray."

He wanted to follow in his father's footsteps, and somehow he knew his parents expected him to follow a schedule of success. "I don't remember particularly wanting to be in the public service as such. I think that from the early days I was planning to be a lawyer because that was what was scheduled for me to do. Dad had been a lawyer first. I can't remember when I decided that was what I was going to be. That was just something I had in my mind all along."

Robertson remembers his father as an extremely sociable, busy man who involved himself in the affairs of state during the week and spent most of his weekends combining business with pleasure out in the woods and fields he loved so passionately. In 1926 he became chairman of the State Commission of Game and Inland Fisheries, a commission he had created himself through a proposal in the state senate a decade earlier. The job permitted him to indulge his passion even more than usual. In 1926 he was voted Outstanding Sportsman of America by *Field & Stream* magazine. By the time Pat was born four years later, Willis Robertson was essentially an absentee father.

"There was quite an age gap between me and my father," says Robertson. "When I was sixteen, he was sixty. So I really didn't begin to communicate with him until I worked in the Senate Appropriations Committee when I was in law school."

Willis Robertson ran successfully for Congress in 1932, the Depression year that swept Franklin D. Roosevelt into office. That year he established the House Wildlife Committee and became its first chairman. In that role he sponsored the Duck Stamp Bill for game refuges as well as the Pittman-Robertson Act, a milestone in the conservation movement that taxed sporting goods to finance conservation measures.

Eager as he was to conserve the environment, Willis Robertson proved himself even more eager to conserve a sound fiscal policy. He became for that reason an opponent of the New Deal, a posture that estranged him from most of his fellow Democrats and in particular from Harry S. Byrd, who was to dominate Virginia politics for thirty-five years. Byrd and Robertson had grown up together, served in the state senate together, and were elected to the House together. Now, however, Byrd became an ally of Roosevelt and the permanent and virulent enemy of Willis Robertson.

Willis Robertson was reared in a rural environment of hard work as the son of a Baptist preacher, and he wanted his sons to realize that bucolic life had its rigors for many. Lexington had sailed smoothly through the Depression, unlike many of its more industrialized neighboring regions, and life for the Robertsons, if not affluent, was comfortable.

"The senator was the soul of integrity," recalls a former Lexington resident, "and the Robertsons really didn't have any money. He never would have taken any money on the side. But Pat didn't have any family money to fall back on. Of course being the son of a senator opened some doors, but there wasn't any money."

"My father's salary was $10,000 a year, a modest sum," recalls Robertson. "But in the Depression we had the cook we paid seven dollars a week, and a maid we paid five dollars a week, so twelve dollars a week was awful hard to get. For a family with an income of no more than $10,000 we lived very well. And in our lives we didn't experience the Depression. We drove a Dodge or a Plymouth. In those days, a Dodge or a Plymouth cost $700 or

$800. Everything was relative in the economic sense. Those who had wealth were really very well off. Those prices were so low and services were so cheap. Those who didn't have worth were in trouble. I think the two colleges in Lexington and the fairly stable economy pretty much stabilized things."

The Robertson boys didn't learn until their teenage years that there was a difference between life in a village surrounded by farms and life on the farm itself. Hence the elder Robertson decided that a summer with one of their Scottish relatives farther up in the valley might instill the merits of frugality into his mischievous son. One summer in the middle of World War II, when Pat was thirteen years old, he worked on a farm from six o'clock in the morning to as late as nine o'clock at night for $15 a month. He recalls "haying, sacking potatoes, and shocking weeds in the boiling hot sun all day long. I chopped the wood for the fire; we didn't have electricity in the kitchen. The range was a wood stove. We fed the livestock and slopped the hogs. It was tough, tough work, but my father would say to the farmer, 'You need to work him harder.' "

By his own account the lessons of this and similar summer experiences were lasting. In his father's household, he recalls, no trait was valued more highly than frugality: "Money was to be saved and not wasted. Waste in government was a sin. Deficit was a terrible thing. Up to this day I will spend a little time thinking whether I should use a Kleenex or a paper towel to wipe a particular spot—which might cost more."

During this period the senator had gradually distanced himself from Senator Harry Byrd and the spending policies that had characterized the Roosevelt era in the late 1930s and had earned a reputation either as a "skinflint" or an advocate of judicious spending policies, depending on one's political perspective. He was outspoken in his criticism of the New Deal as a policy of free spending and as a critic of the power of the federal government in general as the ever-encroaching predator of states' rights. ("I remember one picture that was taken of my father with his fist pounding down and a caption quoting him saying, 'I defy the federal government!' ") A student of the economist Beardsley Rummel and the arch-enemy of budget deficits, Willis Robertson was among those responsible for the pay-as-you-go tax system that financed World War II. The "Scottish" principles that the elder Robertson was having his son learn on the farm were simultaneously being inculcated in the House of Representatives.

Senator Robertson was known in Lexington as the man who could arrange whatever you needed in Washington without delay. Old family friends tell stories of which the following is typical: "A friend of my sister's was from Lebanon and her permission to remain in the United States was denied, even though she was about to be awarded a scholarship to Cornell. My sister contacted Senator Robertson and it wasn't but a little while before her visa was extended."

Robertson's father remained a somewhat distant presence throughout his life. When Congress was in session, his father was in Washington, and when the pheasant were in season, his father was in the woods. His mother, by contrast, was almost always at home and her concerns were primarily religious in nature. For many years she had been a popular Washington hostess, a vivacious member of the Congressional Wives Club. By the time her sons were in their teens, however, the wife of her hometown pastor had led her into a deeper fellowship with God, and as a result, she turned her back on what had formerly seemed so alluring. Instead of dinner parties with the current luminaries of Capitol Hill, she was now more inclined to prayer meetings with members of several local churches in Lexington.

"She was a very beautiful woman, very gracious," Robertson says. "Sparkling. She was quite a person for entertaining. When she met the Lord she decided she found something a great deal superior to what she had before. She thought the other was pretty vapid and artificial."

When he was in the eighth grade Robertson's parents decided that a military environment might tame the fractious behavior of their son and accordingly sent him off to Baltimore for a taste of tough military discipline at the McDonough School. Typical of the tight regimentation there was a 6 A.M. formation outside the barracks before marching to breakfast. Regimentation was not at all to his liking at that age, however, and he was beginning to exhibit a precocious independent streak. Sneaking out from time to time with like-minded "inmates," Robertson managed to get into a racetrack on a neighboring street and even to get to Washington for further skylarking. Because of his intense dislike of the school, his parents decided to keep him home for high school.

Entering Lexington High School in 1943, Robertson continued testing the limits of adulthood and found it easier at home than in the narrow confines of the military academy. A former schoolmate recalls that Lexington High was "a very small school where everybody knew everybody else. The teachers would take time with you, but they were strict, compared to today, and you had to sit up and say 'Yes, ma'am' and 'No, sir.' Nobody wore blue jeans and the girls all wore dresses."

His classmates remember Robertson as bright but unassuming. "He was no smart-aleck," recalls one man, "but he was very bright, very quick. But there were a lot of bright kids. If he had been out in a country school, he would have been more outstanding, but with two colleges, Lexington was an academic community."

By age thirteen his best friend, Charlie McDowell, had introduced him to smoking and girls. He and two or three older classmates would devise ways of taking out girls that had been left behind by students at Virginia Military Institute, where strict curfews were in effect. Driving was legal at age fourteen and he had friends with cars. As he recalls, "We would go off on the highway someplace, park, and do what we could do. My mother never said anything about my being out until three o'clock in the morning. I would never have permitted even my own children to do anything like that."

Teenagers in Lexington didn't do much cruising in automobiles because gas was rationed from 1941 to 1945 to three gallons a week. The roughest place in town to hang out was the pool hall, where they sold beer. Billiards were fine, as played by the upper crust, but pool was another matter. Mothers often warned their sons about the dangers of being associated with the pool hall.

Robertson's father was prone to occasional lectures, which did little to compress the expanding social horizons of his son. His parents also doubted that he was being educated adequately, and so back to military school he was sent. This time, however, the choice was the McCallie School in Chattanooga, Tennessee. The military aspect of McCallie was more subdued than at McDonough, but it nevertheless had rules against most of the diversions that interested Robertson, including smoking. He circumvented that restriction by feigning an interest in horseshoes, because he noticed that playing horseshoes would kick up enough dust so that the billows of tobacco smoke would be effectively camouflaged. As he recalls it, the activity was the usual teenage mimicking of adults.

Academically, he was a standout in the verbally oriented subjects, particularly French, history, and English, and he won a medal in French upon graduating in 1946 at the age of sixteen. His natural interest lay in history, however, and he knew he would major in that in college.

When the time came for college, the natural choice was the elegant and distinguished Washington and Lee University, the institution for which his hometown is chiefly known. Founded in 1749 as Liberty Hall Academy, it was given its present name shortly after the death of General Robert E. Lee, who had assumed its presidency at the close of the Civil War. Near the main buildings of the college, which are fronted by a graceful colonnade of a dozen tall pillars, stands the Lee Chapel, the focus of many symposia, lectures, and cultural events. Beneath the chapel is the tomb of Lee, who became Robertson's prototype of a Southern gentleman.

"One of my heroes then and now is Robert E. Lee," says Robertson. "He was a magnificent gentleman who was held up to me as being more or less the ideal man. He was gracious, trained, and a perfect gentleman. He was always a man of great honor and dignity and was known for his kindliness toward people. A magnificent leader in battle and a strategist, he was equally gracious in defeat. He was particularly a model of what a Southerner would consider chivalry or some would consider gentlemanliness. The concept of a Southern Christian gentleman was instilled in me as the ideal."

Robertson avoided the usual adolescent musings of "Who am I?" and "Why am I here?" because his entire life had been molded around the ideal of public service. It never occurred to the young man to consider another occupation. His parents had effectively taught him that his destiny lay in serving others, and Robertson set out to find the proper road to fulfill his service. In college the road demanded proficiency in languages and history.

Living at home, Robertson steeped himself in American and European history as well as in his minor, English literature. In his junior year, when he was nineteen years old, he won a Phi Beta Kappa key. He graduated with almost a straight A average. Though he did well in a variety of subjects, including human biology, his preoccupation with history remained a dominant intellectual passion.

He recalls being particularly impressed with the Napoleonic era, during which Prince Metternich established a practical balance of power that was the foundation of an enduring peace among the major nations of Europe: "I don't know if Metternich was cynical or whether he was infinitely pragmatic and realistic, but he, in recognizing the tendency of nations to try to take territory away from others, set up power blocks that would prevent that from happening. It was a much wiser course than this utopian dream that brought about the League of Nations and the United Nations. The United Nations was started in a wonderful idealism, but it overlooked the essential human nature. By now it has become a useless debating society.

"In my early college days I would have thought that the League of Nations was a good plan to keep peace together. But I learned about disarmament treaties and how we began to scrap battleships and do away with our arms. But I think it was Winston Churchill who discovered that every wise nation has prepared for war because the history of mankind shows there has been more war than peace and the best way to ensure peace is through strength. In my young years I was idealistic enough to hope we would live in some kind of peace, but I have subsequently realized the flaws in that hope."

By living at home he claims he managed to have the best of both worlds: the partying, football outings, and other fellowship that went along with belonging to a fraternity, together with enough privacy to concentrate on studying at a level that would have been impossible if he had been boarding at the fraternity.

"If I had an exam, my mother would knock on my door and wake me up. She would set an alarm and knock on my door at 4:00 A.M. and say it was time to study."

His father, meanwhile, continued to apply his emphasis on fiscal responsibility both in the Senate and at home. His monthly allocation to his son was only $40 ("That was his nature—'Scot' Robertson"). Still, he admits to "living a great deal more lavishly in college than most people would have approved of, since the life-style of a young fellow in a fraternity included considerable consumption of alcoholic beverages and parties with all kinds of girls."

On one occasion when he double-dated, as he frequently did, with his best friend Charlie McDowell: "I had my father's car, and Charlie was driving his family car. I was bumping him and he went rolling down the street. All of a sudden he said, 'Enough,' and slammed on the brakes. His back-end bumper raised up and I crumpled the grille on my car. That was in college. My father was very forgiving on that. I was surprised."

Robertson was proud of his father's reputation and would trade on it in a genial way from time to time. Among his college chums there were several other sons of well-known men. A classmate reports that he was out driving one day and was caught speeding. Robertson explained to the officer that it would be unpatriotic to give them a ticket, since Robert E. Lee (the great-grandson of the general) and Fred Vinson (son of the Chief Justice of the Supreme Court at that time) were with him in the car. He added that his father was Senator Robertson. The police officer answered simply that he himself happened to be George Washington, and calmly wrote out the ticket.

CHAPTER TWO

Searching

Since Willis Robertson's professional life kept him in the nation's capital for much of the time, and because Gladys Robertson now found it more important to spend her time in Lexington, where Pat was now in college, there was some distance emotionally between father and son. However, as he approached adulthood, Pat's relationship with his father seemed to become closer, and they discussed weighty matters from time to time. "I wrote a speech for him that he gave at the University of Virginia when I was in college. He was interrupted so often by applause, he didn't understand what he'd done."

With the doors of communication open between the senator and his son, Pat began to find that his father's strong views influenced his own perceptions of the ideas he had been taught in college: "I was the child of my father. He began to be very uncomfortable about some of the programs that were extensions of federal power to the states. Interstate commerce, for instance, was legislation that forced farmers to kill their little pigs. He was for states' rights and he felt there was an encroachment of the federal government on our liberty. I absorbed a great deal of that thinking and I didn't fight about that when we began.

"My father had a fabulous memory," recalls Robertson. "He'd talk about the previous governors and other matters of state politics. That was part of life. He was always discussing the various congressmen, the political scene, governors, strategies, and things in the news. I was much more liberal than he was when I was growing up, especially in relation to blacks. I was much more open toward assimilation to the blacks in society than were the Old Guard Southerners. I was uncomfortable with the massive resistance that went on, the unwillingness to allow black people into the school, and segregation in general, which put one class of people down. They had a feeling of white superiority. That was their culture and it was a blind spot, although those people were mostly Christians who just couldn't accommodate the emerging status of blacks.

"In the college environment I was in, we weren't crusading for social issues, we were just trying to do well in school, get a diploma, and have as much fun as we could on the way. The social protests of the sixties just weren't a part of our environment. We had a nice thing going. We were considered gentlemen. We wore coats and ties. We spoke to each other on the campus and we had a code of honor. We had some campus politics, but other than that we just weren't absorbed in national issues.

"I remember debating about communism. I was very concerned about the spread of communism; I thought it was tyranny then and I think it is tyranny now. I was reluctant to see the beginnings of government encroachments into our freedoms. Freedom is very, very important. The concept wasn't crystallized for me until I really met the Lord, but perhaps what was dormant just burst into flames. I remember arguing with my friend McDowell and another guy over whether the Chinese were Communists or weary farmers. I said there was no way those people were Communists. But then one of my friends on a government mission was killed in Korea by some of those agreeable farmers and I began to see my tragic error of classical liberal thinking.

"We weren't terribly concerned about morals in those days. It's a funny thing. If anybody in the college was married and running around, we thought it was totally reprehensible. But if one of us was single and running around, it was good, clean fun. I don't think there were great debates over which it was, but there is something innate in me that says marriage is a very sacred institution that should be preserved."

College opened up new vistas in Robertson's thinking, and he explored a variety of topics both in and out of the classroom. "We talked about literature. We talked about art, and we talked about music," recalls Robertson. "We talked about culture; it was an artistic environment. But I don't recall talking much about religion or the social policies of government at the time.

"I had tried literature, and I studied the poetry of Eliot and the poetry of Yeats and the various philosophers. I was a little puritanical in terms of somebody like D. H. Lawrence, who exalted the physical sex act almost into a religion. I thought this was just insane. Somehow exalting adultery and physical sex over propriety offended my conscience, and I wrote so in a paper. I couldn't get away from my religious training as a child."

To take a break from his serious musings, Robertson became the self-proclaimed leader of the party crowd. "There was no question about it," he recalls. "I guess we change our standards to suit our own life-styles, and so I didn't feel there was any clash between my upbringing and my college life-style. I never questioned my life-style, but I had a sense of not belonging. I felt that, in all the parties and drinking parties, at the fraternities and all the Washington, D.C., bashes, I always knew it wasn't quite right. I always felt I really belonged someplace else, but I didn't really know where that someplace else was.

"God? Who was He really? I had joined our Southern Baptist Church in Lexington as a boy—just like all the other boys. But the experience had been primarily social, not spiritual. Time was spent in Sunday school and church, but I never did really understand what the church was all about. It was so easy to drop away from it when I left home.

"I knew there was something. In all the parties and discussions and frolics, I never really felt at home. When I went to Europe and was partying over there, I never felt at home. Even in my hometown of Lexington, I never felt at home. I felt like a stranger. It was as if somewhere there was a place where I needed to be or something had to happen."

This sense of not belonging probably existed because Robertson had yet to find his own dreams and inclinations. His course in life, predetermined largely by his father's example and the military atmosphere of his education and hometown, led him through college and the ROTC program and into the United States Marine Corps and the Korean War.

While in the Marines, Robertson recalls being transferred from Quantico, Virginia, to Camp Pendleton, California. He hitched a ride on a military transport plane, telling the officers in charge he was on Marine Corps business. He turned in a $165 voucher for travel expenses. Years later this dishonest act haunted Robertson and he sent the Marines a check for the $165.

Though Robertson doesn't shrink from the mention of his youthful misdeeds, he has reacted forcefully to an accusation that he tried to avoid combat duty during his service in Korea by asking his father to intervene on his behalf.

During the summer of 1986, Democratic Congressman Andrew Jacobs, Jr., of Indiana, hearing Robertson make a speech supporting military action by U.S.-backed rebels in Nicaragua, recalled comments from former Republican Congressman Paul McCloskey, Jr., that labeled Robertson a "hawkish conservative" who had avoided combat service. Jacobs asked McCloskey to provide further details, and subsequently received a six-page letter from McCloskey, who was then a lawyer in Palo Alto, California. In January 1951, according to McCloskey, he left San Diego on the USS *Breckinridge* along with Robertson and 2,000 other marines. The ship stopped at Yokosuka and Kobe, Japan; Robertson disembarked at Kobe. "My single distinct memory," McCloskey wrote, "is of Pat, with a big smile on his face, standing on the dock and saying something like, 'So long, you guys, and good luck,' and telling us that his father had gotten him out of combat duty."

Several months later, continued McCloskey, Robertson and five other officers who had been pulled off the *Breckinridge* with him were reassigned to Korea. McCloskey wrote that Robertson had served as "division liquor officer," flying alcoholic beverages in from Japan for his contingent.

Robertson did leave the USS *Breckinridge* in Kobe and was later transferred to Korea, where he served at First Marine Division headquarters as an assistant adjutant. His duties included transporting classified codes between Korea and Japan. He was stationed near the 38th parallel, separating North and South, and near a battle site known as "Heartbreak Ridge."

"Not only did I not use influence to avoid combat in Korea," says Robertson, "the record is clear that I served in the combat zone near North Korea. General Victor Krulak, the former division chief of staff of the First Marine Division, says he personally served there and that it was 'in combat.' Major Sawyer, aide to General Shepherd, affirms the situation to have been so dangerous that the aide to a general and his driver were killed. There were land mines and the possibility of artillery fire.

"Marine officers in the chain of command who have knowledge of my service in Japan and Korea have denied, under oath, any knowledge of any political influence being used to alter my service. Pete McCloskey has had to back away from testimony that he has alleged against me. His only defense in the libel action is based upon conflicting and contradictory hearsay evidence from the then-young Marines who, thirty-six years after the fact, are attempting to piece together vague recollections. On the other hand, those Marines who were closest to me by way of friendship and duty station have confirmed my version of the events in question."

After McCloskey's accusations were aired, Robertson promptly issued a statement declaring the charges to be a blatant attempt to damage his efforts to make a bid for the 1988 Republican presidential nomination. "I may become a candidate for President of the United States," said Robertson later. "It is important that I demonstrate the falsehood of these stories."

In late October 1986, Robertson launched a counterattack against his accusers. He filed two libel suits for $35 million each in District of Columbia Federal District Court.

Robertson felt strongly about McCloskey's charges because as a man who might possibly be President of the United States, it is important that he have the respect of men and women in the armed services, of whom he would be Commander in Chief. He reasons that some would question the propriety of his sending soldiers into combat if he himself had shirked combat duty. As to the charge that Robertson served as "the liquor officer," McCloskey based those charges on remarks by Lieutenants John Gearhart and Christopher Lindsey. Both Gearhart and Lindsey have emphatically denied having ever made such a statement to McCloskey. Gearhart wrote McCloskey in 1981 that he had made no such statements about Robertson, but McCloskey chose to ignore the clear, written refutation of this claim and went ahead and restated it in a letter and in the national press in 1986.

McCloskey and Jacobs assert that there was no conspiracy to libel Robertson. Yet Jacobs has admitted in sworn testimony that he and McCloskey worked in concert and sent unsolicited letters containing accusations concerning Robertson to a wide variety of reporters.

Jacobs and McCloskey filed a motion to dismiss the suit. The Federal District Court of the District of Columbia found that while Mr. Jacobs could be dismissed from the suit, there was sufficient evidence of malice for a jury to consider Robertson's complaints against Pete McCloskey. Thus the court rejected Mr. McCloskey's motion to dismiss the suit.

Serving in Korea with his college buddy John Warner, now a Virginia senator, Robertson was faced with the most serious questions of his life. "I had friends, one guy who was over there with me got killed. I remember one Christmas leave up on the border of North Korea. They brought up some cases of liquor so we could have a party. I remember getting roaring drunk. It was horribly cold, the temperature was twenty degrees below zero. I was out underneath the stars and, with all the mountains around, all I could think of was 'What is the meaning of life, why are we doing this, why are we here, what is the meaning of it all?' It wasn't so much the horror of death, it was just the same sense of emptiness I had known all my life. I didn't know who I was or why I was on earth.

"I was also frustrated in Korea because I knew we were fighting a no-win war. Politically in the United States, the citizens were in no way supporting the war. It was kind of a thankless job. We were out there all by ourselves in Korea. It's one thing to know people are dead for a noble cause for which you're going to create a land of freedom, but this was a stalemate with a no-win situation.

I thought it was the greatest folly I'd ever seen to waste our energy, our lives, and our money for a situation that was pointless."

According to the plan to follow in his father's footsteps, Robertson entered law school at Yale. The work was demanding, though not exhausting, and on weekends Robertson and his buddies ventured into New York and partied with the energy of pent-up youth.

With his family background leading him into public service, Robertson might have practiced law and later run for public office. "I've always had a political sense," he says, "and I was sure that law and public service were intertwined. But having been somewhat disillusioned with the law, I didn't want to hang around and find out. I would probably have started practicing law and from that maybe run for Congress or the Senate or something like that."

But in addition to endowing him with analytical tools that were useful in business ventures, the law school experience left him with a slowly smoldering resentment of another branch of government: the Supreme Court. During law school this tendency started as a disillusionment: "From the moment I enrolled at Yale law school, I was assigned huge, leather-bound editions of legal cases to study and discuss. I read what lawyers and judges, professors and historians said about the Constitution. But never once was I assigned the task of reading the Constitution itself.

"I really was looking, I was searching. I wanted something to invest my life in and I thought it was pleasure, but pleasure didn't do it. I thought then I would find this noble profession of law, and I went to Yale with great idealism. I thought that this was a high, wonderful calling of brilliant men sending down fair decisions for us all to live by. It was a great thing that I could help bring justice to the world of law.

"I remember the shock I had in class a few weeks into the term when we had studied a court decision. When it was over we were analyzing what the judge had said. The professor then said there was a possibility that the judge was bribed; what he was saying was merely an attempt to cover up the man's decision. I thought, 'My heaven, you're talking about a judge getting bribed and that this process has been nothing but a cover-up to imply rational closings of an illegal act.'

"I remember one of our leading professors was a great guy, but I saw him drunk at a party with a couple of other professors who were leading lights in the world. The idea that these men, who were supposedly at the top of their profession, were so unhappy with their lives that they poured themselves into a bottle was incredible."

In the student body at Yale, students came from top schools to study. They were taught not to be swayed by the aura of finality in law, but rather how to analyze a case.

"We would analyze cases of the Supreme Court and many times show the absurdity of what had been written. When we saw the fallacy in the Court's reasoning, it was hard to understand why that body was superior to the President and superior to the Congress.

"We studied by the Socratic method, not case law. The Socratic method molds your mental processes fabulously. It is an attempt to learn 'the law,' an attempt to construct a method of thinking in which you could make the law do whatever you wanted it to do. Needless to say, since I could make the law whatever I wanted it to be, it lost its high place in my thinking. I still maintained my idealism, but I was still searching for something. I wanted something to dedicate my life to. I didn't just want to go through life making money. I didn't want to go through life just having a party. I didn't want to go through life manipulating other people that employed me under the name of a profession. I wasn't looking for a profession. I was looking for a commitment.

"I guess there are a lot of young people who commit themselves to communism or 'the conservative way' or the Democratic Party, and it isn't too long before they find that the leaders of the causes are people who are greedy and selfish and not worthy of the commitment. That's how I felt about the law. I just felt it wasn't worthy of a lifetime commitment. It was an interesting discipline and I learned a great deal, and it still is an enormous value to me in everything I do. It just wasn't the kind of commitment I was looking for."

Despite the rigorous grind of studies at Yale, Robertson made time to attend one of the almost obligatory social events that are planned with the schools dominated by women. Hardly expecting anything but a mildly amusing evening, this decision turned out to be one that would change the course of his life, because at an open house he met his future wife, a graduate nursing student named Adelia (Dede) Elmer.

Dede was a lovely, auburn-haired woman of twenty-four. She grew up in a prosperous Catholic family from Columbus, Ohio, where her father was a vice president of the Hanna Paint Company. After two years at Ohio Wesleyan, she attended Ohio State at Columbus and earned a bachelor of science degree in social administration. A party-loving girl, she was always eager to be in the center of whatever was amusing. As a sorority sister at Ohio State, she allowed herself to be snatched by a group of fraternity boys and held prisoner on the roof of the fraternity house. Tall and attractive, she was elected homecoming queen one year.

"My mother was the religious one," she recalled, "but my father insisted that everyone go to church. It was all very legalistic. My father was essentially antireligious because he was appalled at what he saw as the hypocrisy of it." Nevertheless, out of fear and a sense of duty, Dede and her older brother, Ralph, practiced their faith.

A more serious streak in her had yet to appear: a desire to be in one of the helping professions. In her senior year at college she announced that she wanted to enter nursing. Her parents worried that the presence of so much suffering demanded a tougher type of personality, but Dede had made up her mind and applied to the graduate nursing program at Yale, which she entered in September 1952.

She recalls those days as crowded with a demanding schedule of studying and practical experience at the hospital with little time for relaxation. Nevertheless, her dormitory was the site of an open house to which members of the incoming law school class were invited. She lived with sixty classmates in a magnificent old mansion that had been converted into a dormitory, the first floor of which had dark wood floors and tall windows bordered by magnificent draperies.

One law student with blond hair fixed his gaze on her and smiled when he caught her eye. Unfortunately for him, Dede Elmer could see that he was several inches shorter than she was. He began moving toward her when she decided this was the moment to lend a hand at the refreshment table. Rushing through the crowd to another room, she spotted the table and noticed that no one had thought to light the candles there. That, she thought, was an excellent method of politely avoiding the young man with blond hair. She lighted the near candles first and then leaned over to light the ones toward the back of the table when her hair caught fire.

In the next moment she felt someone clapping his hands on her head, saying, "Don't worry. It's only singed. It would be too bad to burn that hair."

She said, "Thank you. My name is Dede Elmer."

"And I'm Pat Robertson. Would you care to join me for a dance?"

Indeed she would. She also cared to join him for a walk and for a visit to a local beer hall for a drink. Before many months passed, they realized their relationship was to be permanent.

Dede and Pat dated for a year and a half in New Haven before marrying. They knew their parents, particularly Pat's, would disapprove of their marrying. Dede had three strikes against her: being a Yankee, being a Catholic, and being partly Irish. "We weren't particularly religious at that time," she says now. "I rarely went to church, and Pat went only if he won anything at poker the night before."

Dede and Pat began sleeping together. When Dede became pregnant, they decided to marry secretly. They traveled to Elkton, Maryland (which Dede has called "a good place to elope"). The marriage took place on August 27, 1954. However, they have always celebrated their wedding anniversary on Pat's birthday, March 22, because of the strong traditional views they later developed about marriage and the family, in addition to the desire to protect their children. It appears that the circumstances of their elopement have always been a subject of regret and secretiveness with the Robertsons. Their son, Timmy, was born in November 1954. Dede remembers that year as "one big treadmill of work, shared baby-sitting, hospital rounds, study, more study, made triply difficult with the new baby."

Yale was a time of hard work with little time for each other. Pat was studying for exams most of the time, it seemed, and Dede was on the hospital floor or in a clinical situation of some other kind.

After graduation from Yale, Robertson took the New York Bar exam, but because his heart wasn't in it he failed. Robertson was simply confused. His entire life's plan had been disrupted by the disillusionment he felt with the practice of law, and now there was nothing to take its place. The dreams his parents had dangled before him seemed empty and mocking. "You're a born leader," his mother had said, but Robertson felt he couldn't even lead his own life successfully. How could he ever hope to lead others? Even though he was happy in his marriage, Robertson was so depressed by the seeming futility of life that he actually contemplated suicide.

While Dede finished her schooling in New Haven, during the week Robertson worked in New York for the W. R. Grace Company as a troubleshooter. He had worked for the company one summer as an intern assistant to the tax counsel. The company, a multi-industry conglomerate with an emphasis on chemicals, manufacturing, and banking, was largely an international shipping concern in those days. Grace offered Robertson a job and he accepted an opportunity to become a management trainee upon graduation. He had not yet made up his mind about practicing law, but was moving generally toward a career in business.

"I thought if I made a bunch of money I would have some satisfaction. I was told by Peter Grace that if I stayed on for three years, in three months, guaranteed, I would have a good job. I liked the concept of the uncharted wilderness of Brazil, the Amazon Valley, and the great untapped unknown. Maybe I could find adventure and my fortune through one job. It was more a move toward fulfilling my need. If I couldn't get fulfillment through the law, perhaps having a lot of money would satisfy me. And if I could have fame and fortune, maybe one day I could be a philanthropist and give money away to help the poor."

W. R. Grace proved exciting in some respects because it opened new, foreign vistas. He was sent to Peru to analyze the management problems in textile, fertilizer, and cement plants and to acclimate himself to managing in an international environment.

He studied textile plants in Peru, cement plants in Bolivia, and through it all Robertson learned. The young man from Virginia had never seen a cement plant in his life when he was assigned to analyze one, so he learned quickly, studying manufacturing, legal accounting, and financing. While there Robertson also watched and analyzed the economy of a country different from any he had ever encountered. He noticed that W. R. Grace provided jobs, education, and quality leadership to the people of Peru. But he was discouraged when he saw a rich American company in the midst of extreme poverty selling trifles to poor Indians.

"In the cities it was all right," he recalls, "but I knew the people in the rural areas were so desperately poor, how could we try to take profits? I couldn't in good conscience charge them for anything, but we were selling textiles and candy and various things. The thrust was to increase sales in these rural areas, to the Indians, the villagers. Their salaries were maybe $700 a year, more or less. I just didn't have the heart to try to strike even modest profits from transactions with those people. I didn't say a great deal about it because I was a junior member of the team, but there was one man down there who had a feeling for the people. My boss thought he was a bit of a wimp because he didn't drive hard enough, but he had a sense of the country and a sense of the people. Unfortunately he was killed in an aircraft crash while I was down there. My idealism couldn't reconcile doing anything except outright giving things to those people, and of course no business could operate by giving things away. I thought Brazil, the sleeping giant, was the land of opportunity, but the country is still sleeping. It has never reached its full potential."

This was the first step toward a glamorous career in a major international corporation. Robertson busied himself working twelve to sixteen-hour days trying to develop a commercial expertise that would enable him to run a large business of his own.

He had been working in New York for several months and had established himself in a chauffeur's cottage on Staten Island by the time Dede and Timmy joined him full-time in November 1955. Both Pat and Dede were delighted at first with the cosmopolitan character of New York and its contrast to the rural environment of Staten Island, which in the days before the Verazzano Bridge seemed far out in the country.

But at the age of twenty-five Pat Robertson found the pressures of being a junior executive for a New York company excessive. "There seemed to be a certain futility in it," he recalls. "I was thinking, 'Well, I'll just make my fortune myself.' I couldn't see sweating my blood for a big company so they could pay their stockholders some money, even if my salary was $100,000. It seemed like a twenty-year grind, and frankly I thought I would rather own my own business. If there was a chance of real money and if I was going to be successful, I'd rather do it my way than take a salary.

"Working for Grace was tremendous training," says Robertson. "And I wanted, to an extent, to use Grace as a stepping-stone to learn about South American trading and manufacturing so I could then branch out on my own."

Pat and Dede Robertson had a fun, teasing marriage. It was also a relationship between two self-confident individuals who clashed from time to time. They considered themselves intellectuals and talked endlessly about psychology and sociology. "Your id is showing," Pat would joke; Dede countered with critical comments about the man Pat admired, Franklin Roosevelt, but whom Dede called "The Great Mahatma."

Through the years their personalities and ideas gradually merged. "He changed my religion and I changed his politics," says Dede. Indeed, Pat became more conservative and came to question FDR's stature. He had been too young to absorb much about Roosevelt during his presidency, but his impressions of Roosevelt had been mostly favorable: "He was the leader of this country," he says. "During World War II we were all united in a desire to see the Germans and Japanese defeated, so there was a unity in the country. It was the national will to win a war, and therefore we gave him a special place which he might not have had, had we been more aware of some of the other things he did."

Their lives seemed to be full and rewarding. They lived in a modernized cottage, complete with all the physical trappings of success, but Robertson still felt inward emptiness. One day he prayed and promised God he'd use all his money to help the poor. The pledge brought no peace.

The tension he felt began to show at home. "He'd come home and play with the baby, get a beer, ask a question, and play with the baby again," recalls Dede. "He was so restless."

Robertson soon began to be interested in the prospect of becoming an entrepreneur. Together with two law school classmates, he founded the Curry Sound Company, which manufactured speakers. "I have never been fearful of taking moves. I'm always willing to step up to a challenge, to take the chance to try something new. With this corporation I didn't have any qualms at all. It was kind of like 'This is going to be fun, let's go for it.' I knew that being a capitalist, being an owner or an entrepreneur, was where I should be. I didn't fit the role of the pulpit man. I'm not too much of a free spirit or whatever."

This venture ran into difficulty when it became clear that the mechanism had an electrical deficiency that would take tremendous research to rectify. "We had an electrostatic speaker that was extremely good on the high range. It was built with 20,000 cycles of unbroken stability, which made it very attractive. Because it was flexible, we thought we could build it into airplanes and put various speakers on almost any application on which you wanted sound. The problem was it took a thousand volts to drive the speaker. The underwriter's laboratory wasn't too happy with the voltage problems."

This problem coincided with a far deeper one that was developing with Pat's whole outlook. Dissatisfied first with the law, and now with business, he began to grow more introspective and to sense that he was destined for something else.

One day he came home and announced to Dede that he thought he should go into the ministry. Dede had no reaction, but when pressed said she thought it might be fun. "Maybe you could get a nice church, and I could sit behind a beautiful tea service and entertain. We could have a big old manse with rooms to spare. It sounds exciting.

"But," she added practically, "if you're going to go into the ministry, perhaps we had better start going to church to see what it's all about."

The Robertsons began visiting churches. A poor trumpet solo in a Baptist church scared them away, and the Moravian church's "right hand of fellowship"—where people suddenly stood up and started shaking hands at a secret signal in the service—so shook the Robertsons that they crossed that church off their list.

The Evangelical Free Church seemed to agree with them, and the pastor's message agreed with what Robertson had been reading in his Bible for the past year. But when the pastor came to visit and saw the cottage with the huge Modigliani nude hanging over the sofa and the Courvoisier brandy on the bar, he was startled by Dede's statement that her husband was going into the ministry. The poor man left, speechless with astonishment.

But Robertson kept searching the Scriptures and trying to fill the emptiness in his life. Dede was bewildered: she had always considered herself a religious person, but to her mind Christianity wasn't something that had to dominate one's life. It wasn't the kind of thing in which God actually had plans for people. She thought her husband was simply becoming a religious fanatic.

Robertson thought his mother would be pleased when he announced his intention to enter the ministry. She was a devout Christian, often writing him letters about her relationship to the Lord and encouraging Robertson to read his Bible. But after he told her of his decision, her reaction shocked him.

"Pat, something's wrong," she said. "You don't have the slightest idea what you're talking about."

"But, Mother, I thought this would be the thing that would please you most."

"It does please me, son," she said, sitting across from Robertson. "But how can you go into the ministry until you *know* Jesus Christ? You can't know Him. You never mention His name. You've got to accept Him as Lord of your life, Pat. Unless you do, you're going to be just as spiritually empty a minister as you are a businessman. You cannot fill your emptiness by trying to do the work of God. It's like trying to fill a bottomless bucket. What you need is a new bucket. You need to be born again."

After dinner they sipped coffee and Gladys Robertson spoke again to her son: "The pulpits of America are filled with men just like you. They want to do good for mankind. They want to help people, but they're doing it in their own power, and that's worse than nothing. Jesus said, 'I am the way, the truth, and the life; no man cometh to the Father but by me.' There's no use going into the ministry, Pat, unless you've first surrendered your life to Him.''

One week later Robertson had dinner with a man named Cornelius Vanderbreggen, a man who simply and unashamedly shared the gospel with Robertson. Suddenly Robertson understood what had been eluding him for years: Jesus Christ was a personal Savior who died not only for the sins of the world, but for the sins of Pat Robertson.

Pat realized his entire life would be forever changed. From that day forward he would live according to the faith in the Son of God.

Dede was bewildered when her husband returned home and spoke of Christ as a real person instead of the mystical object of veneration to which she was accustomed. ''If you think I'm going to put up with this stuff the rest of my life, you've got another think coming,'' she said. ''I want my children to grow up in a normal home.''

His business partners were equally astounded when one day Robertson walked in and announced he had a newfound faith and wanted to enter a seminary. He had no money to pay off his share of the company's loan, so Robertson prayed for guidance.

In another city a man came home from work and happened to pick up his wife's Bible. In Psalm 150 the word ''organ'' caught his eye and he recalled reading an ad from Robertson's firm about speakers that were exceptionally clear on high notes. The next day he called his travel agent, flew to New York, and by the end of the day he owned 25 percent of the Curry Sound Company.

Robertson was off the financial hook. ''I sold my stock to my two partners, got out of the business, and wound up in the seminary. I finally found the peace I was looking for and I found a real answer to life. I found something worthy of the dedication of my life wholeheartedly, forever, and no amount of stress would be too much in this endeavor. I found what I was looking for and out of that I got back everything I wanted—the chance to start a number of businesses. I had the chance to go all over the world. I had a chance to help the poor and needy and help those who are hurting.''

Pat Robertson often refers to his mother when he is touting the merits of intercessory prayer. "I was a grown man, a husband and a father. By all worldly standards well on the road to success and wealth. But back in Virginia my mother was assaulting the very throne of God, anticipating my salvation. Then God's answer came, and I began to feel a painful emptiness. My world, with its so-called sophistication and glamour, brought neither peace nor satisfaction. That's when I met Jesus Christ."

Dede didn't understand. When Pat decided to go on a retreat to a Bible camp, she suggested he was mentally ill. "I recognize schizoid tendencies when I see them, and I think you're sick," she told him. "No normal man would walk out on his wife and her small child when she's expecting a baby any minute to go off in the woods for a retreat."

All Robertson could say was, "I'm sorry, Dede. I know the timing isn't perfect, but this is something I have to do." Within a few days he was gone.

When he returned from the retreat, Robertson waited to see what he should do next. As he and Dede waited for the birth of their second child, Pat found a position at *Faith at Work* magazine in New York. The position paid nothing.

Robertson's mother-in-law, who came to visit for the baby's birth, added to the commotion: "How do you expect to support two children?" she demanded. "And don't tell me about God! I'm a lot older than you and I've belonged to the church all my life. I could teach you a thing or two about God, but I don't think you'd listen. I don't care if you are the son of a senator. I think you've turned into some kind of religious oddball, and if Dede had any sense, she'd come home with me and leave you for good. Imagine! A man with two children and two degrees working for nothing at a religious magazine! It's ridiculous!"

Robertson felt led, finally, to enroll at New York Theological Seminary in Manhattan. While in seminary he worked as an assistant pastor at the Bayside Community Methodist Church in Queens. He and his family found a two-bedroom apartment in that borough and the provocative nude that had decorated the wall in their Staten Island cottage was replaced by a more presentable van Gogh.

That entire school year the couple saw very little of each other. Pat's life was impossibly busy, torn between responsibilities at the church, at home, and at school. The two young children, Tim and Elizabeth, were caught up in their children's games and didn't feel the rising tensions in the household, but something was going to give—and soon. Pat and Dede fought over the fact that she worked, leaving their son and daughter with a baby-sitter. They fought over the fact that Dede did the cleaning. They fought over most of the details of life. She would challenge Pat to stop reading the Bible and start practicing his Christianity. As she recalls it now, she deliberately set out to destroy the gains she perceived her husband making in his spiritual life.

As if matters weren't bad enough, their son, Timmy, suddenly developed a high fever. They could only cool his body with wet sponges and call the doctor. The doctor was delayed, and Timmy's temperature approached 105 degrees. Quietly, Pat stopped sponging his son's body and began to pray. The little boy's body stiffened, on the verge of a convulsion. Robertson realized, in near desperation, that he had come to the end of his abilities. Even Dede, a nurse, could do nothing but join her husband in prayer. But as they prayed, without a sound, the boy began to sweat and the fever broke. The experience of such utter helplessness stayed with both parents, as did the lesson that there are limits to our abilities to control events, and that turning crises over to God is the wisest course in any event.

But at the end of that year Dede miscarried what would have been the couple's third child. With Dede sick in bed, Robertson found that not only did his regular work fall on his shoulders, but such chores as changing diapers, washing clothes, and doing dishes fell to his lot. With such a succession of difficulties, Robertson nearly rebelled. Soon, however, he began to see his ministry had its place at home too.

Although tensions were sometimes high during this period, Dede also became more aware of Pat's strengths. As she reports in her book *My God Will Supply:*

"I don't think I have ever known a more honest man. In dealing with the churches where he worked as a student, Pat paid close attention to the details of honesty. He was supposed to put in a certain number of hours for his paycheck; whenever there was a question as to whether an hour belonged to the church or to Pat, the church got the benefit. In school, whenever he was writing a paper, he was careful to footnote ideas that were not his own. He was a man of principle even when it cost him. For example, he just did not believe in raffles. One day I entered a raffle held by the residents of our apartment building to pay for equipment on the playground. I won. But Pat made me give back my loot. The neighbors, I must say, thought we were crazy.

"For a while," Dede recalls, "my illness brought us closer together. But then, inevitably, as I began to regain my strength, Pat started to work once again and to work and study pretty much around the clock." The isolation began to prey on Dede's mind. To find the companionship of other adults and to supplement their income, Dede took a job as a nurse from three in the afternoon until eleven at night.

The situation seemed to be approaching another crisis when, in the summer of 1957, Robertson's mother offered to pay their expenses for a vacation. Pat chose the Word of Life Inn, a small Christian camp located deep in the Adirondack Mountains of New York State. While they were there, Robertson one night volunteered to stay with the children so that Dede could attend a service alone. As she sat quietly and heard the message, it seemed as though the speaker was talking only to her. His message was on "hard-heartedness," and Dede felt her attitudes undergoing a profound change. Although she still felt some small disappointment over her earlier dreams of a more glamorous life, Dede began now to better understand her husband's religious intensity and to realize the importance of relinquishment.

From that point on, Dede lessened the pressure on her husband. She began to see the wisdom of simply letting go, of relinquishing her own worry and simply trusting God in any situation. With the help of Harald Bredesen's wife, Gen, her new attitude had its good effects on Pat as well.

One morning, as Pat rushed out of the house to yet another meeting before breakfast, she stopped him in his tracks. "Pat, stop constantly chasing after the things the Lord is willing to give you! Sit down and eat your breakfast." He did.

* * *

As Robertson finished seminary, the school officials began to put pressure on him. "You need to have some sort of a job lined up," they urged. By then the couple had a third child, Gordon, who was born on June 4, 1958, and Robertson's mother-in-law joined in with the criticism too: "Imagine having two degrees and no job!" Robertson had been working with Harald Bredesen as an associate pastor in Mount Vernon, leading a Bible study group for Jewish Christians, and was considering becoming either a missionary or an evangelist.

One day he and Dede approached Norman Grubb, head of the Worldwide Evangelization Crusade. "Here we are," Robertson announced. "My wife is a graduate nurse. I have a law degree and will soon graduate from seminary. We're both volunteering to go to the mission field as missionaries. What would you like us to do?"

"Nothing," said Grubb. "It would be a tragedy for you to get into something God has not called you to. I sense His call to you will be in ways quite different from any others in the past. I believe God has great things in store for you in the future. One day you will thank Him that WEC did not stand in His way by taking you on as missionaries."

Several other opportunities appeared. A large church located on New York's Upper East Side offered the pastorate to Robertson. The large parsonage appealed to Robertson's sense of security for his family, but somehow he sensed that accepting the position merely for security's sake was not right. He declined the church's offer, and when they offered to raise the salary he simply shook his head.

Another church, one in Brooklyn's Bedford-Stuyvesant, at that time second only to Harlem as the worst black slum in America, offered a position as pastor, but a friend of Robertson's, Dick Simmons, was led to accept the position.

One day Dede bundled up Timmy and took what she hoped was her first and last trip to Brooklyn to visit the Simmons family. When she came back she was distraught and disheveled: "That place is the filthiest, ugliest, most germ-infested and disgraceful place I've ever been in," she said. "How anyone in the world could live there is beyond me. If I were Barbara Simmons," she continued, hurrying to the shower, "I'd walk out for good!"

As Robertson sought his place in the ministry, Dede was confused. To her, not knowing where she was going was harder to bear than anything. Her life so far had not been what she had imagined it would be when she married the son of a U.S. senator. She had long buried her dreams of a luxurious home, but the limbo Robertson placed the family in wore on her nerves.

When her brother became ill Dede took the children and went home to Columbus to nurse him. While she was out there, Robertson read a Bible verse that would change his life. "Sell all that ye have, and give alms," challenged Luke 12:33, so Robertson promptly sold the beautiful Early American furniture, the pictures on the walls, and the silver on the buffet. All that remained were some wedding presents, a seven-year-old DeSoto, a baby bed, a few pots and pans, and Dede's clothes.

He gave most of the money he earned from his sale to a man who ran orphanages in Korea and gave the rest to Dick Simmons to distribute among the poor in Brooklyn who had been dispossessed of their homes and were literally living on the streets. Robertson told the apartment manager to cancel his lease, and he piled the family's few belongings into the DeSoto and moved into the Brooklyn brownstone occupied by the Simmonses.

The next week Dede tried calling Robertson. The operator told her the phone in the apartment had been disconnected and the forwarding number was that of the Simmonses' apartment in Brooklyn.

"Pat, what's happened?" she demanded hysterically when she finally had him on the phone.

"I sold the furniture," he replied.

"You what?" she screamed. "Pat, what have you done this time?"

"Didn't you read my letter?" he asked, puzzled.

"What letter?"

"The letter where I told you God was speaking to me through Luke 12:33."

"Pat, I don't even know what Luke 12:33 is! Why have you

sold the furniture? Why are you living with Dick and Barbara?"

"But you wrote back and told me I should do whatever the Lord was telling me to do. And he told me through Luke 12:33 to sell the furniture and give all the money to the poor."

"You gave the money away too?"

"Well, yes, that's what the Scripture said."

"Oh, Pat, I didn't read that verse. I never look up verses that people scribble down like that."

"Honey, I'm sorry, but you should have looked up that one, because it's too late now."

"You mean everything's gone?"

"Yep, and I've given all the money away and moved in here with Dick and Barbara."

Nothing from Dede Robertson's previous life could have prepared her for the life that awaited her upon arriving in Brooklyn. "This wasn't exactly what I had in mind," she recalled. "I knew this wasn't going to be the luxurious parish house that could have been ours on the Upper East Side. I knew the accommodations would be simple. But this place I never expected."

This was a tough neighborhood where knifings and other violent crimes were commonplace. The "manse" itself was large, but the Robertsons and the Simmonses were not the only tenants. Thanks to the compassionate and outgoing nature of Simmons, various difficult people came to live there, including a spastic who dribbled and threw food on the table during meals and a large unemployed laborer who wandered the halls in the middle of the night singing at the top of his lungs. Next door was a brothel.

Ruby, the madam of the brothel, once had an exterminator come to her place. The various and assorted vermin beat a quick path to the Robertsons' brownstone next door, and Dede became quickly acquainted with rat traps, roaches, and even bedbugs. Dick once tried to poison the rats, but they only crept up into the walls to die, so the stench was unbearable.

One night Dede awoke Pat with her screams. "They're all over me! They're crawling all over me!"

Robertson held his frightened wife. "Honey, you're dreaming," he reassured her. "I don't see anything on you."

Dede began thinking that the parish house on the Upper East

Side might not have been God's idea for Pat's ministry, but it certainly was closer to Dede's idea. Nevertheless, she bundled her three small children into the top-floor rooms of this decaying brownstone and braced herself for a long siege of discomfort, if not danger. For once she was grateful that her parents were still well out of reach in Columbus; they wouldn't have to know just how low her fortunes had ebbed.

Robertson and Dick Simmons, meanwhile, were spending their days going about the neighborhood talking about the power of God to anyone who would listen, which generally meant the down-and-out, the unemployed, the desperate. Some of these would wind up confirming a religious commitment; others would go away with some comfort and good cheer; still others would gaze at them with the bemused air of people who sense they are in the presence of fanatics.

One afternoon Robertson and Simmons set up speakers and stood preaching on a street corner, fully expecting to draw a crowd. They didn't. No one even glanced their way except for a few people who were drawn momentarily to the windows of the tenement buildings.

Back at the manse, tensions were rising, and Dede was usually at the center of them. Dick Simmons had what Robertson called a "stubborn streak" when he made up his mind about something, and he let it be known that he was the spiritual head of the household and therefore in charge of discipline. One day was proclaimed to be "bath day." Dede was perfectly pleased to take regular baths, but much less pleased to have someone announce to her what her schedule should be in that regard. Robertson was more willing to accept the leadership of Simmons, but Dede's temper flared, and she prevailed.

Simmons was also in charge of food. His salary supported the entire household, and imagination was required in order to feed the group. Vegetables were scavenged from the local produce center and carefully stretched out to provide meals for everyone.

At one point Robertson, with Dede in tow, took a short trip to Lexington to "tell what great things the Lord had done" for him. Dede was secretly praying that someone in Lexington would be able to talk some sense into the husband she thought had gone off the deep end. Going to Lexington to see Mrs. Gladys Robertson, though, did not comfort her.

Mrs. Robertson never quite approved of the girl her dear son Pat had chosen to marry. She disapproved of Dede's being Catholic, and even after Dede converted to Robertson's religious beliefs, Mrs. Robertson still found fault with her daughter-in-law and delighted in exposing small errors Dede made. Perhaps she was dissatisfied that her son had married a Yankee with no blue-blooded connections. Gladys, after all, had married her distant cousin and was assured that his genealogical roots were as pure as hers. Dede, however, was from a family with new blood and new money—a combination Mrs. Robertson found hard to bear.

While they were in Lexington, Robertson was asked to fill a radio spot vacated by a vacationing pastor. For fifteen minutes a day for one week he spoke on the radio while his family listened at home. Dede learned something new about her husband. "Pat, you were very, very natural," she told him. "This is a side of you I didn't know existed."

Throughout this period Robertson's emotions were moving in several directions at once. He had made up his mind to follow what he discerned to be God's will, but the human side of him was in full rebellion. Both he and Dede wanted a more normal existence for their small children. Finally he sensed that this current ministry wasn't really what was in store for him, and he hated the uncertainty of not knowing what his future was and when it would arrive.

The manse in Brooklyn wasn't the sort of place that could easily be fixed up for grandmothers to visit, as grandmothers are wont to do. The first of these arrivals was Barbara Simmons's mother, a strident segregationist from Louisiana. Her only word for the dominant racial group in Bedford-Stuyvesant was "nigger." Not a shrinking violet, she created several embarrassing incidents around the house. Finally Pat fully expected a race riot after he heard his five-year-old son, Tim, using the word among other children out on the street. All were relieved when the day came for grandmother to take the train home.

Even more disturbing was the appearance of Dede's mother. Dede met her at Grand Central Station, which was halcyon com-

41

pared to the environment the older woman was about to visit. At first her shock was so profound that she said nothing. Expecting her disbelief to be leavened by some pleasant surprises, she instead observed and heard some things that unsettled her further. She saw the rat traps that had been installed to combat the constant intruders of that species. She heard about the bedbugs that had left large red welts on the skin of the Simmonses before they could figure out the problem.

By the end of her stay she had an announcement: "Dede, I'm leaving in the morning for Columbus, and I want you and the children to come with me. There's no sense in your staying on in this squalor."

Robertson recalls that he felt his stomach tighten. But Dede, in a gentle yet firm voice, answered, "Mother, for the first time in my life I realize that if I leave Pat, I would not only be leaving my husband, but leaving the Lord. God is more important to me than anything else in the world, and I cannot turn my back on Him."

To Robertson this expression of full commitment on Dede's part was a major turning point for the whole future course of their life together and his ministry. He says, "I remembered something I had learned—commitment always precedes revelation." Though he didn't realize it beforehand, this commitment by Dede opened the door to the next phase of the Pat Robertson story.

Today Dick Simmons believes that Robertson's time in the slums of New York prepared him for his present ministry: "It was there that God sensitized his heart to the horrendous needs of the cities of America. Pat is not just an ivory-tower idealist. He was down there. When he was struggling to try and find God's will for his life, he was actually considering becoming a street worker, getting a Volkswagen bus and going all over the boroughs preaching on the streets and ministering to the poor and needy. When he moved in with us I had my salary supporting him and his family plus my family, two missionaries, a cerebral palsy victim, and a fellow just out of a mental hospital.

"So it's one thing to be concerned about slums. It's another thing to sleep and have rats watch you eat and realize that there is a danger of a baby being bitten by a rat and killed. It's not a misuse of public funds to exterminate rats, as some people might think. Pat's a man who could make very realistic decisions.

"Pat has seen firsthand the gross abuse of the welfare system—we knew one man who boasted of having fathered sixty illegitimate children in the slums of New York City. Now there are three generations of children coming up as fodder for the criminal justice system. The church has let the government take responsibility for the poor, but the government isn't teaching responsibility and the churches are now sitting empty."

While living in Brooklyn, Dede tried to escape but found the opportunities limited. "Our children were without a safe and interesting place in which to play," she writes in her book *My God Will Supply.* "The backyard was solid-packed dirt, with dust constantly blowing off the top; there was not a blade of grass anywhere. The children tried playing in that yard but soon gave up. So as often as possible I made an escape—to a park, a library, a museum, a friend who lived far away. People in the commune didn't appreciate my being away so much."

The people in the commune also didn't appreciate Dede's constant emphasis on eating high-protein foods. She tried serving her soybean dishes, but often the others in the house rebelled against eating something so unglamorous. The conflict was everywhere—in the kitchen, in the parlor, and in their rooms. No wonder Dede tried to get away as often as possible.

But eventually she came to the point where she suspected that being in Bedford-Stuyvesant was a lesson in obedience for her family. She was from a moneyed family, her husband from a prestigious one, but together they had come to identify with the reality of suffering.

One afternoon Tim was out in front of the brownstone with his tricycle. Dede had been giving Tim more freedom to go about the neighborhood, and often two or three little boys would knock at the door to play with Tim and his tricycle. Somehow, with two or three boys riding the only tricycle on the block, it became an airplane in their minds. One boy would ride on the handlebars as navigator, another would sit on the seat as pilot, and still another would stand on the rear platform as a tail gunner.

On this afternoon Dede heard crying and a crash so she rushed outside to check on the boys. They were all right, but the tricycle was totaled. The front wheels and handlebars had separated from the rear wheels and axle.

"I'm sorry, but it's broken for good," she gently told her son. "There's no money to buy a new one. I'm afraid you won't have a tricycle anymore."

Timmy wiped his tears and corrected her. "No, Mommy. *They* won't have a tricycle anymore. They're my friends."

God used this simple statement to reveal to Dede that there was power in Tim's childlike meekness. By giving freely of his possessions to others, he had attained a level of greatness Dede had yet to find.

During the time spent in Brooklyn, Dede grew and matured spiritually. Previously she had noticed a rebelliousness in her nature that now seemed gradually to wear away. In the past she had always held on to the belief that if things got too rough, she could take the children to her parents' home in Ohio and support them with her income as a nurse. But now she knew that she could never leave her husband. "That was a preparation time in the eyes of the Lord," she recalls. "God knew we would soon need to be a true team as never before. I had surrendered my own natural authority to Pat, the authority that comes because I am a capable and well-trained woman. As soon as that surrender occurred, we became a team."

CHAPTER THREE

On the Air

On a visit home to Lexington, Robertson's mother showed him a letter from George Lauderdale, a former schoolmate of Robertson's. The postscript was for Pat: "There is a television station in Portsmouth, Virginia, that has gone defunct and is on the market. Would Pat be interested in claiming it for the Lord?"

The possibility of the television station dangled tantalizingly before his imagination. He thought this might be part of what destiny had in store for him, yet he had no idea how it might come about. As Dede reminded him, he didn't even have enough money for a television set, much less a station. Throughout this period of frustration and discouragement, he fortified himself with the daily discipline of prayer and of "waiting on the Lord" for fresh indications of what the next step in His plan might be.

Before leaving for New York, Robertson pulled up at a red light and noticed that the driver of the car next to him was none other than George Lauderdale. They went for coffee and Robertson inquired about the television station. "How much does it cost to erect a station like that?" Robertson wanted to know.

"Oh, between $250,000 and $300,000."

Robertson continued to mull over the possibility and prayed

for wisdom. He began to sense that God was giving him a specific direction to offer $37,000 for the station, so he wrote its owner, Tim Bright, a note to that effect.

In a few weeks he had his answer from Bright: "For the equipment, building, and land I want $50,000. For the equipment alone I want $25,000." Robertson's heart leapt. His figure was right in the middle.

Robertson spent a few more days praying and considering the possibility. Finally he was convinced that there would be a Christian station in Tidewater and that he was the man who would see it through.

The big turning point—when they left Brooklyn and knew that they were to go to Tidewater—did not actually come because of some new insight given to Pat but because Dede hit a new level of surrender to God. First he announced that the building that had housed the brothel next door was for sale and he was trying to decide whether or not to turn it into a mission. Then he popped the big question: Would she be willing to stay there if he decided that it was right for them?

She did not want to raise children in that neighborhood, yet she had determined that she wanted to yield to God's will for her life. She told him yes, she would do it, and she believes that all the circumstances leading to their move away from Bedford-Stuyvesant began shaping themselves at that moment.

Dede was glad to escape the brownstone, so even though she had no idea how they would get there with only $70 in the family purse, she helped Robertson pack the family belongings in the DeSoto and a five-by-seven-foot U-Haul trailer. They ate a sparse breakfast, said their last good-byes, and paused for prayer with their friends. The Robertsons were on their way.

On their arrival in Tidewater, Pat and Dede had $70 to establish his beachhead in the world of broadcasting. By any rational analysis he was embarking upon a fool's errand. Were it not for his sense of vocation, his own analytical faculties would have militated against such an audacious move. Never had such a lofty ambition been based on such meager resources. One powerful source of opposition was the chairman of the Senate Banking and Currency Committee, the practical, worldly Senator A. Willis

Robertson, who requested from members of his staff an analysis of the likelihood that such a broadcasting venture would succeed.

The elder Robertson besieged Harald Bredesen by telephone, pleading with him to intercede with his son and to dissuade him from the foolhardy effort and have him follow a more conventional route. "Try to bring him back to his senses," he told Bredesen. "Where's he going to get the $275,000 to buy that station? . . . And even worse, the $500,000 a year to run it? Try to bring him back to his senses."

With so little in the family purse, Pat and Dede proceeded on simple faith alone. First they lived for two weeks with a woman who had fixed up a guest room for preachers. Then they saw an apartment complex with a "For Rent" sign in the front yard. The apartment could be rented furnished or unfurnished, but since the furnishings cost an extra $10 a month, the Robertsons opted to live without furniture.

They moved into the downstairs apartment the week before Thanksgiving in 1959 and splurged to buy a turkey. When George Lauderdale and his family joined the Robertsons, they found the turkey dinner they had expected but in an unexpected setting. There in the middle of a bare living-room floor was a trunk decorated with a silver candelabra salvaged from Robertson's sellout yard sale. The Robertsons passed out place mats to sit on. "It was the most thankful Thanksgiving we had ever spent," recalls Robertson.

Shortly afterward they decided to visit the defunct station that embodied Robertson's vision for the future of his family and the future of Christian broadcasting. Nothing in the vandalized building validated his lofty ambitions. The building was located at the edge of a slum and on a dead-end street stopped by one of the saltwater marshes common in the Tidewater area. The place gave new meaning to the term "godforsaken." The brick building, surrounded by high weeds, reeked of urine. Robertson was amazed that a television station on the forward edge of technology could look quite so woebegone. He climbed through a broken window to enter the studio and kicked his way through broken glass, tubes, and other debris. Vandals had snatched the tubes from the cameras and other equipment and smashed them against the walls. The ceiling had been ripped out and insulation scattered throughout the building. The floor was littered with beer cans.

Driving away from this scene of desolation, the Robertsons had little to say to one another. Dede knew that complaining was out of order by now, and Robertson knew that he was going to purchase the station no matter what happened. Their patience was further tried by the fact that Tim Bright was nowhere to be found.

As Robertson worked on locating Bright, Dede tried to run the skimpy family budget with grace. The family purse was nearly depleted, but Pat was determined to be self-sufficient and not ask for money. At this point George Lauderdale suggested that Robertson preach at some of the small churches in the Tidewater area.

This job, while inspiring, did not always offer the compensation for which he had hoped. In one church he received nothing but a heartfelt smile and a handshake from the head of the church board. At another church, however, one of the deacons approached him and, after admitting that he had no money, said that he wanted to help.

"What do you do?" asked Robertson.

"I sell farm supplies."

"Great!" said Robertson. "Can you get me some soybeans?"

"How do you use soybeans in television?" the man wanted to know.

"We eat them."

"You mean you have animals on your television show?"

"No. I'm going to eat them myself."

The man shrugged and simply gazed in bewilderment, but later that week he appeared at the family home with a seventy-pound bag of soybeans in the trunk of his Chevrolet.

In Mount Vernon, New York, Dede had been introduced to the possibilities of the simple soybean as a total concept of nutrition. For the first time since her nursing-school experience she began to think very seriously about nutrition and was amazed to realize that the simple soybean provided the kind of low-cost but high-energy nutrition that her family needed.

It took a determined effort, but the family ate soybeans for weeks and were thankful for them. When the children complained, Robertson took down his Bible and read from Numbers

11, where the Israelites were fed with manna from heaven. "This is God's manna," Robertson explained.

Timmy dropped his head and stared at the mush on his plate. "I think I'd rather have the manna," he muttered.

Dede bought some whole-wheat flour and baked whole-wheat bread. They bought a huge sack of cheap oatmeal and someone gave them a sack of peanuts from Suffolk. Occasionally they would go on a spending spree and buy some peanut butter and bologna, a real treat. In December, Robertson's mother sent the family a Virginia country ham. They laughed. There they were, too poor to afford bologna but eating country ham worth $3.50 a pound. They mixed it with soybeans and found it "delicious."

Tim Robertson recalls those early days in Tidewater: "I developed a lifetime aversion to soybeans, but my mother and father created a good environment for us as a family. Mother had such a sense of style; she could have lived in any shell of a house and would have been able to transform the inside into a very lovely place with very little money and garage-sale furniture. She had a tremendous talent for that. We never felt poor or deprived, and it was not until I was older and met kids who were members of country clubs and played golf and tennis that I began to realize that maybe at earlier points in my childhood there had been a large gulf existing between them and me. But I never noticed it."

Before their last dollar ran out, Dede was able to obtain a job as a nurse in a local hospital. Weeks had now gone by and the Robertsons felt no closer to actually obtaining the station than they had been in New York. Robertson was tempted to believe his father had been right after all. He decided to engage the help of others.

As he has learned to do throughout his career, Robertson solicited the prayers of others for his venture. Accordingly, he had prayer cards printed that asked for specific prayer toward a specific objective: first, for the wisdom to know how to start a television station; second, for God's blessing in the negotiations to buy it; third, favor with the Federal Communications Commission; fourth, a nationwide ministry on radio and television, and so on. These prayer cards went out to anyone who met the Robertsons or was willing to distribute them.

* * *

By Christmas the family was still eating soybeans and the station was still a dream. After Christmas, Robertson sensed God wanted him to relinquish worry about the situation and relax until after the first of the year. In early January, Robertson picked up the telephone and called the accountant employed by Bright.

"It's strange you should call today," said the accountant. "Mr. Bright has just arrived in town and is over at the station."

That same morning Robertson strode into the rubble-strewn building and found himself in his first important negotiation as a broadcaster. Shaking hands with Bright, he announced his sense that God wanted him to buy the television station. Bright scratched his chin and asked how much God was willing to pay. Robertson replied that the offer was $37,000, provided the station was free from all debts and encumbrances. He added that he wanted a six-month option from Bright promising that the station would be available to Robertson at that price anytime within the next six months.

Bright responded that the tower alone cost him $100,000 to build and that the two and one half acres of downtown real estate was still valuable. Nevertheless, he said, trying to get the full proposal from Robertson, "What do you want to give me for the option, how much earnest money?"

Robertson replied that he wasn't going to give him anything for the option. Bright said, "I don't like God's way of doing business." By now, however, Bright was amused enough by this unconventional approach to a business negotiation that he seemed to want to continue.

So Robertson had one more request: that Bright show him how to run the station. Robertson pointed out that the equipment was in sorry shape and there was no guarantee that any of it really worked. Bright assured him that everything was in good condition and confidently pulled the switch on a transmitter.

A tremendous ball of fire exploded out of the transmitter and traveled out the transmission lines. Both men were pale and shaken by the experience, but Bright continued to profess confidence in the equipment. He explained there was some moisture in the transmitter, which had been sitting idle for several months. Entering the control room, Bright put on a record and a slide and said, "If you'll trot down the street and ask someone if you can peek at their television set for a minute, you'll see that we're on the air."

Robertson went down to Bowens' Grill and asked the proprietor if he had a UHF receiver, and if so, would he turn it to channel 27. It was there he saw his first image on channel 27, which eventually became the flagship station of the Christian Broadcasting Network.

Robertson uncrated his law books that night and drew up option papers that he hoped Bright would sign. He typed them out on his portable typewriter and met Bright the next day at the accountant's office. By now Bright was asking Robertson to tell him more about Christianity and Robertson readily obliged.

Before long Bright was displaying considerable interest and announced that he didn't feel very good about his own life. At that point Robertson asked him about the option and Bright said he just couldn't do it, although he offered to think it over for a couple of weeks. Before they finished the conversation, however, Bright blurted out, "Pat, do I have to sign that option?" Robertson told him that he did, hoping that Bright wouldn't ask if he had the money in the bank. He pulled the option papers out of his pocket. As Robertson recalls the incident, "Bright took one strange look at me and hastily scrawled his name on the bottom of the option. Then he grinned and said, 'Your boss sure does know how to drive a business deal.'"

Robertson was delighted that he could now buy a television station at ten cents on the dollar, but he still had to figure out how to get the ten cents. Having majored in corporate law, he was able to draw up the incorporation papers himself and file them with the state of Virginia. He then received a cash contribution of three one-dollar bills in the mail and decided he needed a bank account.

An hour later, inside the large glass-fronted office of the Bank of Virginia, Robertson tried to explain to a young woman at the new-accounts desk that he wanted to open a bank account under the name of Christian Broadcasting Network, Incorporated, chartered January 11, 1960. The Board of Directors consisted of Harald Bredesen, Bob Walker (an old Robertson friend), George Lauderdale, and Pat and Dede. When the woman asked how much he wished to deposit, Robertson reached into his coat pocket and pulled out the three wrinkled dollar bills. In the back of his mind he could hear Dede giggling at this grand gesture, but the bank officer showed no emotion. "You'll need a checkbook, which will be $6.00," she said. "Do you want to pay for it"—she smiled—"or shall I take it out of your account?"

Robertson tried to be businesslike. "Take it out of the account." Dede would be rolling with laughter, he thought. His company, brand new, had its own account and was already three dollars overdrawn.

Still remaining to be negotiated, however, was a debt of $44,000 Bright's station owed to RCA. Bright had agreed to sell the station free of debt, but he told Robertson that he would have to be the one to negotiate a reduction of the debt with RCA. This negotiation presented Robertson with a daunting prospect and his faith began to falter.

His entire family, with the exception of the baby, had the flu and everyone was running a miserable high fever. Their money was almost gone and the possibility of going hungry loomed in the near future. Robertson was at the point of going back into law or business, but two days before his self-imposed deadline he received a call from the pastor of the Hillside Avenue Presbyterian Church in Queens, New York.

The pastor, Paul Morris, said he sensed that Robertson was probably feeling discouraged. Morris wanted to come down and bestow a blessing on him. Robertson eagerly welcomed him, and the following evening Morris arrived at the door of the house and wrote out a check for $8,000. He handed it to Robertson, who, after a quick glance, thought the check was for $80 at a time when he needed $250 to pay his back rent. A wave of disappointment swept over him, but then he looked again. The decimal was *after* the last zero, not in between. Robertson was so moved he broke down and began to cry.

"Where did this come from?" he asked. "You don't have this kind of money."

Morris wouldn't say from where the money had come, but

simply said that he sensed God wanted him to give it all to Robertson with no strings attached.

Robertson then drove up to New York and found the RCA office at the top floor of 30 Rockefeller Plaza, where he met with the manager of the credit division, Sam Twohig. He told Twohig that he was trying to organize or establish a faith-oriented television station, but Twohig didn't seem at all interested. He simply told Robertson that RCA wanted the $44,000 owed by Mr. Bright.

Robertson explained that he didn't have any more than $37,000 to work with and that RCA and Bright would have to find the money out of that in some way. Twohig seemed to relent a bit. He told Robertson he would meet with his advisers and agree with them on a negotiating position. He added, however, that RCA would have to have at least $25,000. Like Bright earlier, he never asked whether or not the $37,000 was in the bank.

After he left the office, though, Robertson called Twohig. "Mr. Twohig, I believe I represented the Lord very poorly in our talk this afternoon. Twenty-five thousand dollars is just too big a price to pay in these old obligations."

Twohig laughed and said, "Well, Mr. Robertson, since you're acting for the Lord, you go ask him for some more money. I don't think RCA will negotiate any lower."

Robertson drove back to Portsmouth and sent Twohig a letter stating that he would be willing to consider a payment of $22,000, half the original obligation. Twohig's letter of response, however, indicated that his committee of advisers refused to go lower than $25,000. Dede told her husband that he should feel thankful that RCA had come down $19,000 from the original figure. Robertson wasn't encouraged, though, because he didn't have $22,000, $25,000, or $44,000. The negotiations then became a waiting game.

Robertson busied himself trying to refurbish the station. Weeks went by, and Robertson decided he would write Twohig a long, carefully reasoned letter to explain that RCA should simply donate the equipment to the Christian Broadcasting Network, Inc. The response from RCA stated that the company didn't feel that they could donate the equipment but that they would be open to any reasonable offer.

Robertson then replied with an offer of ten cents on the dollar: $2,500. RCA countered, saying they would settle for $11,000. The negotiation process focused once again on Tim Bright. Robertson made an offer to buy Bright's interest for $10,000 plus any accrued taxes and the cost of repairing the equipment. The haggling went back and forth and Robertson held his ground. Finally, Bright said, "You know, I've come to the conclusion that God really is in this, and rather than haggle over the price, I think I'll simply deed over the land, building, and tower, and all my equity in the equipment for nothing."

From Robertson's point of view, God had made the original offer impossible so that a better offer could come through—an outright gift. Two problems still remained: the $11,000 owed to RCA and the commitment for $31,000 the FCC demanded to demonstrate that Robertson had the funds necessary to put the station on the air.

Shortly after the negotiations with Bright had concluded, the manager of a local radio station made an offer to rent space on the tower. He agreed to pay rental income amounting to $6,000 a year, and also to turn over $7,200 worth of broadcasting equipment—a total of $13,200. This money would more than satisfy the commitment to RCA, but without the commitment for $31,000 it would be impossible to obtain a license.

Then an individual appeared who seemed to be the answer to their urgent prayers. A man who had a business near the station took an interest in the station project and expressed a desire to invest money. In due time he made an offer to purchase the property for $31,000 and lease it to CBN for $1.00 a year for twenty years. Robertson went home that night in a mood of elation and couldn't wait to tell Dede what had happened.

Dede, however, conveyed her suspicions to her husband. "He'll own the station and everything in it," she pointed out.

"Dede, when you don't have anything, you can't afford to look into the future, you have to step out on faith day by day," Robertson objected.

"Are you sure this is faith?" Dede said. "Or is it desperation? You may get the money, but this man is going to wind up ahead. You'll have no freedom at all."

Robertson wouldn't listen and ended the conversation in a fit of temper. The following day he signed the contract, in which the local businessman agreed to lend him the money completely secured by all the property. With the contract in hand, Robertson was able to apply for the FCC license.

After waiting two months, the FCC decided that it would grant the license even though it didn't appear Robertson had enough money to make the station operable. The government was anxious to get more UHF stations on the air so it didn't insist upon its own regulations. However, the blow Dede had foreseen soon struck.

The local businessman entered the station, where the Robertsons and several guests were gathered for a Thanksgiving dinner, and demanded to know, "Who put up the partitions in the control room? If I'm going to put up the money in this place, I want to know what's going on around here."

Robertson was stunned. He explained nervously that they simply needed an audio booth. "Why would we have to contact you about something minor like that?" he asked.

The businessman declared that he owned the building and Robertson wouldn't be able to make a single change without his permission.

"I can't do business like that," said Robertson.

"Then I'm not going to put up any money for you," the man raged.

"But we have a contract."

"Then tear it up. You've deceived me and that constitutes a breach of contract." The man walked out and slammed the door. Out the door with him went Robertson's hope for enough money to pay RCA and buy the new equipment he sorely needed to go on the air by the end of the year.

At that point discouragement seemed to be coming at him from all sides, and Robertson recalls that a feeling of hopelessness began to settle over him. "Up to that time I had been proud we were living on faith. I boasted that we were going to rely solely on God for everything, but now a few swift blows had made a shambles of my faith. I was actually beginning to question the goodness of God."

In some cases it seemed that it was Pat who was trying to help Dede move forward spiritually, and in other cases it was clearly the other way around. Their lives didn't seem to move forward until they were clearly a mutually supportive team. He was leading her toward new levels of surrender to God. In other cases she was the one out in front, trying to restrain his driven state of mind with the kind of spiritual insight that is frequently expressed as "Let go and let God."

Once, when they were visiting the station in Portsmouth, she could see his discouragement about making a viable enterprise at such an unpromising site, and she sensed what she believed to be a nudging from God to tell him that it was up to God to create the station. The point is that he shouldn't regard this as his own burden but should release it to God.

Dede tried to encourage Robertson by saying they were no worse off in Tidewater than they had been in Brooklyn, but Robertson argued that at least in Brooklyn they didn't owe anyone a lot of money. "We may have been little fools up there, but we've been big fools down here," he muttered. "Down here in Dad's backyard."

Even money for food was a problem. "Pat and I would normally go down to the Circle Restaurant," recalls Dede, "and they served a buffet. It was all you wanted to eat for $1.50. A lot of times I had the $3.00 and sometimes he had the $3.00. It depends who had the $3.00 whether we ate or not. It was really that close, financially, a lot of times. We were all working on a very minimal salary. We averaged eating one good meal a day, usually at lunch. That's where we discussed most of the business and our plans."

Robertson decided to sell the station to pay the bills. Two things convinced him he was making the right decision. First, a telephone call from Mrs. William L. Lumpkin, the wife of the pastor of the Free Mason Street Baptist Church in downtown Norfolk, inviting Robertson to help lead a weekend with the young people of the church. After the weekend Robertson was offered the position of minister of education at the church. With no income from any source other than Dede's wages from nursing, Robertson accepted the offer.

The second confirmation was an unexpected, unsolicited offer by the Northrop School Board to buy the station for $35,000. This would have allowed Robertson to pay off his debt to RCA and still come out with a profit of $24,000. This was tempting, so he called the members of his board of directors to gain their approval for the sale.

Harald Bredesen, however, suggested another board meeting and recommended they hold it in Washington concurrent with a meeting of a group known as the Full Gospel Businessmen's Fellowship International. Upon arriving, Robertson held a meeting with the board and poured out his heart, explaining that he was deeply in debt and that the school board offered a way out.

To Robertson's astonishment, both Bredesen and Walker opposed his decision to sell and Bredesen told Robertson the circumstances were exposing Robertson's pride.

"Pride!" Robertson exploded. "What do I have to be proud of? I'm broke, hungry, disgusted, and thousands of dollars in debt. I'm ridiculed by reporters, ministers, and humiliated in public because of my blunders. You have the audacity to say I'm proud? If I'm all that proud, maybe I'm not the guy to do this."

But Bredesen continued. "You're too proud to ask anybody for help," he said. "You're also afraid that people will think you're a religious fanatic, so you have been sitting on your testimony."

He was saying, in effect, that Robertson was hesitant about going forth in the fullness of his own convictions. Bob Walker concurred with Bredesen's analysis, but he offered another perspective. "Maybe Pat's motives aren't a hundred percent pure, whose are? But Pat, as much as any man I've ever known, has sought to hear the voice of God and be led by Him. He has staked his whole life and his family's, too, on his conviction that a man who really wants to hear from God and be led by God can indeed be led by Him."

The following day they all attended a meeting of the Full Gospel Businessmen's Fellowship. While there, Robertson had the profound but definite impression that God would provide and that he indeed was interested in going forward with the venture. Following that experience he received a telegram signed by a "repentant procrastinator" making an immediate pledge of $500.

After he returned to Norfolk the repentant procrastinator made good on his offer and Robertson was once again drawn back from the brink of giving up his dream.

About this time two young men joined the broadcasting station staff for very little in compensation. The first was Harvey Waff, who was about to graduate from William and Mary and who volunteered to help until he was out of school. "I promised him I would by that time try to raise enough money to pay him some kind of salary," recalls Robertson. "At the same time I was joined by another young man with a masters degree in radio and television from Ohio State University by the name of Neil Eskelin. Several volunteers came to help with whatever needed to be done, and then a woman named Shirley Jones agreed to work as a combination stenographer and piano player. We fully expected to put the station on the air by October 1."

Harvey Waff and executives at RCA both predicted that it couldn't be done. Nevertheless, Robertson made a bold announcement that the station would go on the air by that date. Just after the announcement he received a wire from the RCA Credit Department in New York: "Anticipate receipt of $11,000 under contract prior to commencement of first broadcast." By the last week of September, $11,000 was still lacking, but the group continued a promotional campaign saying they were definitely going on the air Sunday afternoon. This was typical of the faith-oriented approach of Pat Robertson. RCA was waiting to prevent the station from going on the air and Waff kept insisting they would never make it; it would take another three weeks to complete the set.

On Friday afternoon of the last week of September there was no sign of the $11,000. Robertson's reputation was now on the line and he was beginning to think he had inaccurately interpreted God's plan. Just about that time he received a phone call from a minister in Baltimore who had heard he had obtained a license for a radio station. This license had just come through from the FCC granting permission to broadcast using the old equipment they had acquired as a trade for rented space on the transmission tower.

Robertson asked the minister, "How would you like to buy the whole station?" There was a pause on the telephone line.

"You must need money pretty desperately," the minister said.

"We've got to raise eleven thousand dollars by the day after tomorrow."

"How much do you want for the station?"

"Five thousand dollars."

"I'll take it."

The deadline was down to two days and Robertson was still $6,000 short. A tremendous amount of work was still needed on props and scenery so Robertson and Waff worked all day Saturday, a day Robertson had hoped to use for fund-raising.

At the end of the day Pat went home with a deep sense of defeat, but Dede buttressed his sagging spirits, saying, "It was God who promised."

The next morning he got into his car to drive toward the church where he was in charge of the Sunday school. At a stoplight he glanced at the man in the car beside him. It was Jim Coates, an official of the Norfolk Shipbuilding and Dry Dock Company and a strong Christian. Robertson rolled down his window, honked his horn, and yelled, "We're opening the television station at one o'clock. Come by!" Coates replied he'd be there if he could.

When Robertson arrived at church he was met by Dr. Lumpkin, the pastor. "You're excused from your duties this morning," he said, "and I'm going to announce from the pulpit that the station will be going on the air at one o'clock." Robertson didn't mention that he was going to fail in his commitment to put on the show that day unless he somehow came up with $6,000 in two hours.

He went to the station and was met by Harvey Waff. Waff was frantic, neck deep in wires and tubes. Looking up from the control panels with an electric soldering iron in his hand, he said, "I've been over here since before dawn. We'll never make it, Pat. You've missed God. You're too early. You shouldn't have set it for this date. You're wrong." With tears streaming down his face, he immersed himself in the control panel again.

Robertson looked at his watch and saw that it was 12:45. I've got fifteen minutes, he said to himself. A moment later Jim Coates walked through his office door.

"Jim, we've got a problem. I've never asked anyone for money and I'm not going to do it now. But do you know anybody who's got $6,000 to lend us? We can't go on the air unless we have it in hand."

"Are you asking me to lend it to you?"

"No, I just wanted to know if you knew anyone."

Thinking for a moment, Coates said, "I know one woman who might do it."

"How about calling her?" Robertson suggested.

Coates dialed the number, but no one answered the ring. Coates just stood there, pondering or praying. Finally he looked up and said, "I'll lend it to you."

"Do you have that much money available?"

"I've got some real estate investments and a few other things. I can borrow it from my bank tomorrow."

Robertson looked at his watch. It was exactly one o'clock. He ran out of the control room shouting, "We've got the money, Harvey, now put us on the air!"

It still took two hours for the technical problems to be worked out, but by three o'clock that afternoon the first halting and shaky signal of WYAH-TV appeared on television screens. It was a picture of Pat Robertson standing in prayer.

CHAPTER FOUR

On the Brink

There's a category of television programming that could be politely termed "the divine comedy." Such was the category of the first programs of the Christian Broadcasting Network. One evening Robertson announced that a group of men was going to perform some hymns (a local group, not very talented, but extremely earnest).

The group began singing a hymn with an extremely broad range and built up to their very highest note. The audience leaned forward in expectation, but suddenly the transmitter went dead and there was silence both in the studio and throughout the world of Christian television. Everyone on the staff, after recovering from their stunned state, began bustling about frantically trying to figure out what had occurred. Finally some astute engineer opened the doors behind the transformers and looked between the two electrical poles that carried the voltage for operating the transmitter. There he saw a tiny mouse—completely shriveled from the electrical shock. Robertson called, "Cut the power," the power was cut, and he reached in and pulled out the errant mouse. The power was soon on again, and the Christian Broadcasting Network was back in business.

Robertson tossed the mouse into a basket as he came before the camera and apologized to any patient remaining viewers. It was during this period that Robertson acquired his noted capacity for instant decision-making. At times those qualities would save a situation, though on other occasions events just seemed to conspire in his favor.

Among the earliest ministers who contributed to the programming was the Reverend John Stallings, president of the Christian Deaf Fellowship of America. They scheduled a program with the title "The Deaf Hear," and Stallings began communicating on the show in sign language while also speaking the words. Suddenly there was a tremendous flash, and sparks and smoke began to emanate from the control room. Amid all the smoke, Harvey was waving frantically for Robertson to come. When he arrived Waff explained that the picture was still being transmitted but that all the sound was gone. Stallings, meanwhile, was continuing with his presentation. Robertson shouted, "We've lost the voice part of our transmission. Can you keep going until we get it fixed?"

Stallings nodded with a smile and continued in sign language long beyond his planned presentation. It was a "first" for the television industry—live interpretation for the deaf and, in this case, the hearing as well.

The early studio was very primitive. The only audio board was ancient, the one television camera tilted sideways, and the station had been literally built on a garbage dump. One staff member's filing cabinet was pulled from another dump, sanded, painted, and placed in his office. Someone donated five gallons of orange paint, and soon the studio was transformed from dull gray, black, and white by bright splashes of blazing orange paint.

"Our production budget—which included sets, paint, and everything—was only $125 a month," recalls an early producer. "It was a real poverty situation. All we had was someone with a microphone, a blackboard, and a piece of chalk."

But it was all they needed. Robertson, equipped with those items, began to talk and pray and teach people who listened. And called. And supported the ministry.

All the sets were constructed back to back, against one another, inside a room that was only twenty-seven by twenty-seven feet. Since the majority of the programs were live, it took constant innovation to keep everything in action. Robertson, like all the other members of his staff, did everything that needed to be done. Sometimes announcing, sometimes working the camera, sometimes sweeping the floor. Since they had only one camera, he couldn't cut from one set to the next. Viewers therefore would watch as the camera went swinging past two or three sets to go to the one that was scheduled next. Robertson, meanwhile, would be hustling one group of performers out of the studio while the others were moving in.

He recalls, "While one man was standing in front of the camera, preaching or singing, just a few feet away from him another group would be trying to get ready for the next program." The doors would bang open and close. Gusts of wind would blow women's hair or send the sheet music out of the hands of the musicians and across the room. One night a distinguished preacher was a guest and someone opened the door. The wind blew away his sermon notes and the poor man tried to continue preaching while the staff, trying not to be seen on camera, hustled around the studio picking up his notes. "It was at times like that," recalls Robertson, "that I thought I should be showing what goes on *off* camera rather than what we were showing. The interest level might have risen considerably."

On one of the shows Neil Eskelin played the ukulele and talked to Mr. Pingo, a squeaking teddy bear. One evening they decided Mr. Pingo should become an astronaut. The staff fashioned a moon out of papier-mâché, and the plan was to blast Mr. Pingo off the earth and then lower him onto the papier-mâché moon in a capsule. In another part of the studio the choir was squeezed in waiting for Mr. Pingo to finish landing on the moon. The launch, however, though highly realistic, used too much stage powder and the entire studio was filled with blinding smoke. Eventually all the members of the choir were choking and gagging and Eskelin had to shout over those noises at Mr. Pingo to make him hear.

In his continued search for ways to create innovative Christian programming, Robertson began to feel that reaching children was the key because children absorb many hours of television every week. Stepping into this vacuum were two young and pixieish-looking evangelists with the names of Jim and Tammy Bakker. "The thing that attracted me to them was their ability with children," Robertson recalled. "Tammy, only four feet, ten inches tall, looked like a kid herself, and they had developed a puppet routine that drew kids to their meetings in droves." Jim made an announcement over the air that they wanted to have a Halloween party at the studio and children swarmed into the station.

Robertson was not only the teacher-host-originator of the show but at one time ran cameras and swept up at the end of the day as well. His present knowledge of what is happening in the studio comes from years of doing it himself. Once when producer John Gilman was directing a program, a ceiling light was not quite in the right position and Robertson realized it. He waited until the camera cut away from him and began grimacing and pointing to the offending light overhead. When the camera cut back to him and he was still gesturing upward, Robertson simply looked up and said, "Praise the Lord."

While others often became rattled by the pressure of a live television show, Robertson was always under control. He was famous for being exactly on time—never a minute early—and this often aggravated his directors. Once Robertson walked into the studio and onto the set with five seconds until airtime. "Quick, someone get me a Bible," he shouted, and a husky cameraman grabbed the first Bible he saw—a hefty twenty-pound family edition. He threw it through the air at Robertson, who caught it just as the camera came on and the show began.

Robertson drew the Bible to him and straightened the ruffled pages. Though everyone around him was choking with laughter, he amazingly kept his dignity and his composure.

Broadcasting was limited to 7:00 P.M. until 10:00 P.M. each evening and eventually was expanded, first by one hour, then by two hours. The staff never had enough material and had to rely on a few free travelog films to fill in the numerous blank spots in the evening. With live television something always had to be before the camera. Robertson himself was on the air much of the time, sometimes teaching a Sunday-school lesson and at other times doing a program called *Teach In,* on which viewers telephoned in their questions and Robertson tried to answer them. This itself was an innovation since few, if any, shows at that time attempted the format of call-in questions.

The lack of money was an even more serious obstacle than the lack of programming. The station had no financial reserves and was under constant pressure just to pay for the various vacuum tubes and for the lumber needed to build props. At one point Robertson decided to try the financial adviser approach, creating a committee. "One day I came home and brought the subject up with Dede," he recalls. "I told her Norfolk was full of wealthy men who would be delighted to help the ministry. What we need is an advisory board, wealthy men, professional men who will meet with us and help us solve our problems, especially our financial problems."

Dede was skeptical. She said, "You think these men could help you spend what you don't have?"

Robertson wouldn't listen to her and created a list of highly respected businessmen in Norfolk. He arranged for a breakfast meeting at a swanky hotel and prepared a formal outline of his needs and plans. "There was a great deal of discussion, complete with 'Mr. Chairman, I propose . . .' and all that kind of thing," Robertson says. "But when it was all over, I got nothing out of it except a bill for a meal the station couldn't afford." After several attempts, Robertson decided to let the advisory council die.

The number of hours he spent at the station and on the air created a strain with the church where he had a job as minister of education. He was at the station as much as twelve hours a day and finally one of the deacons informed him that the church needed to have him full-time or have his resignation.

Robertson protested that he was putting in over forty hours a week for a $100-a-week job. "We realize that," responded the deacon, "but what do you think about when you shave in the morning?" Robertson chose to resign. Only two days after leaving the church two strangers came to visit him and announced themselves as members of the Park View Baptist Church. They needed an interim minister for several months while they searched for a permanent pastor.

"The television ministry consumes most of my time," Robertson explained, but the men said the church would be content for him to perform activities that required only a half day on the job. Robertson accepted and spent six months at the Park View Church. As he interprets this in retrospect, it was another example of how God shut a good door in order to open a better one. The salary from that church proved necessary during that period since part of it was needed to pay the high school students, the part-time secretary, and others at the station.

Before leaving the church he obtained permission to use its mailing list and sent out a letter asking for prayer partners for the television ministry. Just before his final day at the church one of the recipients of this mailing, a philanthropist named Fred Beasley, who had made a fortune in the ice and coal business, invited Robertson to his office to discuss using some of the television sources for educational TV programs. When Robertson walked through the door, Beasley felt led to offer Robertson a salary so he could devote all his time and energy to the television station. The multimillionaire asked Robertson how much he and his family needed to live on, and Robertson said he had to think about that. When he went back to see Beasley two days later, he told him he needed the modest figure of $100 a week, the same salary he had been receiving at the church.

Beasley told him that he didn't think $100 a week was a living wage and he decided to be more generous. He also offered to lease him a house near the TV station rent-free. Robertson readily agreed to this opportunity.

Dede, however, was furious when she took a look at the house she was offered. Cracks in the floor in some places separated the boards by a quarter of an inch, and since there was no subflooring, a winter wind would be enough to cause the curtains to wave. "We'll just have to yield ourselves to the Lord," Robertson said.

"But I can't stand it," his wife answered, "nor can I yield myself to the Lord in a slum house with one closet upstairs and one closet downstairs and a neighborhood where our children are liable to pick up every disease in the world."

Robertson was still remonstrating when Mr. Beasley's smiling nephew walked in. "I hadn't seen this old place since it got painted," he said. "It looks great, doesn't it?"

Dede scowled at him as Robertson said quickly, "We can't begin to tell you how much we appreciate your uncle's generosity."

"Most ministers wouldn't be satisfied to live in a place like this," said the nephew, "but you're different."

Sensing that his wife was about to explode at this well-intentioned remark, Robertson hustled her out to the car while repeating his profuse thanks to Mr. Beasley's nephew.

The neighborhood was comparable to Bedford-Stuyvesant in Brooklyn. Next door was a woman who, while her husband was at sea with the Navy, lived with a cousin and five children. Their home was the site of many wild parties, replete with the indiscreet behavior common to sailors. Across the street lived a teenager who after a few drinks would walk out under the streetlight at midnight and scream obscenities. A graveyard lay just over the back fence, and the ground was as hard as the baked clay at the Brooklyn manse.

The children adjusted well, but Dede soon found that her mental attitude was influenced by the fact that she was pregnant again. She was also irritated by Robertson's constant giving, particularly after CBN had managed to secure a $12,000 loan, and he suggested donating $1,000 of it to a Korean missionary. How could he simply give away borrowed money? Dede couldn't make sense of it, but she knew her husband would simply say that if God had brought them to a strong enough position to take out a loan, they should be willing to help others who were in need. Robertson's propensity in this area has lasted through the years. As an organization, CBN tithes and gives money to other organizations in need.

Robertson continued working hard and Dede was beginning to feel the strain on him was too great. He worked twenty-hour days and she began to feel that he was neglecting the family. But in April 1963, just before their fourth baby was due, Elizabeth and Gordon came down with measles. In the midst of their sickness, Dede packed her suitcase and headed to the hospital to give birth to Ann.

But Robertson couldn't find anyone to take his shift at the radio station and he couldn't even visit Dede during her five-day hospital stay. When he was at home he had to nurse two sick children, and when Dede and the baby finally came home, postpartum depression set in.

When Dede had recovered from childbirth and the mental aftereffects, she was at peace in her home but she still didn't like the rough neighborhood. One evening she and Robertson were at home when Elizabeth scrambled through the living room calling for help—and fast! The Robertsons rushed outside in time to see Tim surrounded by a gang of boys who were banging his head against a concrete wall. Robertson dispersed the crowd, but Dede realized all her children were in danger for as long as they lived in that neighborhood.

Another time a storage shed attached to the house mysteriously caught on fire and the fire chief strongly suspected arson. Robertson and his wife began to pray for the provision to leave the house behind. "We probably could have endured more, but we asked the Lord to supply us with a new place to live," says Robertson. The couple knew that their time of testing, when they learned how to have peace in the midst of insecurity, was nearly at an end.

"How will we know when it is time to move?" Tim asked.

His father explained, "Faith is a gift from God, but at turning-point times in life you don't dare make a move without it. So you ask for the gift of faith in the situation you face."

The Robertson family tolerated this environment for two years. When they could stand no more Robertson went to see Mr. Beasley with the idea of asking for a gift of some land to build on.

Beasley's response was to tell him about an empty house he owned in the country. "Why should you build when I've got a perfectly good empty house just sitting there?" he asked. "It's been boarded up for five years."

When Robertson reported this to his wife she said, "The house is bound to be so bad that nobody has wanted to live in it for five years."

But when curiosity got the better of them and they drove out to see the house, they were overcome by the beauty of the place. The house appealed to Robertson's long-standing yearning to be a Virginia country gentleman. It was a *Gone with the Wind* style of mansion with four white columns and a ring of enormous magnolia trees surrounding it. It was located on property owned by Frederick College, which had been founded and was financed by Beasley. The college supplied water in addition to lawn mowing and garbage collection services. Within two days a friend offered to help move them, another offered to help with the painting, another offered to help with the carpentry work, and by mid-September they had moved into the spacious home that was to become the one in which their children remember growing up.

Although all was quiet on the home front, the financial strains of the ministry would not let up. Once again Robertson was tempted to get out of the business altogether because he simply couldn't think of a means to cope with the financial dilemma. Up to this point he still found it distasteful and humiliating to go around asking for money. He wanted to avoid, by any means possible, selling commercials. It occurred to him that he might give out financial reports every day over the air, but he felt this was "simply begging in disguise. That was worse than straight begging."

Frequently CBN did not have enough money on hand to meet the payroll. There were times when the accounting department distributed paychecks and asked employees not to cash their checks until Monday so that on Monday—maybe—there would be enough money to cover their checks. Everyone, from Robertson down to the janitorial staff, survived on simple faith. The risks always paid off. Every Monday the money to cover payroll was in the bank; every year the money to grow somehow came in.

The answer to the chronic problem of too little money came through what is now known as the *700 Club,* the name of the television program that has brought Robertson worldwide fame. The plan was to ask 700 people to "add their faith to ours" by contributing $10.00 each month. In order to generate the pledges, he decided to hold a telethon. The whole telethon process was one that Pat Robertson found very painful, but there simply seemed to be no alternative. They put telephones in the studio and invited guests to sing and talk about their faith while telephone pledges were being recorded. By the end of the weekend they had monthly pledges that far exceeded any they had ever received before. It seemed to be a confirmation that this plan was the right one.

"We learned to do it," recalls one former staff member. "We had no videotape and it was strictly Pat on the microphone, but people were excited about his vision and those phones kept ringing. Pat isn't a ranter or a raver, and somehow you just don't believe him, you believe *in* him. We gave him our lives twenty-four hours a day and we still feel that way."

The early telethons were healing-oriented. Despite the disagreement of doctrine between Robertson and other religious leaders, he believed in the healing power of the Holy Spirit and he was not going to compromise his belief.

The local telethons progressed quickly to regional telethons, then to banquets, public appearances, and later to direct mail. The base of support had broadened. With Jay Arlan, the Bakkers, and a new television engineer from the local NBC outlet, Bill Gregory, his staff gave Robertson the sense that his enterprise was rolling forward with top-flight talent.

The accounting ledger, however, did not reflect the same optimism, and by autumn of 1965 the station needed $40,000 to cover its needs. Creating the quality television programming that Robertson really wanted had expanded the budget to an annual $120,000, and to meet that budget meant they needed pledges amounting to quadruple the original $2,500 a month that had resulted from the first telethon.

This time they staged a telethon that far exceeded any previous fund-raising effort and phone calls were coming in from throughout the Tidewater area. By 11:00 P.M. Sunday night, just before they were scheduled to sign off and conclude the telethon still $40,000 short of their goal, Jim Bakker appeared before the camera and delivered an appeal so charged with genuine emotion that the program director, out of embarrassment, tried to prevail on Robertson to intervene.

Robertson sensed that something unusual was about to occur. He turned to Arlan, the program director, and said, "No, hold steady." Immediately the phones in the studio started ringing until all ten lines were occupied. All over Tidewater people were calling in saying that they had felt guided to make contributions. Robertson decided to continue the telethon into the following week and asked people to pledge labor, mortar, bricks, and other materials to build a bigger studio.

In addition to meeting the financial needs of the station, this particular telethon brought a deeper dimension to the operation. The people manning the phones were in many cases bricklayers, bookkeepers, and other nonclergy people. They were listening to the stories of helpless, desperate people from throughout the area who were seeking prayer for their problems. Hundreds of people were being led to the faith over the telephone and there was a tremendous sense of victory in the air. People who were alcoholics were claiming that they felt the first release from their problem and the accompanying depression in many years.

"There was no way in the world it could have been contrived on the air," said one former staff member. "We had people call in and say, 'I hope my wife is listening. Tell her I'm coming home and I'm sorry I left her.' We had people call in drunk who prayed and became sober."

In 1966 CBN held a telethon that subscribed its budget of $150,000 and raised enough over budget to purchase a $30,000 transmitter. Apparent answers to prayer began to flood in, tying up their telephones twenty-four hours a day. An eighty-four-year-old man called in to say that he had been blind for three years and wanted them to pray for him to receive his sight. The man's name was mentioned and about twenty other prayer requests were mentioned over the air.

The next morning, when the blind man's landlady came in to wake him, he opened his eyes and stared at her, suddenly able to see. Story after story of this kind was mentioned on the air and an atmosphere of excited rejoicing filled the studio. Not only was the financial situation improving, but the sense of spiritual victory and the attendant excitement were an overpowering experience for thousands of people watching and listening to the program, which was simulcast on radio and television.

Those with spiritual, physical, or other needs would call in their requests, the requests would be prayed over and read on the air. When an answer to prayer was reported or someone was led to the faith by telephone, the audience could rejoice together. In all these programs there was no script, but everyone who managed the show seemed to be depending on God's direction.

One man, named Harry Van Deventer, had been blind for years. He was playing the piano in the studio, and one night he got up from the piano and, tapping along with a white cane until he reached the middle of the studio, where the camera was focused, he asked if Robertson and the others would pray for him. When they did he opened his eyes and began looking around, shouting at the camera, "I can see! I can see!"

Robertson became quite convinced that a new era in communications had been established by virtue of the sum total of these ordinary tales of pain and release from pain. A reporter called, asking, "What's going on over there? Do you have a Second Coming taking place? People have been calling the newspaper saying it's the most exciting thing ever to happen in Tidewater."

Robertson replied, "All we're doing is broadcasting from six until midnight, reading prayer requests, praying on camera, having testimonies, and announcing what God is doing."

"You mean people are getting excited about that when they could be watching *Gunsmoke*?"

To Robertson and his viewers nothing could have been more exciting. He had apparently tapped into a vein of hunger and longing for difficulties to be resolved that lay in the hearts of many Americans. The potential for television to meet these needs was obviously explosive. For CBN, at least, it was the turning of the tide.

The *700 Club* was originally designed as a late-night show and it ran from 10:15 until midnight—or until the host decided to close it off. Robertson was often the host, and the producers of the show gave him a free hand with the show's format. He had the liberty to add something new or remove something even as he prepared in his dressing room.

A program like the *700 Club* had never been done before. The concept of a Christian television talk show was new and untried, but Robertson had a gift for making it work. His warmth, his knowledge, and his uncanny ability to speak "off the cuff" won audiences.

The whole idea of the this format, with a television host who interacted with the viewing audience via telephone counselors, was unheard of. Up until the dawn of the *700 Club* all television had been one-way. The idea of using telephone counselors was revolutionary. The format was new and exciting because for the first time people could see the gospel message come full circle. The message went forth from the speaker, someone would call in from the television audience, and Robertson or another host could then relate to a listening nation what had happened in someone's life.

This format has been widely imitated, but Robertson admits it was no brainstorm, it was merely an effort at experimentation until a successful formula was reached. Interestingly enough, the format was first tried on the CBN radio station in Bogotá, Colombia. A radio announcer asked people if they had a problem to call in and then the announcer prayed on the air for the caller. People who called in were tremendously encouraged.

The *700 Club* quickly became the heart of CBN's broadcast world. For twenty years it has been a constant broadcast about Christ and about the cluster of values associated with believing in Christ: dedication to family, prayer, compassion for the personal problems of others, and so on. It has evolved over the years from an almost exclusively prayer-oriented format to a livelier magazine format that comprises news, commentary, interviews, and occasional entertainment.

And at the heart of the *700 Club* is the multitude of personal problems that are discussed and prayed over endlessly. A bank of telephone counselors are constantly at work in the rear of the studio, the phone jangling audible to the TV viewers and the counselors busy producing sheets of paper describing the particular malady or social problem afflicting the caller on the line.

Similar sheets arrive daily from prayer counselors located in other areas of the country. In a typical message a woman writes, "I have just remarried after my divorce several years ago, and my son and daughter refused to attend the wedding. I love them deeply and find their attitude to be a constant source of distress. Please pray at CBN that this relationship will be healed and that my marriage will be a successful one."

The heart of the *700 Club* is prayer. Even for nonbelievers an offer to pray for someone appears to create a link and a sense of gratitude that is otherwise unobtainable. When there are actual answers to prayer, the sense of uplift that is created is doubled and for many people the desperation of life is lessened or eliminated altogether and replaced by hope and health. It is this phenomenon that explains the tremendous success of the *700 Club* and similar programs.

Through the spontaneity of programs like the *700 Club,* which covers topics ranging from hospitals to the military, Robertson and other hosts are able to tie everyday occurrences to religious issues. Whatever the story, the producers make every effort to ensure that someone who listens can be encouraged, entertained, or enlightened by hearing a real-life story of God's miraculous working.

From a tiny UHF station whose signal would barely reach across the Chesapeake Bay, Pat Robertson launched a revolution in Christian television. His risks were enormous, his vision panoramic, but Robertson considered his efforts only small steps of faith.

As a television manager, Robertson was less than orthodox. He felt that the format and procedure should be flexible enough to accommodate a spiritual dimension. This meant that if he or someone else wanted to continue one feature beyond its predesignated time schedule or insert another feature before it was scheduled, they would tend to trust the sense of what they should do rather than what they had already planned. This occasionally created personnel problems, and in the case of one program director these problems were more than she could handle. In an effort to create more rigorous procedures, the new program director set out to change the existing methods, but unfortunately adopted an insensitive hypercritical approach toward Robertson and other station personnel who were already feeling various kinds of pressure. After several months the entire staff was boiling in discontent.

This dissension coincided with Robertson's belief that they needed a new radio transmitter that would enable them to get closer to being a first-class operation. A top-of-the-line transmitter powerful enough to reach across Hampton Roads Bay to the towns of Newport News and Hampton would cost $19,000.

It seemed like an impossible sum. Every piece of equipment had to be bought and paid for with cash. CBN had no substantial credit rating, and what little credit rating they had was not good. Many times the crew would need an electronic part and it would be miraculously provided just before airtime.

Robertson went on the air and told the audience he had established a deadline of about one month to obtain a down payment of $10,000. A staff member, however, volunteered on the air a day or two later that "all we need to do is trust God to perform a miracle on this old transmitter. If God wants the message to get out, He'll perform a miracle to see that it gets out." Robertson's approach to this Pandora's box of problems was simply to keep going.

He just wanted to get up in the mornings and move on. He later crystallized this practical approach in a book called *The Secret Kingdom* as the "law of perseverance." "With hindsight," he says, "it is amusing to know how the Lord forced us to use everything He'd given us to its very limit before He provided something new. Had He led us otherwise, dumping on us too quickly the responsibility for worldwide ministry and a budget of tens of billions of dollars, we would have crumbled. But He was wise enough to lead His people according to His laws even before we were able to know and articulate them."

For several key members of his staff it is this quality of perseverance, which his critics might term obstinacy, that put him through each of these crises. In the crises just mentioned, which combined financial disarray with internal staff dissension, the simple process of waiting and plodding on ultimately smoothed everything over.

Though Robertson spent most of his waking hours down at the station or involved in other aspects of CBN, his children remember him as a loving and caring father. "We had active, regular family devotions," recalls Tim. "Dad read the Bible to us and we prayed together as a family. The thing that spoke the loudest to me was the example my parents set. Dad was always completely uncompromising in his own personal life when it came to matters of the faith.

"From a very early age it was quite clear what was the expected course. 'This is the course and this is the only course that really works and brings happiness,' they told me, but it didn't mean I never went through a period of trying to ignore it. I never rebelled against my father, nor did I ever doubt that God existed, that He loved me, or that He was the Savior of the world; it was more like I didn't want to acknowledge the call that knowledge was going to place on my own life."

The Robertson family blossomed after they moved to the country house. Robertson enjoyed wrestling with his sons and teaching the girls how to ride their two horses, gifts from a cousin. He took his sons camping out under the stars and Tim recalls one particularly nasty camping episode when their dog tangled with a skunk.

"Other kids probably thought we were strange because we didn't have to be doing things, we simply enjoyed sitting around being together," says Tim. Although there were other families nearby, more often than not the Robertson children kept busy doing their chores on the property or simply spending time together. "We were all competitive," recalls Tim. "Whenever we played games there would be huge family fights because we all wanted to win. We all have serious goals to accomplish and we don't like to lose."

CHAPTER FIVE

On the Move

Contributions from farther afield in the Norfolk area also began to trickle in. In the case of the transmitter, the wherewithal to purchase it was supplied by one mysterious donor from Texas who sent Robertson a check for $10,000. The transmitter, once installed, gave CBN Radio the most powerful FM signal in Tidewater, Virginia. By Thanksgiving of 1963, Robertson had acquired a new building designed to hold the new transmitter together with the expanded radio facilities. The new transmitter immediately quadrupled its audience and a year later it had become the most popular station in the area. By the beginning of the following year, Robertson had hired a program director who had been ABC's top announcer, having handled programs such as *Breakfast Club* and *Paul Harvey News*. He had also been program director for Billy Graham's radio stations.

Now Robertson felt he was beginning to succeed and that the forces were mounting on his side. Until then, in addition to the simple financial inadequacy and the challenge of creating a type of programming that had never existed previously, he had sensed the specific and direct opposition of organizations that held seances and appealed to church people to believe in reincarnation and other doctrines that are not accepted as a part of mainstream Christianity. In fact, he and other Christian leaders believed that Tidewater, as headquarters of the Edgar Cayce Foundation, was a hub of spiritualist activity. People phoned in from throughout the area asking for prayer for relatives who had been drawn into occult activities. But now, after two years of difficulty, that, too, seemed to subside.

In 1961, when Robertson bought his first UHF station, UHF was considered a "sleeping giant." The television industry was unkind to UHF, and most television sets did not have antennas for UHF stations. Only a few even had UHF tuners. But with the advent of FCC regulations in the sixties that encouraged UHF stations, television sets were required to offer UHF tuners and antennas.

In the latter part of 1966 came two agonizing personal events. Robertson's father, having won reelection in 1960 with the biggest majority ever given a senatorial candidate in the history of the state, was suddenly defeated by a coalition of blacks, young liberals, and labor. To the younger Robertson this came as a considerable surprise: "Not only had my father been one of the most popular men in the state, but by virtue of his seniority he was one of the most powerful men in the Senate. He was chairman of the Senate Banking Committee, one of the ranking members of the Appropriations Committee, and floor leader for the Defense Appropriations Bill, which controlled the federal budget. It was difficult to understand how he could ever be beaten in his home state."

Pat was heartbroken. On election night his father appeared to be a broken and defeated man. After half a century in public service, the elder Robertson had been cast out of office by those he sought to serve.

Pat Robertson had not worked steadily on his father's campaign, although he had written one speech that reportedly was the hardest-hitting speech of the campaign. Nevertheless, he sensed that his father did not share the deep faith he and his mother shared, and Pat had a premonition that his father's pride was something that probably needed to be pruned. "My father was a good man, a noble man, scrupulously honest and a devoted public servant. I knew that he was the kind of person that could never allow himself to be bribed or to be demeaned by scandal or to use his power for selfish ends. Nevertheless, during his later years he had drifted from the idea that God must dominate his life."

At about the same time he began to have some trouble with Jim Bakker. Bakker had been a hard worker in the telethons and the youth ministry in addition to serving as a weekend radio announcer. One Saturday night, however, the program director ordered Bakker to go on the air, but Jim said he was exhausted. When it came time for him to go on he simply didn't show up. Robertson decided to discipline Bakker by fining him $100 because he felt the chain of command could not be violated with impunity. At that Bakker simply said, "I'm quitting," and walked out. Robertson not only accepted that as final, but called a couple who had previously applied for a job and told them to come in right away to work.

Bakker, meanwhile, came back, almost literally on his knees, pleading to have his job back. Robertson recalls, "Thursday morning I was sitting at my desk when Jim Bakker walked back into the station. His face showed he had spent several sleepless nights, and his eyes were red from weeping."

Robertson, even before Bakker returned, began feeling that Bakker should not have been allowed to leave and therefore accepted him back. This created an awkward situation with several considerations. "Just pay the fine, Jim," Robertson suggested. "I've levied the fine and the staff will expect me to make it stick."

"Pat, I just don't have the money," Jim explained. "I guess that's one of the reasons I walked out. It was easier to quit than to admit I was broke."

Robertson eventually gave the $100 to Bakker so the fine could be paid. No one knew the fine was paid with Robertson's own money.

But another problem loomed large. That afternoon Robertson was expected to meet the couple he had hired to replace the Bakkers—and now he had no job for them. Feeling slightly embarrassed, Robertson explained the situation simply and honestly. To his amazement, the other man breathed a tremendous sigh of relief and said that what he really wanted to do was build. Robertson nearly leapt from his chair with excitement. "We're getting ready to build a new station and have been through eight sets of plans from the architects and not one of them has been able to give us satisfaction," he said. Within a couple of days the new man sketched everything to Robertson's complete satisfaction: halls, offices, a prayer room, and two huge studios. Plans were announced to break ground for the new Radio and Television Broadcasting Center.

Once the *700 Club* was fully established, Robertson drew up the appropriate financial statements necessary to apply for a loan at the major bank in the area. Six years before they had been turned down for a $5,000 loan; now they were applying for a loan for $225,000. As had other circumstances, events seemed to conspire in his favor. On the very afternoon that Robertson applied, the Federal Reserve Board lowered the amount of reserves required to be kept by member banks, thereby releasing millions of dollars of loan money. By June 1967 construction for the new facility began.

Through the tough times Robertson never forgot that the reason for CBN was people. Because he cared about people, he never intentionally hurt anyone. There were times when he had to fire employees, but he seemed willing to go the second mile and give the second chance. He wanted to be fair. But if the situation demanded it, he reasoned that the ministry came first.

Unproductive employees were not tolerated. Sales staff who could not or would not sell valuable airtime were given time to reevaluate, then dismissed if they couldn't produce. CBN was a business, and tough business decisions were frequently required, but it was also a ministry. The ministry just happened to include the business of television and radio. If Robertson and his staff had not given careful attention to the business matters of CBN, they would have been out of business in a very short time.

When the *700 Club* began curious people in religious circles in Tidewater strained to watch the growth or demise of the show. What they saw surprised them. The quality of the show steadily increased, equipment was added, and CBN expanded its audience by buying more airtime for radio and television.

As the audience grew, so did viewer contributions. CBN was financed, not by large donors, but by ordinary people who regularly gave $10 or $15 a month. Churches also provided support; many churches and concerned businesses bought thirty-minute intervals of television time. Often businesses who received on-the-air recognition of their support were surprised to find that supporting CBN literally paid off. This "advertising" convinced Robertson that advertising was the best route for CBN stations.

In the beginning many advertisers had bought advertising time on the fledgling station simply to help the ministry. None of them thought they were going to have any tremendous return from their investments. Few people believed the CBN stations had a viable audience.

The CBN staff had to learn one important principle: in advertising, if a television station makes money for the client, then the client will make money for the television station.

Not only did advertising bring about changes, so did the programming. The scheduling of the late sixties was innovative and quickly progressed from being primarily religious to a lively mix of family entertainment and religious talk and information. CBN was producing music videos years before the current craze took form, and call-in shows were commonplace at CBN in 1968, long before Phil Donahue and Oprah Winfrey.

Robertson was on the air about fifty hours each week doing programs that were innovative in the eyes of both religious and secular broadcasters. On Sunday afternoons Robertson broadcast a show called *Panorama,* which analyzed world and local news in the light of the scriptures.

In 1968 the station set up a campaign headquarters and began to cover local election issues. The staff assembled expert commentators and the station put on its own election report. Even then political and social issues were an important part of the programs offered on CBN.

Shortly after the format change the attention of the counselors working on the *700 Club* program moved toward young people. For a time over half of those calling in were teenagers and many were being converted. Not long after that Robertson met a young man with long hair and a psychedelic shirt named Scott Ross. Somewhat to Robertson's surprise, Ross told him that he was a Christian. Later in the summer Robertson called Ross and asked him if he would like to go to work for the *700 Club* directing youth-oriented programs.

Ross had come out of the rock music culture in New York and had been the emcee for various rock concerts, including those of the Beatles and the Rolling Stones. In the course of his career he had taken huge doses of LSD. In spite of this past life, or perhaps because of it, and because of his current commitment to the faith, Robertson felt that Ross was just the person to evangelize teenagers. One of Robertson's mottos has always been, "When fishing for trout, use trout bait."

Ross also had a black wife, which posed a potential problem for Robertson's conservative Christians of the Tidewater area, on whom he depended for support. Taking the chance, however, Robertson hired Ross and told him to go forward and try to reach teenagers in any way he knew how. One of Ross's first moves was to bring in a rock group from Virginia Beach and put them on the air. This was not a Christian rock group, but a group that was still part of the drug culture in the area. Ross would come on the air and ask, "Does God love these people?" and the group would play their music loudly. Periodically Scott would break in with the gospel message in language that teenagers could understand. All of this created an uproar, not only among members of the television audience, but among people in the studio as well.

Radio broadcasts had actually been a part of CBN since early 1962. The earliest radio station was situated in a garage and had a homemade antenna on top of a creosote-soaked pole. Electric sparks would create a brilliant display whenever a gust of wind came along. When Robertson turned on the transmitter for the first time, he immediately burned out the transmission lines because the antenna didn't match them properly. They learned later that the transmitter was the very first type of FM transmitter ever manufactured.

Robertson found managing a radio station much easier going than managing a television station. An abundance of record albums could be obtained free of charge. Within three months this new station, WXRI-FM, was providing stiff competition to the other AM and FM stations in the Tidewater area, to the point where it was ranked number five in popularity among the more than twenty radio stations. Among those that WXRI-FM passed in popularity were the large NBC and ABC stations in that area.

During this period Robertson also acquired five FM radio stations in central New York State almost for free. Scott Ross, who eventually ran the stations, reminisces about how Robertson obtained them:

"It was a hot afternoon in July 1968 when I bumped into Pat in the hallway of CBN. In his hand he held a letter. 'Interesting, Scott,' he said, handing me the letter as we passed.

"Interesting indeed," Ross continued. "Even as I read, my heart gave a little jump. The letter was from Blackburn & Company, the nation's largest radio and television broker. My eyes raced ahead. There were five stations linked into a little network. An unusual network, too, because they overlapped.

"Today FCC regulations would prohibit this. You could drive a car from Buffalo, New York, to Albany and never be out of range of these overlapping stations. It turned out that the facilities were for sale. They were currently owned by a telephone company, but a recent court decision required it to sell."

In the letter the broker said that the stations were worth $600,000 but he thought they could be sold for half that amount.

" 'A good price,' said Robertson. But I knew," says Ross, "that Pat and his associates had about zilch dollars in the bank. I put the letter on Pat's desk."

Robertson just said that he flatly was not interested, that he had nowhere near $300,000 available. A week later, though, Robertson called the broker back and made the surprising proposition that the owner of the stations simply make them a gift to CBN. The way it would work was that the Continental Telephone Company would receive a tax-deductible receipt for the market value of $600,000 and CBN would guarantee the broker a cash commission of $15,000. The broker promised to take the offer to the telephone company for a reaction.

By coincidence, the comptroller of Continental happened to be the brother-in-law of Neil Eskelin, CBN's first program director. When the comptroller saw the proposal it was immediately approved. On January 1, 1969, CBN Northeast began broadcasting its five-station network. The signal could be heard from Toronto to Vermont, and from Massachusetts to Pennsylvania.

"Upstate New York," remembers Ross. "Dozens of colleges and universities. All those kids. We could talk to students at Cornell and Syracuse and Rochester and Rensselaer and Colgate. We could talk straight. We could let it all hang out. It would be something brand new."

By 1968, CBN had developed an innovative radio program that outclassed all others and soon tied the American Top 40 for the top syndicated radio show in the United States. Robertson's program was a collage of contemporary inspirational music, with a lot of fast patter. In 1968 no one had thought of such a concept with religious music, but soon the idea caught on and today most religious stations copy the format. Robertson recalls, "It was sort of rock it and sock it."

Many traditionalists around Robertson saw it as something a bit too brand new. One was John Stallings, who had hosted CBN's television program for deaf viewers.

"At the time when Christian rock music was invading the nominal churches and the old hymns of the church were definitely out, even in broadcasting, radio, and TV, the other music was substituted.

"Those of us who were older protested the change, some by letter and phone, but my close relationship with Pat gave me an opportunity to protest to him personally," said Stallings. "At that time a cloud of uncertainty hung over this drastic change." Robertson told Stallings, "My children like it, and I see nothing wrong with it. We must have music our youth like."

"It was then," recalls Stallings, "that I saw another Pat Robertson. . . . I saw the man in a different light, for his total ministry was in danger. . . . He bit the bullet and made an unpopular decision."

Robertson's long-standing desire to reach people in other countries as well as in the United States and to use broadcast technology to spread the word took on a new dimension in the late sixties.

Robertson was already contributing a portion of the profits of his ministries to various forms of missionary activity around the world, including a radio ministry on a Bogotá, Colombia, station run by Sixto Lopez, a South American whom Robertson had met in New York.

Then, in the fall of 1967, an opportunity for international expansion of CBN operations came, once again in a postscript to a letter. "The radio station where I have my program is for sale," Lopez wrote in his P.S. to Robertson. "Would you be interested in it?"

The timing seemed right. After convening Vatican Council II, Pope John XXIII had created a new climate of amity between Catholics and Protestants, and the atmosphere for an evangelical ministry by Protestants was more promising than ever.

The actual negotiation, however, was not easy. The station was owned by a man who looked like a stereotypical "bandito," complete with slicked-down hair and a pencil-thin mustache. In Robertson's view the Colombian had his eye on what he viewed to be the money of a "rich gringo." When Robertson discovered that the lawyer he had brought to represent him was being paid a retainer by the seller as well, negotiations became more difficult. The two parties finally reached a settlement and Robertson agreed to a $5,000 down payment at the signing of the contract. The next day, however, he discovered that the contract demanded payment even if the government did not authorize the transfer of the station license. Robertson suspected that the owner of the station, fully aware of the loopholes in the contract, might attempt to derail the license transfer at the Ministry of Communications.

As usual in such situations, Robertson sought a quiet time before he came to a decision. During that period he had a strong sense that he could get the seller to agree to reasonable terms. When he went back to close the negotiations he was astounded to find that instead of wrangling, the owner meekly consented to all the changes in the contract and gave Robertson terms that were even more favorable than he and his lawyer had dared ask for.

They redrafted the contract and agreed to a 50-50 relationship in the station for a six-month period. Then all Robertson had to do was raise $25,000. He went on the air with a telethon explaining that they would call the Bogotá station Nuevo Continente (New Continent), and would his viewers supply the needed money? They did.

Nuevo Continente was but one link in CBN's early expanding chain of holdings. Despite occasional financial setbacks, Robertson managed to acquire other radio stations and several UHF television stations as well, the latter being grouped together under the name CBN Continental in 1979. In fact, it was on the television industry that CBN was to make its most dramatic impact and through which it would experience its greatest growth.

The next task involved getting new equipment for the stations. Robertson was becoming irritated by having to limp along from what he called "one piece of junk to the next." He asked his chief engineer, Bill Gregory, to create a list of quality equipment needs so negotiations could begin. Gregory huddled with a salesman from the RCA Corporation and produced a price for the required equipment of about $3 million. Robertson by then had a very favorable relationship with RCA, but considerable negotiation was still necessary.

The key person for RCA in these negotiations was John Kunkel, the top credit man for RCA's Broadcast Division, who came to Portsmouth with another RCA official, Ed Tracy, vice president of sales. Both men were curious about what Robertson had in mind.

Because CBN simply had no money to speak of, Robertson's role as negotiator on behalf of the organization was somewhat difficult. Nevertheless, he outlined a proposal that would give the network a very low down payment, a year's moratorium on payments, a long-term payout, low interest rates, complete flexibility in the timing of purchases, and a legal escape in case the necessary down payment never materialized.

A Willis and Gladys Churchill Robertson in Salem, Virginia, 1922.

Pat Robertson, about one year old.

At home in 1933.

Pat's brother, Tad, in Lexington at age four.

At the wedding of Pat's cousin Mary Churchill Walker, Petersburg, Virginia, 1943.

The cadet at McCallie.

The 1945 McCallie football squad. (Robertson is seated in the second row from bottom, first on left.)

Pat Robertson (*second from right*) was one of the first two men to receive a commission in the U.S. Marine Corps upon graduation from Washington and Lee.

In Korea.

Robertson (*on left*) in Korea with John Warner (*center*), who was later to become a senator from Virginia.

In Berlin at the dedication of a statue commemorating U.S. servicemen in World War II, 1964, with Senator Robertson and Senator John Stennis (*on left*).

Dede and Pat at Pat's parents' home in Lexington, Virginia, 1957.

Dede with Tim, Elizabeth, and Gordon in Lexington, 1959.

The family on church steps in Virginia, 1961.

Robertson at the Berlin Wall, 1964.

On the set of the *700 Club*.

With his father at CBN birthday dinner.

Pat Robertson in the early seventies.

Robertson's last *700 Club* appearance. *From left:* Susan Howard, Ben Kinchlow, Pat, Tim, Bob Slosser.

The Robertson family on the *700 Club* "Resignation Show." Cutting the cake is Scott Ross.

Announcement tour, Des Moines, Iowa, October 2, 1987.

On the campaign trail with Americans for Robertson Director of Communications, Constance Snapp.

Bedford-Stuyvesant, Brooklyn: Pat Robertson announces that he is a candidate for the Republican nomination for President of the United States, October 1, 1987.

At the Brooklyn announcement. *From left:* Gordon Robertson, Tim's wife, Lisa, Tim Robertson.

Demonstrators at the Brooklyn announcement rally.

Roosevelt Grier, aide and former pro football star, at the Brooklyn rally.

The triumphant New Hampshire announcement rally, October 1, 1987.

Kunkel was astonished at such a proposal and explained that he was accustomed to granting a credit concession of one kind to one customer and another kind to another customer. He had never been asked to grant every credit concession that had ever been given simultaneously to *one* customer. He observed that if CBN defaulted on a contract like this, RCA would have to sell equipment for twenty years to make up the loss. But Kunkel then approved the proposal.

"You people must have really impressed him," Ed Tracy said later. "He's one of the toughest credit men in the business, and he gave you everything you asked for!"

With matters of payment and credit terms settled, talks then centered on the price of the equipment package. Robertson told Tracy he wasn't prepared to go over $2.5 million. Negotiations continued into the night. "Pat," Tracy finally said, "there's one last thing I can do. I'll give you a $58,000 trade on your old transmitter. That would make the deal stand at $2,528,000. I just can't go any lower."

"If you drop the $28,000, we've got a deal," responded Robertson.

"Damn it, Pat," Tracy shouted. "You're the most obstinate so-and-so I've ever seen. You win, it's a deal." Robertson had just negotiated a $600,000 reduction in price, together with the best credit terms RCA had ever heard of.

Following the successful negotiation with RCA, Robertson entered a phase that could best be termed "empire building." He began to fix his mind on CBN becoming very big, very fast. The first opportunity came via a call regarding a super-powered station that would be capable of reaching people in the Soviet Union and in the Arab countries from a point within Israel. Robertson dispatched a representative to Continental Electronics in Dallas, a company capable of selling a station with that kind of power. Before the subject of beaming from Israel was raised, however, the representative explained that a radio station would be available in Costa Rica with a million watts on AM compared to a mere 1,000 watts on the station reaching eight countries out of Bogotá, Colombia.

"For a million dollars," he said, "you could own the most powerful radio station in the western hemisphere, with the capability of reaching half a billion people in North and South America—in addition to others via shortwave to Europe and Asia."

Robertson then flew to Israel to inspect another million-watt AM station that was being offered together with a half-million-watt shortwave station. He was more excited about this station opportunity than any previous one. Years ago, while in Westchester County, New York, he had felt called to become a missionary to Israel. That call had persisted over the years, and Robertson's sense of history, together with his awareness of the possibility that God might be shaping events for rapid conclusion, created the exciting prospect of a broadcast evangelism from Israel. He negotiated with a succession of government officials in Jerusalem and left his proposal with Michael Arnon, secretary to the Israeli Cabinet, who promised to give it careful consideration.

Shortly after that trip, expansion potential increased in the United States. Television stations in Boston, Baltimore, and Atlanta were put up for sale. And there was even the possibility of acquiring the largest of all radio stations in America, WOR in New York, which might be purchased for roughly $30 million.

A man for whom $30,000 was a staggering sum two years before was now contemplating a total purchase of $42 million. Becoming extremely bold and self-confident, he made up his mind to pursue that amount of money. The stage was therefore set for Robertson to become bamboozled on a grand scale.

From out of nowhere Gene Ryder, a member of CBN's board of directors and a former editor with *The New York Times,* called Robertson on the phone. "Something wonderful has happened, Pat," he said.

"What's that, Gene?"

"I believe we're going to get our money to put CBN in Costa Rica," he said enthusiastically. "At least $5 million, maybe ten."

"This is fantastic," Robertson shouted. "Where from?"

"It's going to sound like a fairy tale," Ryder warned. "You know I haven't seen my real father since early childhood when I was adopted by the Ryders. I recently learned that my father's name is Greathope [not the actual name] and that he is in a nursing home in Texas, dying of brain cancer. He is married to a fifty-three-year-old woman named Lucy, who was the nurse for Mrs. H. L. Hunt prior to Mrs. Hunt's death. I flew to Dallas and was reunited with my father. My stepmother, Lucy, is extremely close to H. L. Hunt. She told me that Hunt was a member of the First Baptist Church in Dallas and active in various patriotic ventures, and so I asked her if she thought he would be willing to lend CBN $5 million so we could expand the ministry into Costa Rica."

Ryder paused for breath. "Lucy agreed to approach him on the matter and she has just called me back. Hunt wants to make an outright gift to CBN of $10 million!"

Robertson reports that he almost turned cartwheels in his kitchen after the news. After that he was on the phone with Gene Ryder almost daily. Ryder, in turn, was hearing from Lucy Greathope at regular intervals. In December, Ryder reported, "The amount of money has grown, Pat. The sum that she is going to get for us is now closer to $40 million."

"Gene, I just don't understand. What kind of power does this woman hold over this man?" asked Robertson.

"I can't keep this from you any longer, Pat. It wouldn't be fair. Lucy Greathope is actually the illegitimate daughter of H. L. Hunt. That's how I can assure you this money is coming. He's set up a trust for her. The sum is something close to $40 million—and she wants nearly all of it to go to CBN."

"How did all this come to pass?" asked Robertson.

"At first Lucy didn't know who her father was," Ryder said. "Then three years ago her mother was killed in an accident. She left a letter stating that H. L. Hunt was Lucy's real father. When Lucy confronted Hunt with the letter, he readily admitted having fathered a child. He even joked, saying, 'All these years I thought you were a boy. Now I guess you're going to blackmail me.'

" 'No,' Lucy told him, 'I don't want any of your money. I just want to be your daughter.' This impressed Hunt, and later he asked Lucy to nurse his wife when she was dying. 'Hap,' as she now calls him, is turning over much of his fortune to her, and she has come to us for legal advice on how to use it for the Lord's work."

Robertson was stunned at the magnitude of the bequest. In

agreement with Dede, he took seven days to pray and to consider its ramifications. Although no one at CBN knew of the situation, Robertson subconsciously began to change his perspective on running a ministry. No longer did it seem important to take the time to check even the most insignificant decisions, nor did the little $1.00, $5.00, and $10.00 contributions which had been CBN's lifeblood now seem so important. Robertson's original insistence that CBN operate wholly on a cash basis now seemed merely the prelude for an abundant new provision.

Robertson rented a motel room in Norfolk to spend time in prayer and serious thought. Gene Ryder drove down from his home in Boston to spend the night with Robertson. Paul Morris, a new staff member, and Dede joined them on the first evening.

"Pat, this is the full story," began Ryder. "Lucy has just heard from Hap that the total amount of the trust fund is $113 million. She wants to give CBN $100 million, but we're not to say a word about it until the deal is finalized."

"Gene," Dede spoke up hesitantly, "I hate to interject any kind of negative note here, but why does this have to be kept secret? It seems that the things of the ministry should always be open and aboveboard. We should be able to check this out with all those involved."

With uncharacteristic vehemence, Ryder turned on Dede: "Can you imagine what could happen to CBN if all this got out now? Not only would we rob our partners of the blessing of giving, but we would be besieged for handouts!"

Robertson agreed with Ryder's logic, and he also considered that if they did too much inquiring it would appear as though they didn't trust Lucy. The whole deal could be lost. Ignoring Dede's apprehension, Ryder turned to Robertson and said, "Lucy is coming to Boston next week. She wants to meet you so we can draw up the final papers for the transfer of funds."

The three left Robertson alone to spend the week praying and considering the incredible offer. The following week he met Lucy Greathope at Gene Ryder's beautiful home in the outskirts of Boston. She was a simple woman, utterly lacking in worldly pretense.

They stayed up until midnight hearing the woman's fantastic story. "Hap came to my apartment Christmas Day," she said, "and we stayed up late that night reading the Bible together. God has brought us into the most beautiful spiritual relationship imaginable, and I want to glorify Him by putting this money to work in His kingdom."

Robertson sat enthralled by the woman's story. In the past he had always been quick to investigate dubious stories, but Gene Ryder was totally confident in his stepmother's story. "How can we help you?" asked Robertson.

"Write this down," she directed, "and work out the details. I want to give $100 million to CBN—no strings attached. It is to be an outright gift, and you can use it in any way you want. I want to give $2 million to evangelist Lester Rolloff in Corpus Christi, $1 million to Oral Roberts University to set up a scholarship fund, $2 million to Gene, and $4 million to his children. The balance I want to use to set up a trust fund to support my dying husband and our adopted son, who is slightly mentally retarded."

Robertson slept very little that night, working most of the time on the legal documents necessary to complete the transfer of funds. The next morning Lucy added another chapter to the story: "I guess I should tell you the whole story since it looks like we're going to be doing business together. This $113 million is in cash, but Hap is also leaving me the controlling interest in the Hunt Oil Company, which is worth about $300 million. The shares have already been endorsed over into my name. Hap is afraid his sons and his sister, Hassie, will quibble with one another when he dies, so he's leaving it in my name with the stipulation that I not sell it. As soon as the stock is mine, I want to put it into a foundation that will send the gospel around the world."

It was a dream come true for Robertson. He and Ryder worked all morning around the kitchen table drawing up plans for the "Worldwide Gospel Foundation." On the way back to the airport Robertson turned to Ryder and said, "What should I do? We'll need a lawyer."

CBN engaged the services of the finest law firm in Norfolk, and the firm put their entire secretarial staff to work on the transaction. The CBN staff worked around the clock for more than a week, drawing up wills, trusts, charitable bequests, and foundation papers. They not only investigated the laws of Texas and Virginia, but all the federal tax forms and schedules as well.

Robertson called a meeting with his staff and vaguely hinted about the windfall that was expected. "I want you to dream up what you would do with your department if money was no object," he suggested. The managers were dumbfounded. They were thinking in terms of minor growth and adjustment, but Robertson was planning for world outreach with limitless dollars.

Accordingly, CBN made a few plans and hired new staff members in anticipation of the money. Robertson then gathered his papers and flew to meet Lucy Greathope.

She went over the legal papers with a fine-tooth comb, changing bits and portions here and there at intervals. It was obvious that this uneducated woman was no fool but had an intimate knowledge of the law as well as an amazingly astute financial brain.

"I want you to meet me next Wednesday at the Chase Manhattan Bank in New York," she said. "Hap has agreed to be there, and we will finalize the plans for the transfer of funds."

Before leaving Dallas, Robertson negotiated with LTV Electrosystems, the parent corporation of Continental Electronics, for the station in Costa Rica. They now wanted the $1 million in cash before they would let CBN begin operations. Robertson shook hands on the deal, confident the money would be in by the next week.

For the next week there were daily conversations between Ryder, Lucy, and Robertson. She was talking to Hap every day and he was ready to make the transfer of funds. There were several horrendous crises, only narrowly averted. Robertson felt he was on a roller coaster with no safety belt to hold him in.

"Pat," Dede said one night, "if I didn't know you felt this was right, I would strongly suspect this thing could destroy you. You're so different lately." Robertson didn't have time to be husband, father, president of CBN, and station manager. Future plans were being laid, travel expenses to Texas and New York were adding up, and the lawyers' fees kept accumulating.

Plans were changed again and Robertson was to meet with Lucy and Ryder in Dallas on a Friday afternoon. But instead of meeting Robertson at the bank, Ryder came to his hotel room. He seemed strained and upset. "The woman is grief-stricken for her father," he said. "There are all kinds of problems between him and his children and she's caught in the middle of them. The money just isn't that important, Pat. Frankly, I think we are too involved and we should back off."

"Back off?" Robertson exploded. "What do you mean? She's come to us for advice! I've spent weeks and weeks of my time. We've run up thousands of dollars of debts. The Costa Rica deal hinges on whether she comes through or not. How can you say back off?"

Ryder turned and left, slamming the door. He reopened it and said, "Just leave Lucy alone. I don't want you talking to her anymore."

Lucy called Robertson that afternoon. "Pat, I heard what happened today with Gene. I don't know what's gotten into him. Perhaps it would be better not to discuss these matters with him anymore. You and I can talk about them between ourselves."

Robertson was calmed but remained determined that the situation was not going to break up his friendship with Gene Ryder.

On Sunday, Lucy called. "I've got it."

"Got what?"

"The money. It's been transferred into my name. All the stock and the cash too."

"Where is it?"

"The stocks are in a safe-deposit box in a bank in Dallas. The money is there, too, in the Republic National Bank. There is only one catch."

"What's that?"

"Hap is afraid of the community property laws in Texas. His lawyer has advised him that it might be possible for my husband's brothers to step in and claim part of the estate. Hap wants all the stocks to remain in my name and says the only way to do it is for me to divorce my husband. What do you think I should do?"

Robertson was flabbergasted. If he advised her to take the money, she would have to divorce a husband who was dying of brain cancer. But if he told her to stay with Ryder's father, CBN would miss out on what seemed the one great opportunity to spread the ministry around the world.

"I'll have to pray," said Robertson. "I'll call you back after I talk to Gene."

"There's nothing to pray about," said Ryder when he heard the latest situation. "How can we be a party to breaking up their home? I'm surprised that you even considered any possibility other than telling her to stay with her husband and forget the money."

Robertson called Lucy back. "Our advice is that you not divorce your husband," he said, "but frankly I don't feel as strongly about it as Gene does."

When Robertson hung up the phone Ryder lit into him with fury. "Pat, you've got the backbone of a jellyfish! Dangle a large sum of money in front of you and you're willing to advise a woman to get a divorce from her dying husband in order to get it for you!"

"Hold on, Gene," Robertson countered, "I just didn't feel as strongly about it as you did."

"You're a vacillating coward," Gene roared, jumping to his feet.

"All right, Gene," Robertson said quietly, clenching his fists. Suddenly he realized he was about to have a fistfight with a dear friend over money.

"Gene," he said thoughtfully, "if you wanted to destroy CBN, how would you go about it? Wouldn't you offer a small amount of money—in order to avoid an investigation—and increase it gradually? If the money then fell through, we would be so bitterly disappointed that our effectiveness would be neutralized through resentment. Or worse, if the money did come in at the expense of a marriage, we'd feel guilty using it for the rest of our lives.

"Don't you see what this woman is doing?" Robertson continued. "She's bad-mouthing you to me, telling me not to share things with you—"

"Is that so?" Gene interrupted.

Robertson nodded.

"She's been doing the same thing to me about you," said Ryder.

"Gene, let's take another look at this entire matter. Something's not right."

But, incredibly, all suspicions were wiped away the next night, after their return from Dallas, when Lucy called and said, "Everything's great! I went to Hap and told him I wasn't going to divorce Mr. Greathope. He said, 'I'm glad you won't. I wouldn't have respected you if you had.' It was some sort of test he was putting me through, and now he's satisfied. I get the money anyway. The stock and cash are all mine."

Robertson went into the den, where Ryder and Dede were talking, and told them the news.

"I don't know what to do," Ryder said. "I'm no financier." Then he added wistfully, "I've always wanted to go off in the Maine woods and write poetry. Maybe that's what I'll do. I've never been more confused in all my life."

The next day Robertson received another phone call. This time a woman's husky voice on the other end of the line said, "I'm Mrs. Greathope's bodyguard. Her father hired me to look after her. She wants to talk to you for a minute."

There was a pause and then Lucy's voice came over the phone. "Pat, this is terrible. I've been sued."

Robertson felt weak and suddenly very tired. "Who sued you?" he stammered.

"The two brothers, Bunker and Herb, and their Aunt Hassie. They've got a court order and sealed the safe-deposit box where the stock is located. They've done the same with the bank account. It's all tied up, and Hap has sent a bodyguard around to protect me. What should I do?"

"Lucy"—Robertson fumbled—"I don't want to stick my nose into this. Gene is very concerned as it is because we're already so involved."

"But I need help. You've got to help me, Pat. I've got no one else to turn to."

"All right. I'll contact Gene and we'll fly out tomorrow."

Robertson called Gene Ryder and they made plans to fly back to Dallas. When Robertson arrived at midday he spent the entire afternoon in his hotel room waiting for Gene's call. At 10:30 P.M. the phone rang. Robertson could barely hear Ryder as he whispered on the phone. "Listen, Pat, the bodyguard's here, and I'm really afraid. Something's going on. I don't know what it is, but the bodyguard thinks someone is going to make an attempt on Lucy's life—and maybe on yours and mine too. I'd stay away if I were you."

"Listen carefully, Gene," Robertson said. "We've got to check this thing out before we go one step further. In the morning I want you to go to the bank where she says she has the safe-deposit box. Get the banker to tell you who got the court order to close the box. If there's no court order, or no box, we'll know something's wrong. Call me tomorrow as soon as you can."

Ryder agreed.

The next morning Robertson went down to the dining room in the hotel. There was a line waiting to get in, and Robertson was tempted not to wait, but as he turned to leave he saw a man with a familiar face. The man seemed to recognize Robertson also, but the two passed without speaking. Robertson got back in line and stood directly behind the man he thought he had recognized. When the hostess finally seated them, Robertson was at a table directly facing the familiar man. Suddenly Robertson recalled the face. It was Bunker Hunt, whom he had met briefly the previous fall in Dallas.

Hunt got up and went over to shake his hand. "Hello, Pat," he said warmly. "How are things in Norfolk? What brings you to Dallas?"

"Well," Robertson stammered, completely taken off guard, "I'm here to do business with LTV on a station we're trying to purchase in Costa Rica. How's Herb? I haven't seen him since we played poker together in school."

"He's just fine. Our offices are on the nineteenth floor of the First National Bank Building. Why don't you come up and see him? He'll be glad to see you after all these years."

Robertson's brief encounter with Bunker put him at rest, and he went back up to his room to wait for Ryder's call. At 2:00 P.M. the phone rang.

"Pat, I'm convinced the entire matter is a fraud. It's all a lie."

"Oh, no," Robertson groaned. "How do you know?"

"She refused to take me to the bank. She refused to take me to Hunt's house. She was acting funny, and I faced her with the entire thing. I told her I thought she was lying. I said, 'Why me? Why CBN? Why have you done this to us?' A strange, almost weird look came over her face. You know how kind and sweet she is. Well, suddenly all that was gone, and she began raving that she *was* Hunt's daughter and if we didn't believe her she was going to cut us off without a dime. Not only that, but I think this bodyguard is involved in some kind of dope ring."

"Okay, Gene," Robertson managed, struggling to regain his composure. "I ran into Bunker Hunt at breakfast this morning. He couldn't have been more cordial, and even invited us up to his office to see Herb. I'll call for an appointment."

The group met at 4:30 in Herb's office, and Robertson quickly ran through the entire story from the beginning.

"First of all," Herb said, "there is no Lucy Greathope—at least not to my knowledge. My mother died in the Mayo Clinic ten days after she got sick, and there was no Mrs. Greathope who nursed her. However, let me call just to make sure."

He made a phone call and confirmed that there was no Mrs. Greathope who had nursed his mother. Robertson and Ryder continued to ask about other details in the woman's story, one after another of which seemed to check out with frightening accuracy. At that point they weren't sure who to believe, and Ryder was almost finished with his story.

"So when she told us that you, Bunker, and your Aunt Hassie had filed suit against her—"

"Aunt Hassie?" Herb grinned. "Would you believe Hassie is my father's brother?"

"Oh no!" Ryder slumped in his chair. "She thought Hassie was a woman. She's made the whole thing up from bits and fragments of information gathered here and there."

Herb said, "I'm sorry. People claim these things all the time. Wealthy people get hit with paternity suits constantly, and it's not unusual for things like this to spring up. I'm just sorry you guys got sucked into it."

It was all a fraud. There was no money. No stock transfer. No safe-deposit boxes. Nothing. There was to be no big deal. No giant foundation. No quick and easy way to build a worldwide Christian broadcasting center.

Robertson and Ryder returned to Virginia sick, broken-hearted, and wiser. Robertson was exhausted, but he felt he had learned a valuable lesson. Dede consoled him. "Pat, you didn't compromise. This was simply a gift from a nice old lady. I was taken in by it too. I'm a nurse and should have recognized psychotic delusions when I saw them, but this woman was different."

Robertson, straightening, said, "I was planning as though I were the president of NBC, not CBN, and spending like it too. I lost sight of our original goals, but I'm going to call our staff together and renew our initial objectives and purposes." He later admitted that the incident was the closest he had ever come to "throwing in the towel."

How Robertson handled that incident reveals much about his strength of character, according to a close associate. "Around the turn of the decade, we really had that tremendous financial disappointment. We were counting on that support. It was tragic. But Pat's answer was, come back home and get up the next day and go to work. The one principle that has most impressed me about him—of his "laws of the kingdom"—is perseverance. His challenge to everyone is, 'Don't ever give up.' "

Reaching the World

In the early days of television, going back to the fifties and sixties, most programming was live. Then the industry entered a transition stage in the early seventies. Videotape was relatively new at that time, color was new, and the idea of syndication for any type of programming was a novel concept as well.

"Oral Roberts was running his specials in those days," Robertson recalls. "But the pioneering work then—the thing that brought about the big national television evangelists and nationally syndicated ministries that we have today—was what we did earlier on the air and with computers."

Prior to Robertson's entry into television, a program like the *700 Club* had never been done on a nationwide basis. The *700 Club,* which was to become the flagship program of CBN television, broke new ground in the field of broadcasting in several ways. It was not only the first television program of any type ever to be syndicated nationally, but it also pioneered the whole idea of morning television and of interaction with audiences at home.

"Today," notes Robertson, "our programs are produced in a studio, then edited and released through syndication—generally the feed is via powerful satellites. But it wasn't always that way."

In 1971, Robertson faced what was, in many ways, the biggest challenge of his career up to that point. His "flagship program," the *700 Club*, was bringing innovation to television as on-air telephone counselors interacted with the viewing audience—a revolutionary approach at that time. But his television holdings then included only a small station in Virginia and a fledgling station in Atlanta, and operating both stations left the CBN organization with virtually no capital.

Most businesses have either a big bank loan or they float a stock issue. But CBN was "running on a wing and a prayer"; money to support and expand religious television was in short supply. Moreover, there were basic technical questions facing Robertson: How could he possibly come up with original programming for both stations? And how could he be in two places at once to do the *700 Club*, a show based upon live viewer response?

Pondering these problems, Robertson came up with the idea of syndicating a four-hour package of programs that could be made available to religious broadcasters and to secular stations also.

Syndication was a new concept and a highly profitable one for the burgeoning videotape industry. Programs were videotaped and produced in a studio and then edited, perfected, and released through syndication.

"The major networks were feeding programs to stations on a telephone line, of course, but the entry cost was absolutely enormous," explains Robertson. "So this idea of a block of programs being 'bicycled' on videotape for religious broadcasting was brand new. It hadn't been done with independent stations before, and it created an overnight success. People throughout the nation were excited. That was the beginning of the absolutely explosive growth of CBN during the early 1970s—suddenly, wham, we're all over the country."

Robertson credits much of that "overnight success" to the work of Stan Ditchfield. "He handled all of the syndication. He was the first one to take a program like this out on the road and syndicate it. We were very close during those formative years."

Major independent stations bought the prepackaged programs

from CBN, and Robertson claims it was the first time ever in the religious realm where broadcasters would buy four hours of time on a television station. In fact, this approach by CBN was the "right idea for the right time," undoubtedly helping to save many independent UHF (ultrahigh frequency) stations from bankruptcy when the economy went into a recession in 1974.

The economic recession of the mid-seventies hit the television industry hard, but it was a boon for CBN. "Many independent television stations were going bankrupt, and most UHF stations were in trouble," noted Robertson. "The UHF stations required a special converter antenna and most people simply never got around to making the effort to find the UHF signal.

"It was into this environment that Stan Ditchfield took the *700 Club*, making deals which literally kept a lot of those virtually bankrupt UHF stations alive. He entered into five-year contracts with them at rates which in later years were just fantastic bargains. At the time it was a good deal for the UHF stations, and down the road it was a good deal for CBN," Robertson observed. "Both CBN and the UHF stations prospered, and out of the recession of '74 we were able to grow and prosper and syndicate very rapidly around the country."

CBN's first customer among the so-called secular independents was Ted Turner in Charlotte, North Carolina. "Turner was about to go into bankruptcy in Charlotte, at least he said so, and many others were in trouble. They were very undercapitalized, there wasn't much of an audience, the stations were limited by technology, and the channel legislation was just beginning to take hold. We were welcomed with open arms."

Despite their economic hardships, some station managers initially were reluctant to accept Robertson's programs. "Many managers in those days had an aversion to carrying any religious broadcasting, so they sold us early morning time they thought they couldn't give away. From their point of view, the audience at those hours was too small to be profitable for them," Robertson said.

Nevertheless, Ditchfield and Robertson together made CBN a truly nationwide network. Ditchfield would knock on a station's door, introduce himself and the CBN concept to the station brass, and a contract through which the station was to be compensated would be worked out.

Most UHF stations didn't come on the air until 3:00 P.M., and morning programming on other stations in those early years of television just didn't draw large audiences. Up until the time of the *700 Club*'s debut on the national scene, morning television was the arid, unprofitable time advertisers avoided and about which television programmers grumbled. Thus, many station managers were happy to have CBN pay for the time they usually considered "throw away."

The television stations that signed on with Ditchfield and Robertson were compensated, though usually CBN had to hold a telethon on those stations to raise the money to pay them. One year Robertson did twenty-three telethons for stations around the country while maintaining his regular appearances in Virginia on the *700 Club*! "It was absolutely exhausting," recalls Robertson. "We kept one of the most incredible schedules to hold the thing together."

As another associate remembers, "In 1976 we started doing regional telethons because the local stations were linked via long lines to regional centers, and we did four of these a year. This made a tremendous difference. The first telethon I was involved in lasted twenty-seven days nonstop, from twelve to fifteen hours a day. It wasn't until the late seventies that I had my first Thanksgiving off. Pat knew it was too much. He told me as much after he walked out before the cameras in Houston and said, 'Ladies and gentlemen, I can't tell you how pleased I am to be here in Detroit!' "

According to Robertson, "Before the *700 Club* proved there was a viable audience in the morning, no one had dared to make a move in that market. As ratings grew, however, UHF stations began broadcasting in the morning. And in fact, the *700 Club* literally 'opened up' the early morning market time. Since then, of course, the networks have created their *Good Morning, America*-type shows. But it's clear that a lot of television pioneering was done by Christian television."

Still, the "bicycling" distribution method Robertson and his associates were using in those early days before satellites—in which any given tape might follow a circuit of five or six station plays before it came back to home base—necessarily limited the content of his videotaped CBN programs. Topics dealing with current events had to be avoided on those shows; if not, they were often out of date by the time they were actually broadcast on distant stations. Robertson knew back then that talk shows do better with current information, so he was both surprised and delighted by the *700 Club's* success in its early syndication.

Viewers were impressed by the show's novel "live audience" format. Tapes of the audience's live response would be bicycled to stations in syndication, and even on a delayed basis the response was encouraging. But concept and content also contribute to the show's appeal. The *700 Club* has four basic goals: to give information from a different perspective; to give hope and inspiration so people can face the future; to minister directly to persons through prayer; and to meet the felt needs of viewers.

"We find that testimonies from ordinary people can really touch the lives of people who call themselves 'agnostics' and 'certified sinners,'" says David Clark, marketing manager for CBN. "People are especially touched when the ordinary John Doe tells his story. Their testimony is important.

"TV can be very personal," continues Clark. "It comes into your home, into your bedroom, and it brings God into a person's life without the remoteness of ritual. TV can put you in easier contact with God than going to church on Sunday. But a study done by researchers at the Annenberg School of Communications in 1984 found that people involved with religious TV were actually more involved with local churches. The two were closely correlated. And the study also showed that [religious] programs actually dealt with a lot more social and political material than people thought they did."

As head of marketing for CBN, Clark analyzes the competitive environment and plans the communications approach for the year ahead. Marketing, in general, involves the distribution of goods and services. But CBN follows the model developed by Professor Philip Kotler of Northwestern University, who defines marketing as a matter of "value exchange." (See, for example, Kotler's *Marketing for Nonprofit Organizations,* 2nd ed.; Prentice-Hall,

1982.) "Simply stated," Clark says, "this means CBN contributors must feel they are receiving value in return for their investment, whatever form their contributions may take.

"The *700 Club* ministers directly through prayer. People realize they can have a direct, dynamic relationship with God, and that," claims Clark, "reduces remoteness. The *700 Club* meets the needs that people have to be informed about what God is doing in the world. We deal in information from a theistic perspective. It also inspires people to cope with life and to help others cope with life. If we can give people hope and put people in touch with an Operation Blessing Center, it's all worth it. Watching this show, you see that God is a God of metamorphoses, a God who changes people."

To a significant degree CBN is a journalistic organization, fulfilling Pat Robertson's perception of the need to create alternative channels of communication. Like most journalistic efforts, the focus is on people and, in particular, on interviewing people. The network has had surprising success in interviewing world leaders ranging from Ronald Reagan and George Bush to Middle East figures Jihan Sadat, Ariel Sharon, Yitzak Shamir, and Hosni Mubarak to Ferdinand Marcos and South African black leader Gatsha Buthelezi.

However, in keeping with its policy of emphasis on provoking change in the lives of ordinary people, CBN makes a special effort to channel its journalistic energies toward interviews with "ordinary" people, whether in its religious testimonies, in its features on social issues, or in curious combinations of these two categories. The religious testimony, for example, will often encompass a social dimension whereby a woman who is on welfare and is trying to work and support her family on an income that is below the poverty line finds strength, sustenance, and family leadership qualities by depending on the power of Christ. In addition, guests also include figures from popular culture such as Steve Allen, Johnny Cash, and Pat Boone, as well as other popular figures including Arthur Laffer, Robert Novak, and Norman Vincent Peale.

*   *   *

When Jim Bakker first came to CBN he had the reputation of being a hard worker. He worked long hours, he had some fresh ideas, and he was a real help to Robertson in pioneering the whole approach to television ministry.

But as it all started to grow, Bakker had a change of heart. According to Jerry Horstman, a former CBN staffer who became production manager in 1971, the long hours had stopped by the time Horstman came on board. Another thing that stopped was the children's show that Jim and Tammy Bakker had been doing. Robertson wanted them to do that show, but according to Horstman, they told him that they found the children's show degrading to them and that they really wanted a talk show with the glamour of famous entertainers and other guests.

Horstman, who now runs a training school for religious television producers in Atlanta, says, "The irony was that doing the kids' shows was something they were both very good at—without even working very hard on it. But they quit those shows and I don't think they ever produced any more of the kids' shows after that."

Robertson, he said, was too smart to permit discontent to fester, and he tended to accede to Bakker's demands regarding the format of that portion of the programming. Bakker also demanded to be made a vice president, and Robertson granted that.

Major conflict occurred, however, when secular attitudes, together with financial improprieties, evidenced themselves in the ministry of Jim and Tammy Bakker. Robertson asked Horstman to prepare a cost analysis for doing the television shows and they found that it was costing $100,000 a year to produce the Jim and Tammy variety show out of a total income of about $900,000.

"This seemed way out of line, and we had to take a look at where all the money was going. It turned out that Tammy was having her hair done at the expense of the ministry, that the secretary was also serving them as a baby-sitter, and so on.

"The Bakkers were living in the lap of luxury, and the rest of us were barely making it. Tammy had mink coats, and they lived out on Sterling Point, and only the affluent could even afford to think of living on Sterling Point. Together, they had a salary that exceeded Pat's. Dede got nothing for the time that she put in on behalf of the ministry, and their son Tim was working during the summer—he was working for me for years—and Tim wasn't getting paid.

"I was preparing to go to Pat with my findings about this when I found out that a water heater was ordered by the ministry and was in a warehouse. Then Bakker started arranging to have CBN install it in his house. He expected that he'd be given it because he was a vice president. I went to him and took the position that we should sell it and use the money for the ministry."

Bakker insisted on his authority as a vice president, and Horstman finished his report and went to Robertson, who decided that the situation needed to be cleared up immediately. He called a meeting that included Horstman, both Bakkers, and Bill Garthwaite, another producer. Says Horstman, "The Bakkers were told that they had to start working a forty-hour week, that the secretary could not be used as a baby-sitter at the ministry's expense, and so on. Tammy took it all right, but Jim was really hacked off. But Pat told him, 'Jerry's in charge of production and we're running in the red.' "

In that meeting Horstman had fired the first salvo in what became a condition of open warfare between Bakker and him. "He'd threaten to quit and go on the air and cry. Pat couldn't fire him without creating more dissension. The staff thought Bakker hung the moon. Some of them even prayed for me, saying they thought I was overcome by evil."

Horstman, meanwhile, was becoming steadily more nauseated by the whole Bakker ministry and felt that it was all an act. "He'd be on the air crying, begging for money and telling the viewers that the whole staff was sacrificing to work there, and yet he and his wife weren't suffering one bit.

"Jim would host the *700 Club* for part of the week, and Pat would host it the rest of the week. Tammy would sing sometimes and she would cry on exactly the same line every week. The show was on at night, and Jim would always say, 'I know there's just one more person who wants to call in.' He said they would stay on one more hour if another person called in. I'd groan when he did this, because I had to come in to work the next day and I couldn't sleep all day like Bakker. And of course there was always some kook who would call just to have them stay on the air another hour. And of course there was all the crying. Some of the staff thought it was God's anointing, but in his case, it was just emotionalism."

During 1972, CBN had begun purchasing four hours a day on an independent station in Charlotte, North Carolina, owned by Ted Turner of Atlanta. The station was losing money and the arrangement called for a telethon to be staged every few months out of which Mr. Turner's company would be paid. The telethons proved unusually successful. According to Robertson, "The people in the Charlotte area were marvelous. It was one of the most fruitful experiences we ever had."

Bakker, meanwhile, had become very friendly with the program director of the station and his wife, Sandy and Martha Wheeler. Soon Bakker and the Wheelers went to Robertson requesting that a counseling center with a few telephones be installed in Charlotte, and Robertson agreed. Everyone seemed delighted with the progress in Charlotte.

Bakker was also preparing a break with CBN and had joined with Sandy Wheeler in forming a company incorporated in South Carolina. The purpose of this company was to create programming that would be used in Charlotte to replace CBN.

"After a few months Martha Wheeler showed up at CBN unannounced and said, 'I have Jim's permission to get a list of all our contributors in Charlotte so that we can write them personally. We want to personalize our ministry.' Some felt she shouldn't be given the list, but Pat wasn't there that day and Jim authorized it," explains Horstman.

Then came what Horstman called the "straw that broke the camel's back." Bakker had found his excuse to resign and create his own ministry in Charlotte. It was November 1972 and Bakker wanted to use one of the studios to televise election returns. He insisted on having the studio on election night, but Horstman, as production manager, refused, and Bakker resigned. "They knew I was Pat's boy," Horstman recalls. "They knew I couldn't do what I was doing without Pat's say-so.

"About twenty staffers came to me and said I was being used by the devil. You know, Jim appeals to certain types of people emotionally. He was warm and he did a lot to promote hero worship. Pat never did that. If you worked for Pat, then you knew it was a calling, not because you were supposed to regard him as some kind of hero. Pat was often perceived to be closer to certain people than he actually was. He spent a lot of time with the Bible instead of socializing. He'd play a little golf once in a while but not with the staff. That made it easier to make the tough decisions about staff changes."

Without delay Bakker wrote a letter to all the supporters on the Charlotte mailing list that Martha Wheeler had obtained several months before. The letter suggested that Jim Bakker was being forced to resign because there were financial improprieties at CBN, that people weren't being treated fairly, and that other people were using his studios, leaving him unable to produce his shows. The Bakkers mailed the letter the day they quit.

Wheeler, the program director, was already working on Turner. He told Turner that CBN was ripping the partners off and that Turner couldn't be a party to that, but the truth was that they had started their own ministry.

Robertson, meanwhile, had purchased a station in Atlanta that was not a financial success, and he decided that it would help if CBN solicited local advertising. One day Robertson told Ted Turner of his intentions.

As Robertson recalls it, "Ted Turner was trying to keep me from running commercials in my Atlanta station, and we had a rather heated exchange. He got very mad and stamped on the floor at a brunch in Dallas and told us he would break his contract with us in Charlotte. So the station manager called Bakker and installed him in our set with our donor base. It was very painful, because I really felt a great love and affection for Bakker. The people in Charlotte had been so gracious to us. I was sorry that they might get hurt and exploited and used. So that way Bakker spun off a second network that was pretty much copied after what we were doing."

According to Horstman, Turner has animosity toward Robertson. "Turner made a vow that we'd never be successful in Atlanta. He spent money to buy programming and then sat on it just so CBN couldn't get hold of that programming. And in fact CBN never was successful in Atlanta."

Shortly after the dispute over CBN in Atlanta, Bakker went on the air in Charlotte. Horstman says he was just a new Christian at the time and that he and Stan Ditchfield, Robertson's syndication manager, were prepared to go to Charlotte and remove the sets and generally create havoc there. "But Pat wouldn't allow that. We thought we were doing Pat a favor, but he just preached to us about the way that we would do it versus the way that God would do it."

The Bakkers' program in Charlotte failed after a few months, and Turner's station there eventually went off the air. The Bakkers joined the Trinity Broadcasting Network in California. Differences with Paul Crouch, the president of Trinity, led to another parting of the ways. Bakker then returned to Charlotte and created what is now the PTL Network.

In the earliest days of the Christian Broadcasting Network, Robertson thought of himself not as a syndicator or a programmer but simply as a station owner. As noted, he owned a television station in Virginia, and later one in Atlanta, and syndication, exciting as it was to become, was for him incidental to owning the stations. Much of his life revolved around working at the stations—in the hot studios, with sensitive equipment, and with television audiences. He never once called himself a "televangelist"; he considered himself, then and now, a station owner. "My first job was president of the TV station." He smiles. "I was manager."

Robertson did make all the final programming decisions in those days, but eventually he learned to delegate responsibility to those who could handle the job. Wise persons around him advised that he take the position of visionary planner rather than CEO. Robertson felt comfortable with leaving the job in the hands of capable people, but he admits that there are certain areas that he likes to keep close tabs on. "Peripheral things won't necessarily destroy an organization, but crucial elements could bring down the house if overlooked," he observes.

In corporate enterprise, money—for basic maintenance as well as desired expansion—is always among those "crucial elements." Although the operating budget in 1973 was not more than $3 million, CBN began to add stations: Portsmouth, Charlotte, Visalia (California), Baltimore, Chicago, Houston, Philadelphia, Louisville, and stations in Florida. Little by little what was a tiny venture became twenty stations, then forty, then a hundred. "Before long it was a hundred and ninety-five," says Robertson.

"In 1975 our budget was $9 million and in 1976 it was $22 million. It was very dramatic growth, and it was just an enormous job to build a national network, to service them with videotapes, to get out there personally to them all. I went to all those cities myself. It was a huge undertaking," Robertson relates.

It was a huge undertaking on a shoestring budget. With his programs on nonprime time on most of the syndicated stations, CBN's revenues were raised primarily through the owned and operated stations. On those stations CBN programming filled prime time and viewers supported the religious programming faithfully. But in 1974 and 1975, with no stock and no bank loans, the ministry had to borrow money from contributors to raise the capital to continue the expansion.

Robertson was not afraid to take calculated risks. Once the city of Portsmouth announced that CBN owed the city taxes. CBN disagreed. City officials insisted, so Robertson said, "Let's do the biblical thing. Let's pay double what we owe." The officials were stunned. Eventually the excess money was refunded, but although CBN really couldn't afford to pay the extra tax, the risk Robertson took was well worth the goodwill the gesture earned his ministry.

Somewhat later, after the growth of the network, Robertson decided to build two new studios in Portsmouth—a decision some thought to be in the realm of risk more foolhardy than calculated. "Why are you doing this?" asked a friend. "We're already building one studio larger than the largest local network affiliate. Why in the world would you need two?"

But Robertson knew what his vision demanded. At a time when all other local stations still offered their local spots and commercials in black and white, Pat wanted color. He needed color cameras worth $3 million and he approached RCA with a deal they would have refused any other man.

Robertson arranged to have the equipment sold to him at a 50 percent discount as a contribution to the ministry. The balance of the payments were to be stretched out over ten years, and the first payment wasn't due until a year after the equipment's delivery. All for a TV station no one had ever heard of.

Tim Robertson describes his father as an "astute negotiator" with a keen competitive spirit. "He sets goals for himself and he has to have them," explains Tim. "He doesn't back down. He's gotten leasing deals with companies that never make leasing deals. He once got Doubleday to literally give him a television station. Many people talk about deals and never close them. He closes them."

Regarding that station in Dallas, a former associate tells the extraordinary tale of how Robertson acquired it. "Not long after we lost the Charlotte station, we were going through some financial setbacks and it seemed like the only thing that was making money was the station in Bogotá, Colombia. Well, we had a meeting with the comptroller, and we were trying to figure out what to do.

"Pat left the meeting, saying he was going out to seek the Lord, so we all had to wait until Monday morning to see what he found out from the Lord. When he came back he said that what we should do is give away the station in Colombia to the nationals down there. I'll never forget the face of the comptroller. He said, 'But that's the only thing we have, the only thing that's in the black!'

"Pat continued, saying that we should give them $5,000 in cash to effect the transfer. The comptroller said, 'We don't have it!' Pat said, 'Then we'll borrow it if we have to.' The comptroller said, 'Let's give away the stations in upstate New York instead.' Pat said no, and he went ahead and gave the station in Colombia away." The associate offered that story as a demonstration of Robertson's adage that "You can't outgive God."

Several months after making this gift to Christians in Colombia, Robertson and this associate were driving in Dallas at eleven o'clock at night when they saw a brand-new television station. "Pat decided he wanted a tour," the associate recalls, "but I said, there's no way they're going to let us in at this hour. But of course Pat knocked on the door and they let us in. It turned out to be owned by Doubleday in New York and it was a beautiful place, and Pat said a prayer that we would get that place or one just like it.

"We already had a station in Dallas, and one day we hired a young man whose father was president of the station owned by Doubleday. Shortly after that the president showed up and said that the Doubleday board had decided to sell the station, which was losing a million dollars a year, and that Pat could have the first shot at purchasing it.

"Pat said, 'I'll tell you what. I don't want to buy it, but tell your board they can give it to me and take a tax write-off.' The other guy laughed but agreed to tell his board. He told them, and they gave us the station! Pat had obeyed God at a time of desperate need and given away a radio station, and in return we got a TV station worth several million dollars. And after a year or two, Dallas became a real revenue producer for CBN."

Another associate recalls, "It's hard to forget some things, such as how he took time to pray about decisions. I came to him in the early seventies because a group from Philadelphia wanted us to do some production work and was going to pay us for it. We caught Pat in the hall—the hall was often the place to get hold of him—and I said, 'Pat, Stan Ditchfield and I really think we should do this, and we have to give them an answer by five o'clock today.' Pat said, 'No, I'm not going to make a decision by five today. If God's in this, we won't be forced to make a decision by five today.' Three months later the Philadelphia group went broke and everybody that was in it took a beating. I saw this over and over with Pat."

"He's very fair," Tim Robertson claims, "but he is also a very, very determined guy. If he has to get something done, he'll go in there and get it done. A lot of people don't have his sense of urgency, but if he has a need to get something done, he'll do it right then. He's not a procrastinator and he doesn't sit around and analyze a problem eighty-five different ways."

"I used to be 'hands-on' because we were a small group and we all had to roll up our sleeves," Pat Robertson recalls. "It was day-to-day in the studio, with constant decisions and instant activity. We didn't have the luxury of a chief executive officer. We were struggling for survival. But once things were established and good people were brought in, I developed a different style of management."

An executive who had been dispatched to improve production management at the station in Atlanta called in the employees one by one to explain what he expected of them. Unknown to the executive, one of these was Tim Robertson, then a teenager who impressed him as being lazy. "I called him in," the executive recalls, and I said, 'If I don't see a dramatic change in your work, you're gone.' He was very polite and said, 'Thank you, sir. I'll change.' After he left, the station manager said to me, 'Hey, do you know who that was?' I said no. He said, 'That's Tim Robertson, Pat's son.'

"I said, 'Does it make a difference?' and the station manager said he didn't know. I said, 'We'll find out. If it makes a difference, then I'm in the wrong place.' Well, Tim never complained and I never heard a word from Pat. Tim stayed with us until he finished school and turned out to be one of the best workers I had. He learned and absorbed and eventually became a director."

Still, not much is hidden from Robertson, either on the job or off. "He knows the business so well," says local businessman Conoly Phillips, "he can tell if the lowest guy in the outfit is doing his job as well as the vice president right under him. But as middle management has grown, people have buffered this sort of thing. Pat now understands more. He has really mellowed. He's seeing the global picture and he's a little more tolerant of things, although on certain issues he never wavers."

Those who know say Robertson is an iron ruler who replaces weak links in his chain without a moment's hesitation. Without a doubt Robertson will not tolerate moral weakness in his staff at CBN. "He has a strong temper and a commander temperament," says one former staff member. "He could dress you down properly in front of your peers, but if you look at the context, he's results oriented and feels if you're not doing the job, you should get out of the way. He can also be very long-suffering, and I've seen him give some people a lot of rope. But he can move precisely and quickly if he needs to dismiss someone, particularly in the area of improper conduct."

Once it was reported to Robertson that a CBN staff member

had been seen smoking a marijuana cigarette. Robertson checked out the report, received an independent confirmation, and called the errant employee to say, "That's it. I don't want to see you at work here."

On another occasion, when CBN cable employees began to attend conventions of advertising and cable executives in Las Vegas, a few reports of social drinking disturbed Robertson. "Pat is very anti-alcohol," says Phillips, "and he expects the best behavior on the job and off." Yet, a neighbor from Lexington claims Robertson is typically easygoing about the alcohol question. At lunch with him one day she ordered a beer. When it came, she recalls, "I offered to drink a toast to him. He just laughed."

Among the things Robertson does takes seriously is television that is highly family oriented. CBN programming, which runs twenty-four hours each day, is designed so that any family could watch at any time with no embarrassment to either parents or young children. All programs are carefully screened.

As the home station grew and syndication brought in an ever-increasing audience, Robertson became more and more interested in helping his station gather every possible viewer. He learned to play the "ratings game" and recalls that he was once "absolutely enamored with rating books. I would take them home and read them as some people would fiction. I just enjoyed it; it was like a chess game. I tried to figure what I could do to move programs into position to take out the ratings of other stations."

He learned about demographics. Shows that appealed to eighteen-year-olds had to lead into shows with a gradually more adult appeal. He learned which programs appealed to a male audience and which to females. As Robertson himself puts it, "I would sit down and look at the time men came home from work in Texas, how many shows were on the air for women, and what would happen if we put on a show that would appeal to children as well as to men."

Despite his self-study of the many nuances of the broadcasting field over the years, Robertson remained constant to his philosophy of decision-making, the essence of which is found in the biblical proverb counseling to "trust in the Lord with all thine heart, and lean not unto thine own understanding." He interprets that to mean that, to the extent a person's heart is fixed on "personal wealth or other selfish motives," wisdom will not be available. He adds, "Neither you nor I have any knowledge of the future. We cannot, with any degree of certainty, say what will happen to us, to our surroundings, or to our world, one or twelve months hence. Only Almighty God knows what might happen. But that doesn't mean we forsake common sense or wisdom. It means we have to depend on God and then use the senses He has given us to aid us in moving from one place to another."

Robertson's ability to move in significant ways was demonstrated during the summer of 1976, a time when Bicentennial fever had reached a peak and CBN staged its first nationwide special. The program, called "It's Time to Pray, America," was the largest simultaneously released production from a Christian organization and reached almost the entire American population over 228 television stations, 300 radio stations, and the American Forces Radio and Television Service.

Billed as "the largest prayer meeting ever held in the United States," this hour-long special was also the largest broadcast undertaking ever attempted by CBN. It featured Chuck Colson, the Watergate conspirator turned Christian, on a hotel roof overlooking the White House; Johnny Cash at a Bicentennial celebration near Buffalo; and a host of other prominent sports, entertainment, and evangelical figures.

At about that same time, with the network built up around UHF and VHF affiliates, Robertson stepped out and took another risk. He purchased property in Virginia Beach, Virginia.

Working with the owners, Robertson once again utilized his bargaining savvy and bought the land for nothing down, paying interest only for two years, with the balance to be paid off over twenty-three years at 8 percent simple interest. Some of the land he paid $20,000 for is now worth $300,000.

But why did he take such a gamble? Why leave the network to concentrate on something else? The answer to those questions is found in the vision Robertson had for another phase of ministry: the satellite network.

Following the purchase of land in Virginia Beach, excitement continued to mount during the latter part of 1976 and throughout

1977 toward the completion of the first satellite earth station. In August, CBN made broadcasting history by using two satellites to transmit its West Coast telethon from the East Coast across the country and to Hawaii. And in November, Robertson formalized his commitment to satellites by signing a contract with Scientific-Atlanta to purchase CBN's own satellite earth station, the first to be owned and operated by a Christian organization.

Robertson needed a chief engineer, someone with high-level technical competence, to assume complete responsibility for the NATO transmit/receive earth station in Virginia. He employed Sam Tolbert for that role. Tolbert had experience as a project director on Apollo, NATO, Satcom I, and other space projects, and was to become, next to Ben Kinchlow, the most prominent black person at CBN.

The land was cleared over the summer, under the broiling hot Virginia sun, and by the time winter's snows had melted, the sun shone more favorably on the builder's efforts. The first earth station was completed, and on April 29, 1977, the first transponder on the RCA SacCom 1 was switched on.

Now, with the advent of satellite transmission, CBN could have a low-cost delivery system for taped programs and the ability to broadcast live throughout the nation—and not only to the nation but to the world. Bicycling distribution was no longer needed. Issues no longer had to be screened so they would not appear dated. Now Robertson could be as up-to-the-minute as he had always wanted to be.

"I wanted to be out there the same day or the day after the issues broke," says Robertson. "We were the third syndicator up there on satellite, and the first religious broadcaster in history to have its own earth station with a full-time transponder. It was a very exciting new development."

The CBN earth station was first used for live transmission of a *700 Club* telethon to ten Midwestern and Great Lakes states. Commercial television stations received the broadcast directly from their own earth receive stations or from ground transmission links associated with earth stations. But perhaps the greatest impact of this new satellite technology was to be felt worldwide.

In 1977, CBN became the first religious broadcaster in American history to go overseas with a daily television program. In the Philippines, with Robertson present, the message of the *700 Club* was presented to an appreciative audience.

For about a year Robertson and Stan Ditchfield had been concerned about people overseas who needed to hear the message of the *700 Club.* "Why couldn't we provide tapes dubbed in the native language?" they wondered. Together they went to Argentina and Chile to make such arrangements.

For many at CBN, including Robertson, an emotional moment came in April when a switch was thrown and a satellite picture appeared of singers atop the Mount of Olives in Jerusalem. The Bible says that Jesus Christ will return to earth at the same place from which he ascended, the Mount of Olives, and Robertson and others believed that they were witnessing at that moment the exact manner by which people from throughout the earth would be able to witness the Second Coming. "I had such a lump in my throat that I could hardly talk without crying," he wrote.

Enthusiasm about the satellite continued throughout the year, especially in November when, on the occasion of CBN's sixteenth anniversary, programs fed by the satellite from many parts of the world were broadcast. The show caused Robertson to claim that the whole world has been assigned to CBN as its parish, and soon people in Mexico City, Hong Kong, and cities in Taiwan and Japan were added to the growing CBN audience.

Robertson likened his new satellite to the slingshot of David. As for Goliath, "We are menaced today by giants far worse than Goliath. Powerful interests threaten to overwhelm us with filth, violence, gross sensuality, and drugs. . . . Our sling is a modern-day marvel called a satellite earth station that is capable of flinging the gospel of Jesus Christ with deadly accuracy right into the giant's head and heart. These devices, so simple and so relatively inexpensive, give us access to the minds of the world. At a fraction of the cost of conventional program distribution, they make possible a live, nationwide—and, in time, worldwide—broadcast audience. Today CBN reaches 37 million households and revenue was up 45 percent in 1987."

As a broadcast manager, Robertson is attentive to results and what managers commonly call "the bottom line." He makes quick decisions but usually seeks the advice and counsel of others. His quick thinking is often the undoing of his staff members. Once a man attended a board meeting and passed out copies of a financial report. As he gathered his notes to discuss the report, Robertson interrupted. "This is wrong," he said simply. "These figures don't even add up and this report is wrong." Noting the man's chagrin, Pat smoothed it over on the spot. "Rework the figures and bring the report back," he said. "We'll sit down and go over it later."

Pat Robertson's involvement in the business of broadcasting has been both very successful and, at the same time, unconventional. "At CBN we take our orders from God, and for this reason we regard as perfectly normal projects that the world regards as wild leaps of faith. We keep our eyes on the One who has all power and all resources—the One whose provision is, in fact, unlimited. The world can only look at short-term fluctuations, business cycles, international crises, doom. God's people see abundance, victory, the triumph of God's Spirit in everything they do. They understand the daily outworking of Romans 8:28, which says, 'God shapes everything together into good for those who love Him, for those who are the called according to His plan.' "

In a book written in 1977 called *My Prayer for You,* Robertson adds a couple of subtle spiritual points that reveal his deepest reflections on the delicate subject of divine guidance. First, he believes that a spiritual disquiet penetrates the mind of anyone who is pursuing a path diverging from God's specific will. He says, therefore, that a person should "let the peace of God be a gyroscope."

The other point pertains to the personhood of God—as distinguished from a conception of God as a principle or as a mere set of exalted propositions. With this understanding, the believer goes forward with confidence, not so much because God has provided guidance as because the Guide himself is present.

There can be no doubt that this deep religious conviction has fueled Robertson's success in broadcasting. In its list of the "50 Most Influential Broadcasters of the 1970s," *Broadcasting* magazine included Pat Robertson along with Leonard Goldenson, Phil

Donahue, and other major television personalities. To fully understand the magnitude of Robertson's achievements, it's important to see the mounting significance of cable television. During 1987 cable television will overtake traditional broadcast television as more than half of all Americans will receive television programs over cable wires and satellite dishes rather than over the air.

The cable-TV phenomenon began about forty years ago when an appliance salesman stretched an antenna wire from his store in an Appalachian coal-mining town to a nearby mountaintop, enabling him to receive programs televised from Philadelphia. His purpose was to sell television sets and to hook in antennas since their new sets wouldn't work without them. The salesman obliged them for a monthly fee and soon afterward cable systems became popular throughout the country.

Although cable technology had been seriously limited by the Federal Communications Commission until 1980, when restrictions against advertising were overturned by the courts, perhaps the biggest milestone in the history of cable occurred in 1975 when RCA launched a communications satellite.

The development of communication satellites made it possible for a cable broadcaster to send microwave transmissions and have them relayed over a broad territory. Dish antennas owned by local cable systems could receive the signals and retransmit them over coaxial cables into television sets, thus enabling broadcasters to transmit nationwide to cable channels.

In the ensuing years the percentage of viewers watching commercial network television has shrunk continually and the cable channels have begun to produce more of their own programming. Home Box Office was first, Ted Turner and his Turner Broadcasting System was next, but Pat Robertson was third to convert his network to satellite programming. He knew that with satellite distribution he could cover the entire country for less than the cost of building one new television station.

The Christian Broadcasting Network was the first to offer "basic cable"—that is, the first station that did not charge subscribers to receive its signals. Moreover, CBN was the first that did not initially use commercial advertising.

In the beginning most cable systems had only four or five channels assigned in their twelve-channel systems, so CBN offered the CBN signal free. When, after three years, CBN began to charge for their signals, the network was so popular among viewers that only forty or fifty systems out of 4,000 dropped the CBN signal.

With the dawn of the satellite broadcast age, CBN and the *700 Club* took on a new life. The CBN-owned-and-operated UHF stations were grouped together under the name CBN Continental, and CBN, Inc., became a satellite network.

The CBN Cable Network, created in 1977, claims to be "the nation's leading family entertainer," with nearly 37 million subscribers and growth averaging about 18,000 new homes daily. In an environment in which about half of all American homes have cable television, CBN carries fifteen of the top twenty-five cable programs, not including children's cartoons.

CBN Cable became fully commercial-sponsored in 1981. At the same time it created the family programming format, which provided a means primarily of offsetting the high cost of acquiring entertainment shows that were being currently produced, thereby allowing CBN to compete profitably in the industry. At the time the decision was made to become an entertainment network, it was available to fewer than 10 million viewers, but Robertson and other CBN officials reasoned that the move would draw people who would not be comfortable watching religious programming but who might begin once they became comfortable with the network in general. With that came the decision that the network would sell commercial time so that its operation would eventually be supported entirely by advertisers. The network now serves about 17,000 cities. Of the top eight basic cable programs, five are CBN Westerns.

The key to CBN's cable success, commercially, according to Doug Greenlaw, its chief of sales in New York, is that it's riding on the crest of a national trend toward basic values. He quotes Mark Twain, who said, "history doesn't repeat itself, but sometimes it rhymes," and Greenlaw says now that "it's hip to be square." What seemed upon first analysis to be a disadvantage— the inability to run the more alluring sex- and violence-based programming—turned out to be a key advantage that is helping to make CBN the only basic cable network that's solidly in the black, according to Greenlaw, with the highest rate of return on investment in the cable industry.

Bolstering this position is the willingness of many corporations to play it safe by supporting "family programming" with its advertising while eschewing the potential criticism that could come from promoting programs that a portion of its clientele might find objectionable. Doug Greenlaw points out also that an advantage lies both for advertisers and for viewers in that programs can be watched as a family unit. So, much to their own surprise, the network has competed quite favorably with its reruns of old Westerns, running head to head against such shows as sports on the weekends. The "family programming" fare focuses on classic TV comedies, Westerns and other movies, shows for women and children, documentaries, and religious programs.

In fact, CBN Cable is recognized as the network that single-handedly returned Westerns to national prominence. On weekends more viewers watch CBN shows such as *Wagon Train, Gunsmoke, The Rifleman, Big Valley,* and *The Lone Ranger* than shows on any other basic cable network.

To Dr. Ben Armstrong, executive director of the National Religious Broadcasters, "The leader of the electric church is the man with his hand on the dial. People at the grass roots are becoming involved with Pat and the tremendous growth of what I call family cable, a concept that Pat developed. The fundamental principle is that any member of the family can tune in day or night and not be offended by sex and violence. Before that the parent had to control the child so he couldn't pick up the blue channel. This has eaten into the audience of the three major networks. The focus is the family, and traditional family values are what Pat represents."

Armstrong places Robertson's real significance as a broadcaster, however, further back in time, to those desperate days in the tiny studio in Portsmouth: "Pat Robertson not only founded the first religious television station—the one in Portsmouth—but he has been an innovator in broadcast formats. Perhaps his greatest contribution is the development of the variety-magazine-type show.

"It did more than just entertain people. What it did was complete the communications cycle. Religious broadcasting was a one-way trip ever since the first broadcast from Calvary Episcopal Church in Pittsburgh on January 2, 1921.

"Before Robertson, they weren't as interested in closing the gap between the people and the broadcaster as they were with the listener hearing what they had to say and accepting it. Even the Johnny Carson show doesn't have a device for bringing the listener into relationship with the program. With Pat Robertson's program, people get involved immediately when they have a problem."

Mind and Spirit

Given the stereotype of evangelical preachers since the publication of *Elmer Gantry,* it is difficult for many to conceive of Robertson as a serious thinker. In fact, the image of the evangelical minister as a superficial thinker is perhaps more ingrained than the image of charlatan or huckster. Robertson's books, however, together with many of his television presentations, conflict with the stereotype. His thinking is expressed clearly enough to be widely understood, yet it is often penetrating enough to challenge those with a philosophical turn of mind.

At the very center of Robertson's thinking are the twin ideas of Providence and vocation. His bedrock conviction, echoed in every twist and turn of his career as a broadcaster, is that God has a highly specific plan for the country as a whole and for each individual. To him our task as individuals is to discover signs of that plan beyond particular circumstances. Even though it is possible sometimes to confuse one's own notions and ambitions with the purposes of that superintending Deity, that fact does not absolve the individual from seeking and living out the divine will to the degree it can be discerned. Actual circumstances may appear to conspire against the outworking of that will, but his understanding of faith requires a belief that God shapes ostensibly adverse conditions to suit His purposes.

This viewpoint may be seen as akin to the synthesis of politics and religion attained by Abraham Lincoln. In a book called *Abraham Lincoln: Theologian of American Anguish,* Elton Trueblood wrote, "The sense that there really is a Guiding Hand, which makes possible a genuine calling for both individuals and nations, gave a tremendous new sense of moral strength. It was not enough to watch events and to muddle along day by day. What was much more important, Lincoln came to believe, was the effort to discern a pattern beneath the seeming irrationality of events. He had come really to believe that God molds history and that He employs erring mortals to effect His purpose."

To an important degree, Robertson is a compound of the lives of many people—the people from various walks of life with whom he has had business dealings, the figures from the past whose lives have interested him, but especially the multitude of people who have called in with personal problems that range from poverty to illness, grief, injustice, depression, and failure. He interprets most problems as rooted in spiritual reality, whether in the afflicted individual or in the social environment, so he searches constantly for those mysterious ligaments that will guide people from the problem on the surface to the solution at the core.

His most widely read book is called *The Secret Kingdom,* which he wrote with Bob Slosser. Slosser said that he spent several days in Key West probing Robertson with questions for the final draft. "The whole project really took him years to accomplish," Slosser said, "because he would study and think and act and pray and live out the principles expressed in the book before they were ever written down. I always remember him coming out of the Omni Hotel in Norfolk one day with me and, looking at his hand, he said, 'What did John the Baptist mean about the Kingdom of Heaven being at hand?' He struggled to discover the exact meanings. Every morning he would get out of bed and, after he had finished his prayer time, he would sit out on the porch of that old house in Portsmouth with a yellow legal pad and an open Bible. He would also have a cup of tea in a great big mug. He would read the Bible and take notes in that illegible, left-handed scrawl of his, and then he would think and read and write some more. It was that process, repeated morning after morning, that honed his thinking processes about the laws of the kingdom."

In addition to *The Secret Kingdom,* his most important writings include *America's Dates with Destiny, Answers to 200 of Life's Most Probing Questions,* and *Beyond Reason.* Considered in its entirety, Robertson's thinking may be summarized in two complementary themes: maximum personal responsibility and minimum governmental responsibility.

In *The Secret Kingdom* he expresses his view that the visible world, which presents the appearance of stability, is actually less powerful or permanent than an invisible world, the kingdom. In his view there is a flow of energy between the two "kingdoms" and prayer is the means of unblocking the flow between them. He delineates eight "laws of the kingdom, among which is the 'law of responsibility': Be diligent to fulfill the responsibility required of you. If God and men have entrusted talent, possessions, money or fame to you, they expect a certain level of performance. Don't let them down. If you do, you may lose everything."

With these words he is sounding reveille to fellow believers in God. He long ago abandoned the widespread evangelical notion that salvation is a personal matter that may be confined in a compartment sealed away from the rest of an individual's life in the world. To a degree his attention to emotional and physical healing suggests this viewpoint, since problems like depression and cancer can dominate every aspect of the victim's existence.

Also abandoned is the notion that the individual seeking spiritual comfort and insight can be insulated from the wider world of politics, the arts, and the life of the mind in general. Even though many Christians may disagree on how spiritual commitment must influence their views on those matters, Robertson's view is that Christianity must influence them in some way. People may disagree sincerely about just what that impact should be, but in his view we must not adopt the stance that truth is merely a subjective matter. This not only violates the Gospels but also the basic logical principle that two contradictory propositions cannot be simultaneously valid. We must therefore strive in an atmosphere of mutual respect to determine where Christian truth lies in the economic, political, and other realms of our individual and collective lives.

His conception of faith flies directly in the face of an important intellectual current of our day, and that is to deny or diminish an objective reality behind personal conviction. According to that perspective, any thinking person's conception of reality has equal validity with any other and the greatest offense is to be persuaded so passionately of anything as to exert oneself toward convincing others. It is important to see just how total is Robertson's rejection of such subjectivity.

The spiritual ancestry of Robertson runs straight back to the nineteenth-century minister Charles Finney, who said, "If a man aims at his own interest, he will lose his own interest. If saving his own soul is his supreme object, he will lose it. He must make the good of others his supreme object, or he will be lost." To Finney, therefore, even the substitution of materialistic objectives with spiritual ones is not enough: only a dedication to helping others do the same will suffice. To this spirit of persuasive action Robertson ascribes all the major advances of social reform in the nineteenth century; conversely, it is to the loss of that spirit that he ascribes the major social ills of our own time.

To a degree he has echoed the criticism of certain liberals that many evangelical Christians have actively shunned involvement in social causes. This, indeed, is part of the significance of his political involvement: he is leading a major segment of committed Christians—heretofore avoiding even the polls, not to mention the caucus rooms—toward a militant struggle to spread family and spiritual values or at least forestall their erosion.

He believes that evangelical Christians "have concentrated almost exclusively on personal salvation, neglecting responsibility for intelligent public policy, international affairs, the poor, the oppressed. To whom much enlightenment has been given, much will be required."

The old church concept of "stewardship" may be readily discerned here: believers are urged by Christ in the parable of the unjust steward to work actively to make the maximum possible use of what has been entrusted to them—"To him who is faithful in a little, more will be given." Robertson refers to this in *The Secret Kingdom* as the "law of use."

The old concept of noblesse oblige he believes should be revived because it dictates an imperative for higher levels of personal responsibility. That emphasis didn't start with his study of the Gospels but has saturated his thinking from earliest childhood, largely due to his mother. Noblesse oblige should be the watchword for the nation as a whole and for all those with access, through faith, to the guidance and strength of the Holy Spirit.

Extrapolating this to the level of the nation, particularly regarding America's role as defender of human freedom, he writes, "For multifaceted reasons, we Americans seem to have no stomach for the full burden of leadership and responsibility demanded of someone to whom much has been given. We apparently want the position of power but not all the sacrifices of duty that accompany it. Because of historical and cultural factors, we have not developed a national fiber of noblesse oblige."

Some of what he advocates is common sense that he has developed from his business experience: "A person who has worked his way up to ownership of five stations has a far easier time acquiring a sixth than the person just starting out has in acquiring the first. The former is experienced and knowledgeable. He knows when and how to move. He has access to money markets that the inexperienced, struggling beginner lacks."

This theme encompasses what he sees as the imperative for spiritual renewal and for the personal involvement of citizens in the political process. In his view freedom as we know it in this country can be abused or lost when it is not leavened by a strong ethic of personal discipline. Democracy in particular demands this because, unlike communism, which implies a thoroughly regimented existence, democracy presupposes that nongovernmental influences will effect socially desirable outcomes that are needed.

His views on this subject are not so much grounded in the abstract or the theories of someone else as they are in the personal tragedies and triumphs of the people who telephone the *700 Club* with their problems. The show frequently dramatizes the story of someone who has faced a seemingly unsolvable problem but who overcame it through faith. A recent film segment of this sort featured a black woman from North Carolina who had always refused welfare and worked at the minimum wage all her life. But, through faith and determination, she raised seven children who are all highly educated professional people today. A story like that is vintage Robertson because it highlights the kind of person who regards her own problems as her personal responsibility, not the government's. The link to spiritual roots is evident here as well because of the emphasis on that woman's reliance on God to sustain her in difficulty.

Highly conspicuous in a story of this kind is the connection between the personal victory of an individual and the long-range social victory over the welfare system, a victory that Robertson believes is needed. Robertson is not the kind of conservative that exalts the individual ego and asserts that anyone with enough willpower can overcome extreme afflictions. He believes in struggle but is convinced that God has a plan for each individual life and that God often uses for His purposes people who have failed in the human sense. He sees this in his own life, in which he feels that God had to break down his pride and willfulness by sending him into unsatisfying situations before he was ready to fit into His plan.

He interprets the lives of many other well-known figures as possessing something of this contradictory quality, replete with failures and setbacks ending in extraordinary conquests. To illustrate he offers in *The Secret Kingdom* an interpretation of Abraham Lincoln's life:

"He became one of the greatest governmental and moral leaders in American history. But the achievements didn't come until he had passed through many personal failures, including bankruptcies and endless humiliating labors to make ends meet. The struggles, the battles, the wounds—they equipped him for the environment in which he would make his greatest contribution."

According to Bob Slosser, the president of CBN University, the most all-encompassing "laws of the kingdom" to Pat Robertson—the ones that affect his day-to-day thinking in the conduct of his business—are the "law of reciprocity," the "law of use," and the "law of perseverance."

* * *

First, reciprocity. This is the one Robertson regards as the all-encompassing and immutable law of the universe. He says the words "Give, and it will be given unto you" form a spiritual principle that touches every relationship, every condition of man, whether spiritual or physical. They are pivotal in any hope we have of relieving the world's worsening crises. This principle will not fail. We simply must begin to execute it—individuals, families, companies, nations. Imagine what our times would be like if we treated others the way we want to be treated."

His emphasis on giving has been interpreted cynically by some who say that he chiefly intends this to mean "give to CBN." But his thinking and his own life are so imbued with the "law of reciprocity" (including having CBN itself give away 10 percent of its income) that such an interpretation is not warranted. In the early days of the ministry it became a bone of contention with his wife, who felt that anything new coming into the household would only increase this personal propensity toward giving things away.

Embedded in this idea is something of his sense of Christian paradox and his willingness to try the unexpected: "I am as certain of this as of anything in my life: if you are in financial trouble, the smartest thing you can do is to start giving money away. Give tithes and offerings to the Lord. Give time. Give work. Give love. That sounds crazy. But we have seen how the plan of God is filled with paradox. If you need money, then begin to give away some of whatever you have. Your return, poured into your lap, will be great, pressed down, and running over."

He exemplified this seemingly dangerous idea in the story about giving away the successful radio station in Colombia as a means of recovering from an otherwise difficult financial situation.

Robertson states, "People in debt or in poverty especially need to understand a rule in God's kingdom that I call the 'law of reciprocity.' This is a law of cause and effect, of action and reaction. In the area of money, the law is simple: give, and it will be given to you; good measure, pressed down, shaken together, and running over will be put into your bosom. For with the same measure that you use, it will be measured back to you. When a person begins to give to God's work and to the poor and less fortunate, God begins to give back to him. Regardless of the debt burden, a person should give a very minimum of 10 percent of his income to the Lord. Even if you are at a poverty-level income, you have something you can give to God. Start where you are. Reach out in compassion to those less fortunate than yourself. As a first priority, get into a position to give love, time, energy, and money to other people even if it is only a little bit."

The preoccupation with human suffering, so much a part of the daily life of all ministers, dominates Robertson's thinking. Indeed, it dominates the philosophical thinking of many people: CBN commissioned the Gallup Poll organization to ask 1,500 Americans what is the one question they would like to ask God, and at the top of the list is the dilemma about human suffering. Robertson offers various answers to this complex and mysterious dilemma. He also offers one unequivocal answer: "God will intervene for those who diligently seek Him. Thousands of people can testify that God will intervene to relieve pain and suffering, but this depends on a closeness and an intimacy with Him. Should we then accept everything, and thank God for whatever happens to us—good and bad? God answers this question specifically in the Bible. 'And we know that all things work together for good to those who love God, to those who are called according to His purpose.' It is important to understand that accepting things is not the same thing as being resigned to them. You must accept suffering without becoming bitter, and you can accept it without resigning yourself to it. It is not your 'lot in life' to suffer. Those who do suffer should never quit seeking God's touch and asking Him to set them free."

He is careful not to become ensnared in the get-rich theology of some contemporary preachers for whom the truths of the Bible provide a thin justification for acquisitiveness: "It is important, however, that we not try to equate scriptural prosperity with riches," he writes. "We are speaking of the Lord's blessing, not great material wealth. Some people are not capable of handling money or other wealth. Some would be destroyed by pride. So God prospers according to His wisdom, according to the true need of those involved."

He rejects the widespread notion that people can reap permanent benefits by tapping into spiritual sources of power for selfish motives:

"That which the writers of the many 'success' books call 'positive mental attitude,' or PMA, is indeed important. Because our minds are the agents our spirits use in influencing the world around us, it is patently clear that negative attitudes can vitiate our most valiant attempts. Conversely, positive thinking will lead more often than not to successful action. Unfortunately, such people as Napoleon Hill, who wrote *Think and Grow Rich,* have gleaned only a few of the truths of the kingdom of God. They try to gain the kingdom without submitting themselves to the King. Some of the metaphysical principles of the kingdom, taken by themselves, can produce fantastic temporal benefits. But without the lordship of Jesus these benefits are both transitory and harmful. In fact, many of the advocates of mind over matter ultimately end in hellish spiritism."

He believes reciprocity to be a principle built into the universe and likens it to the physical law that for every action there is an equal and opposite reaction. So, too, he believes, it applies in the social sphere. He writes of an incident just after he arrived in Tidewater: "I remarked to my uncle, a man of admirable maturity, 'The people in Tidewater are so very nice, far more so than I had even expected.' My uncle's eyes twinkled and he spoke a powerful, homespun version of the 'law of reciprocity' that I hope I never forget: 'I tell you what, young man. You will find nice people anywhere you go if you're nice to them.' "

The period just after his arrival there also provided another striking illustration of the law. Dick Simmons, who had lived with them in Brooklyn, paid them a visit and went out with Robertson into an area that had been the scene of recent racial violence. They engaged some young blacks in conversation and eventually several dozen gathered. He writes, "In the middle of one of the city's tensest areas, where violence had already erupted, love and peace and beauty descended. Here were two white men giving love and knowledge and experience—giving the truth of the gospel—to a group of deprived, volatile black youngsters, and what did we get in return? We received love and kindness and warmth back from them."

Suddenly men and dogs came charging out of two police cars toward the youngsters, who responded by hurling curses and rocks at them. Robertson's conclusion: "The 'law of reciprocity' set in. . . . Dick and I had given love; we had received love. The police had given harshness; they had received harshness."

Giving is also the moral tendency in his view that must be present if human problems are to be solved without undue government interference or other forms of collectivism. He would not subscribe to the notion that individual effort will remedy human ills without sacrifices by others. Human weakness is too radical to expect mere self-effort to rescue humanity from poverty, disease, and other ills.

Personal responsibility also involves a strict morality and a disciplined code of personal behavior. At a time when the phrase "victimless crime" has gained acceptance, and when many maintain that private immorality should not be the concern of the community at large, Robertson forges the links between private morality and public policy. Illustrative of his logic is this comment on the subject of drugs:

"The correlation between violent crimes and the use of alcohol and drugs has been well established. At least 54 percent of those committing violent crimes in 1985 had been drinking alcohol just prior to committing the crime. Alcohol and drugs lower a person's inhibitions against antisocial behavior, and the desperate need for drugs on the part of addicts has led to an ever-increasing wave of crime against persons and property, especially in the major population centers. Crime and the misuse of alcohol and drugs in the nation have become two sides of the same problem; therefore, it is necessary to consider them together."

He has written that the "law of reciprocity" may be applied on the national and international scale with spectacular consequences. Were this law to achieve dominance, he asserts, the need for standing armies would be removed because the threat of invasion would disappear; tariff barriers would fall; voluntary acts of kindness would eliminate poverty; crime and pollution and the need for government bureaucracies would disappear.

He makes no secret of his opinion regarding which of the competing political and economic systems most closely approaches the biblical ideal, even though none exactly equates with that ideal: "Although I believe communism and capitalism in their most extreme, secular manifestations are equally doomed to failure, and likely to result in tragic dictatorship, I at the same time believe free enterprise is the economic system most nearly meeting humanity's God-given need for freedom in existence. When greed and materialism displace all spiritual and moral values, capitalism breaks down into ugliness."

In addition to offering analyses of the causes of personal and national shortcomings and adverse situations, he offers a diversity of prescriptions. Much of his advice is reminiscent of the practical precepts set forth in the Book of Proverbs and Franklin's *Poor Richard's Almanac,* particularly his exhortations toward frugal financial management. Consider the "law of use": "Take what you already have and put it to use. Don't wait until you have everything you want. Use what you have. Multiply it exponentially, consistently, persistently. The wonders of the world will explode into fullness."

He believes that people can enter into "the prosperity and abundance of the invisible world by taking maximum advantage of the tendency of things to accumulate rapidly after a certain point." He delights in quoting the financier Baron Rothschild, who termed compound interest "the eighth wonder of the world." Someone who begins with $100, Robertson calculates, and doubles that amount annually would be accumulating slowly for several years; then a take-off phase would commence, and at the end of twenty-five years the original $100 would grow to $1.6 billion.

Once again, what works at the personal level carries implications at the political level, in this case for economic policy. The United States as a whole, he believes, now bears the burden of the same principle working in reverse. The principle can "destroy you if you are borrowing money and paying high interest rates. Vast numbers of Americans are caught in such traps right now, and our government has been suffering under an increasingly impossible burden for years."

Looking back to the Great Depression, he perceives the baleful impact of a spendthrift mentality on the overall economy:

"The American consumer, like his European counterpart, also became a victim of easy credit and inflation. During that era of progress between the Civil War and the Great Depression, huge fortunes were made by a handful of enterprising Americans. The decade of the 1920s was a time of massive accumulation of wealth, but the prosperity was not equally shared. . . . The poor and the growing middle class were using up most of their monthly salaries on necessary goods like food and clothing. Little was left for extra buying, let alone purchasing luxuries. Obviously, once again the solution was credit. Old American values were set aside. Nobody remembered what Ben Franklin had advised during the nation's formative years in *Poor Richard's Almanac:* 'For Age and Want save while you may. No Morning Sun lasts a whole day.' The nation had lost touch with its roots. The people flung caution to the wind. Every dime the workers earned they spent."

He exhibits a willingness to take an economic phenomenon normally relegated to the musings of professional economists, such as the massive national debt faced by Americans generally, and tie it intellectually to moral questions involved in managing a household budget. "The couple who, in their covetousness, are yearning for a new car and new furniture neglect the necessity of waiting for the accumulation of resources necessary to avoid sending compound interest careening into action."

Frugality is another facet of the same gem—another personal quality with broader economic implications. Jokingly imputing the tendency to his Scottish ancestry, he claims that he will weigh the comparative cost of using a piece of tissue versus a paper towel to wipe up a spill on the kitchen floor. He doesn't stint on expenditures for outstanding equipment for the broadcasting facilities, the library, and other CBN requirements, as any visitor there can readily see, but he has installed cost-containment systems equal in sophistication to those at W. R. Grace, the major conglomerate where CBN's comptroller had been a senior financial executive.

Also useful in fulfilling one's responsibility is the "law of perseverance": "Do not give up. Persevere. Endure. Keep on asking, keep on seeking, keep on knocking. The world will keep on responding." Of all the "laws of the kingdom," this is the one that is reflected most often in conversations with staff members at

CBN in their descriptions of Robertson. To them he exemplifies a sense of urgency that is rare, and once he has made up his mind to go forward on a project, only the boldest of staff members would attempt to persuade him to call it to a halt.

Even with the most determined of human efforts, however, failure is inevitable—unless, as Robertson sees it, divine intervention occurs. We can be partakers in the miraculous, he feels. Though he first approached the question of miracles with the critical attitude of the legally trained mind, he is now fully persuaded that human problems can be resolved in ways that are beyond rational explanation: immediate and complete release from drug addiction without withdrawal pangs, reconciliations of seemingly hopeless marriages, sudden provision of material needs out of nowhere, and so on.

His acceptance of the miraculous is part and parcel of his dependence on God in general, since even a minor intervention by God—such as a moment of reassurance—amounts to a miracle. The "law of miracles": "Be humble enough, yet bold enough, to expect and to do miracles fulfilling the purpose of the Lord. Once and for all, become aware of the power of your speech as you walk humbly and obediently."

Unfortunately for some who would like to harness the power of working miracles to accomplish their own purposes, the power is available to be used only for the purposes that God has already decided upon, leaving no possibility of manipulation. Robertson regards many events in his own life as miraculous, including his acquisition of the television station with almost no money, but the precondition was an inner sense of what God wanted done:

"Even now it is hard to describe my inner experience at that time. The persuasion in my spirit was so real that purchasing a station with $70 seemed as possible as buying a bag of groceries at a supermarket. As an official of RCA later told me, 'You sounded so positive that we thought you had the money in the bank.' To those around me who could see only the visible reality, I was on a fool's errand. The things I was attempting were clearly impossible. But God had given me a measure of faith, and my spirit counted God's resources as part of my reality."

The most amazing—or laughable, according to your viewpoint—of all miraculous interventions involves the forces of nature. Robertson says, "For many, when you venture into these areas, you've crossed the line that separates the extraordinary from the absurd. At best, you risk being charged with advocating superstition, magic, or tricks. And at worst, you're regarded as a charlatan." This exactly has been the charge against him for praying more than once against hurricanes that were heading for Virginia Beach. He has been willing to say such prayers in public situations, knowing perfectly well that he becomes the laughingstock among many people. To him a complete conviction of the sovereignty of God should brook no exceptions.

The most famous of such incidents involved Hurricane Gloria, which was heading straight for Virginia Beach in September 1985. In the middle of a telethon, Robertson called a meeting of his staff members. "Either God is God or He isn't," he told them. He then went on the air and prayed that the hurricane be turned away from the Virginia coast. To many staff members, including Terry Heaton, the producer of the *700 Club,* this incident illustrated Robertson's courage, since he knew he'd be a laughingstock. True to their expectations, the incident has since been cited widely as typifying his ministry, or what some regard as his fanaticism.

Robertson takes for granted that people will laugh at him regarding his beliefs. In conversation he might say, "Of course, people laugh at you if you love the Lord . . ." in a casual, matter-of-fact way. Yet it disturbs him that Christians should feel embarrassed about their faith. "The world, for example, sees nothing wrong with a person carrying a copy of *Playboy* or *Penthouse* magazine around under his arm on the street, in the bus or subway. The same with a bottle of whiskey or a carton of cigarettes, with all of its life-threatening ingredients. Yet vast numbers of Christians have been intimidated about carrying a Bible on the street or bus or subway. They're afraid of being categorized as religious freaks, or perhaps old-fashioned and out of step with the world. They are nervous about being discovered in prayer or other attitudes perceived as different."

The final resource that is available to those seeking to fulfill their responsibilities is embodied in what Robertson calls the "law of dominion": "As a follower of the Son of God, assume the authority, power, and dominion that God intends for men to exercise over the rest of creation."

He believes that a revival of faith will enable people to transcend limitations. "For example, it is clear that we are going to run out of fossil fuels, even though at times we experience some relief in the oil and gas shortage. We can't keep burning limited resources forever. But we have some very big oceans, and they contain hydrogen. Sooner or later, God may give to one or more of His people a concept for running cars on such water. He will simply allow a peek into the invisible world to see His purpose. Then a faithful one will speak and act according to the revelation and the concept will take life."

He applies this notion of limitlessness to people trying to escape "any ghetto to which they have been confined, real or imagined. God will make a way. He will provide methods with which to reverse conditions and attitudes. Shortage will turn to abundance, hostility to favor."

If there is one subject in which Robertson's thinking is indisputably outside the mainstream, it is on the subject of lying. His co-host Ben Kinchlow reports that he will frequently stop himself in the middle of a sentence to correct what he suddenly perceives to be a minuscule exaggeration.

To Robertson "there is no such thing as 'a little white lie.' Lies are lies. Yet lying is a part of society. We train our children to lie. For example, suppose you go to someone's house for dinner, and they give you a delicious meal. If you say, 'That was delicious,' you have told the truth and everything is fine. But what if you go to someone's house and they serve you something that is absolutely terrible, and you say, 'That was the most delicious meal I have ever had'? You are lying. You may have done it for a good reason—a white lie—but you still lied. Honestly praise something, or be silent; but do not lie!"

The obverse side of the responsibility coin refers to the role of government, and it is axiomatic to Robertson's turn of mind that government's role should be minimal, not just for the usual reasons that heavy taxation can sap resources that would be better spent on productive activities, but also because interference by the government tends to reduce the sense of individual responsibility among the potential donors and recipients of charitable services.

He regards government as exerting largely a protective role in matters pertaining to the individual rights of citizens, and in those matters he is for a very powerful and firm government. If abortion is being considered, the government should prevent it; if totalitarian ideologies appear to be threatening another country, he favors government action to prevent that. Everything that doesn't fit into this broad category in some way he believes should be left to individuals or to small voluntary groups. He essentially affirms what has sometimes been called the "principle of subsidiarity," which says that nothing should be done by the federal government that can be done by state government, and nothing should be done by state government that could be done by local government, and so on down to the individual.

Here again his focus is on the foundation stones of American government, not so much because antiquity confers validity but because the Founding Fathers seemed to reflect an orientation toward God as an undergirding for human rights and responsibilities. Regarding the Constitution, he comments, "The framers knew the sinfulness of human nature, and they didn't trust it. They had just escaped one tyranny, and they were not about to create another one to replace it."

The assumption here is that the principles of the Bible should so permeate the marrow of the culture as to permit the continuance of prosperity and order with a minimum of restraints. Quoting various Founding Fathers, he concludes, "Our free society depends on one essential element, the self-restraint of its citizens."

Robertson is convinced that a large federal bureaucracy is not only too expensive but can undermine the sense of responsibility that should be borne by smaller units of government, voluntary groups, and individuals. On the one hand, when he was growing up, he loved the lore of Washington:

"In Washington, D.C., as a young boy surrounded by history and fascinated with it, I wandered beneath the ornate rotunda of the United States Capitol building fascinated by the statues honor-

ing heroes of the then forty-eight states. I stood in wonder before
the giant paintings of the great battle scenes of our nation's history, and I read stories from the nation's past in the Library of
Congress and the Smithsonian Institution. As a teenager I accom-
panied my father on visits to various Presidents in the White
House, and during my childhood and young adult years, I sat in
the Senate gallery watching my father and his colleagues make
history, and after crucial votes and debates, I joined them in the
exclusive Senate dining room for their exciting times of repartee
and fellowship."

Once an admirer of Franklin Roosevelt, he later returned to his
father's more conservative view. He has a specific memory of his
father bringing his fist down on the table as he decried the power
of the federal government.

In *America's Dates with Destiny,* Robertson offers the following
analysis of Roosevelt's role:

"The trend toward bigger and more powerful central government really began with Franklin Roosevelt. It all started inno-
cently enough. The President was at 'war with depression.' The
nation's future was threatened on many fronts. Millions were
poor and unemployed. Farms and factories were bankrupt and
closed down. The monetary system had nearly collapsed. People
were hungry and needed both immediate and long-term relief.
Roosevelt began to create federal departments or bureaus to do
the job. He was building an army, but he forgot that the Constitution had already determined the divisions of that army."

He pronounces the Roosevelt program, though well-intentioned and dealing with genuine and serious problems, to have
been a failure—although not one that was recognized as such:

"Roosevelt's strategy didn't work. The crash of 1929 and the
Great Depression that followed taught America that we can't trust
the tinkering of a powerful, charismatic President to restore the
nation's economic health. Roosevelt's New Deal experiment was
ineffective and far too costly. Because of FDR, the Great Depression did more to reshape the existing framework of government
policy than any other single event in recent history. Out of depression came a powerful central government; an imperial presidency; the enormous political power of newspapers, radio, and

later television; an anti-business bias throughout the country; powerful unions; a complexity of federal regulations and agencies designed to control and, in many instances, protect powerful vested interests; and, most importantly, a belief in the economic policies of British scholar John Maynard Keynes, to the end that government spending and 'fine tuning' would supposedly guarantee perpetual prosperity."

Indeed, the trend begun as a response to the Depression continued on into an era of prosperity. Roosevelt's new programs, undertaken as a "war on depression," were adapted in the sixties as a "war on poverty."

"Each Great Society program seemed absolutely necessary and worthwhile on the surface, but just below the surface were serious flaws from the beginning. The Great Society with its all-out 'war on poverty' had produced a maze of agencies, funds, offices, bureaus, departments, and regional representatives within the Johnson administration. At the end of 1966 the federal government had more than $15 billion in aid and grants available to state and local governments, but it was almost impossible to find one's way to the money source through the tangle of 170 separate programs, funded by four hundred different appropriations, administered by twenty-one different departments and agencies, assisted by 150 different bureaus. All too often, federal programs were administered from the top down. The opinions of people close to the actual scenes of battle were disregarded or minimized. The programs of state and local government were often undermined by this sudden flood of federal funding and its army of federally paid and appointed staff. The patient, painful work of local and national charities was often undone and replaced by federal bureaucrats who moved into towns and states like carpetbaggers with no regard for those generous, loving volunteers who had preceded them."

The lesson Robertson draws from these examples are, not surprisingly, essentially spiritual. They hark back to those of maximum personal responsibility, which is something that cannot be successfully usurped by government:

"We must learn from Johnson's Great Society that even the federal government has its limits. What we want for our families and for our neighbors must come from within ourselves. It cannot be proclaimed by a President, passed by Congress, or administered by millions of federal bureaucrats. The problems of poverty, inequality, and injustice are problems of the human spirit. And federal spending, even within limits, will never create a truly great society. The great society begins in the transformed hearts of the people, and it spreads one by one among us until the entire world is transformed. Somewhere along the way, our nation has lost its spiritual direction, and no massive federal program can force upon us what does not come from within. Our only sure hope is to find that direction once again."

In the overlapping areas of security and human rights, however, Robertson believes in an even stronger role for government than ever before. "The dangers faced by individuals from criminals and by the nation as a whole from its determined and well-organized adversaries now warrant a shifting of government resources into those narrower channels.

"Law enforcement agencies must be better funded, and law enforcement officers need to be more adequately trained and supported for their difficult and dangerous tasks. Court systems must be made to work more efficiently. The electronic and print media must become more effectively self-regulated to minimize their contribution to the problem of crime and substance abuse. The churches, schools, and homes of the nation must be aided to increase their effectiveness in education and prevention."

The right of the government to take the lives of murderers is also upheld:

"Capital punishment is unfortunately a necessary corrective to violent crime. . . . [It] is a great deterrent to crime. It is no deterrent whatsoever if it is uncertain and continually delayed. But if those who scoff at society, and who constantly prey on innocent victims, were aware that death would be the penalty for their actions, we would see a dramatic drop in our crime rate.

"Today we place criminals in penitentiaries—places of confinement in which the offender is supposed to become penitent or sorry for his sins. In truth, these places are breeding grounds for crime. In even the best of them, 85 percent of the inmates will be incarcerated again. Society must pay for the anguish suffered by the victims of crime, then pay again each year to hold the criminal in prison, a cost equivalent to an Ivy League education.

The biblical model is far wiser. The perpetrator of lesser crimes was returned to society where he was made to make restitution to his victim. The hard-core, habitual criminal was permanently removed from society through capital punishment. In neither case was society doubly victimized as we are today."

The defense of the national safety is, like the defense of the individual's safety, a proper role for government and one which, in Robertson's thinking, has progressively weakened during the past generation. In the following paragraphs, excerpted from his writings, a picture emerges of his impressions of America's role in the world from his college years in the late forties to the present day.

First, the intellectual appeal of communism, a subject he says was sometimes the subject of bull sessions at Washington and Lee University:

"In America, sensitive young intellectuals—men like Alger Hiss and Harry Dexter White—became convinced that our free enterprise system was wrong and could not be improved. Around the world there were thousands of men and women like them, sincerely longing for a utopian movement under Lenin and Stalin. But the Soviet leaders who initiated, financed, and controlled the Cold War and its bloody worldwide revolution soon proved to be more ruthless, more greedy, and more oppressive than the ruling classes they succeeded."

In part, the intellectual arguments about collectivism may be answered in reference to America's own original experiment with it:

"In the early days of our country, the Massachusetts Bay Colony attempted a primitive form of socialism. Land was owned jointly, everyone was to work together, and then the produce was to be divided to each according to his need. This experiment failed miserably. The people began to starve to death because there was not enough incentive to work. It was only after the land was divided into acre plots and given to individual families that the people began to prosper. That was because they were now working for enlightened self-interest and giving to one another out of their increase."

This view stops short of a 100 percent endorsement of capitalism, at least in its purest form:

"I believe that free enterprise is much closer to the biblical model than any other form of economic system. But wealth contains great spiritual danger. Just as the coercive utopianism of Communist materialism is not of God, neither is a capitalist materialism—based on the amassing of riches for personal gain, with disregard for the afflicted and the needy—right."

Then Korea, where he had been attached to the command group of an infantry division:

"In 1950 Mao signed a treaty of friendship and mutual support with the Soviet Union. That new friendship between Moscow and Beijing led in June of that same year to the Soviet-backed invasion of South Korea by its satellite government in the north. At the close of World War II in 1945, Korea, like Germany, had been divided into zones of occupation. The Soviets quickly moved to consolidate their power in the north. They armed the North Korean government and sponsored the 'civil war' that eventually left 34,000 Americans and American allies dead, along with a million Koreans and a quarter of a million Chinese. With almost no losses of their own, the Russians had managed to retain their sphere of influence in Korea. And in spite of years of warfare, that nation remains tragically divided."

On the "bamboo curtain":

"Early in the 1950s, the United States began to realize the real threat of Communist expansion. Churchill's prophecy of an Iron Curtain extending around all of Eastern Europe had been realized. Now a 'bamboo curtain' seemed to threaten all of Southeast Asia as well. The Soviets worked tirelessly to expand their sphere of influence around the globe. From the very end of World War II the foreign policy of the United States was forced to focus on the containment of Soviet expansion. Under Truman, United States aid was restored to Chiang Kai-shek in Taiwan and to the French battling the Communist Vietnamese nationalists in Indochina."

On the reinforcement of the Iron Curtain:

"On August 13, 1961, just after midnight, East German police backed by East German soldiers blocked all the crossing points between free and Communist Berlin and installed barbed-wire barricades and tank traps as the beginning of a new crackdown against German citizens who were trying to flee to the West. The world watched in shock and surprise as an ugly cement wall was built around Communist-occupied Berlin during those next months. Who will forget the television coverage of those brave young Berliners who gave their lives in attempted escapes over that deadly wall even as we watched?"

On the Vietnam disaster:

"As the leader of the free world, we faltered in our duty to lead in keeping the peace. It became especially critical after the Vietnam debacle, in which our course cost us severely in morale, determination, economic strength, and lives of thousands of valiant youths. From that point on, our neglect went on the downhill slalom. We neglected to keep the peace in Africa, allowing the Communist-led world to take several countries in an unprecedented display of international burglary. We allowed similar conduct in Latin America, where Communists took over Nicaragua and moved upon El Salvador and other countries."

Elsewhere, he writes:

"It was the longest war in American history and we lost it. At least in Germany and Korea no new ground was given up to Communist expansion. The truce Henry Kissinger signed on January 27, 1973, effectively surrendered all of Vietnam to Communist control. Immediately, the victorious Soviet-backed Vietnamese Communists stretched their power into Cambodia and Laos. Already at least three million gentle Asian people in those shattered nations have been slaughtered by the Communist forces that now threaten all of Southeast Asia.

"And, though President Ford spoke hopefully, in fact, 'America's leadership in the world' seemed damaged almost beyond repair. The nation had abandoned almost 30 million people to Communist tyranny. The Soviets had extended their sphere of influence throughout Indochina without the loss of a single soldier, sailor, or airman. Our retreat created a dangerous vacuum in leadership for the entire free world, and the Soviets moved quickly to take advantage of their opportunity. Almost unhindered, the Communists moved into Angola, Ethiopia, South Yemen, and Afghanistan. And from their base in Cuba, the Soviets increased support for terrorism and revolution throughout Central and South America."

The continued weakness becomes evident in other regions:

"The national humiliation of that one final day in Vietnam was relived in Iran on an almost daily basis as terrorists bullied and threatened their American prisoners before the television cameras. For 444 days the world watched and waited while the United States was held captive in its own embassy. That Iranian captivity symbolized a growing sense of the nation's helplessness before her enemies. America, the once mighty world power, had been defeated in Vietnam, outwitted and outmaneuvered by Soviet expansion in Africa, Asia, and Latin America, and humiliated by terrorists and fanatics around the globe."

The onward march of totalitarianism continues into our own time and our own hemisphere:

"In 1979 another dictator was replaced by a Communist-backed revolution in the Western Hemisphere. General Anastasio Somoza of Nicaragua, Latin America's most notorious strongman, was replaced by the Sandinistas, a coalition of freedom fighters that under President Daniel Ortega soon demonstrated its Marxist-Soviet sympathies. From Cuba, an island off Miami, to Nicaragua, a nation placed firmly in the heart of Central America, the Soviets are attempting to extend their sphere of influence throughout the region."

Rechanneling government efforts toward ensuring personal and national safety, therefore, makes up one part of Robertson's philosophy of the government's role. The other part concerns the area of human rights. These issues include some of the most controversial questions associated with his candidacy.

As background to understanding his view on these issues, it is worth noting some of his understanding as to how people should relate to one another. As might be expected, his view is rooted in the Bible, particularly in the teaching of Christ that "He who is greatest among you must be the servant of all."

A window into Robertson's thinking about how people should relate to one another may be found in *The Secret Kingdom,* particularly in his discussions of the "law of greatness": "Resist society's inducements to success and greatness and dare to become a servant, even childlike. True leadership and greatness will follow. The one who serves will become the leader.

"Some people want to be 'great.' They want to drive the biggest cars, employ the most servants, own the biggest houses, and have the most money. These people are not great, just self-centered. The great in our society hate people like Albert Einstein or Mother Teresa or those who, like Florence Nightingale, serve the sick, the needy, and the wounded. These are the great people, because they have given themselves to serve others."

Greatness, he writes, is "the reward of those who are humble, and the secret of greatness is service. If you reflect on it, you see that it fits well with being childlike, but it begins to rub. It goes against the grain of society. That is why we should be serious and careful on this subject. We are dealing with a law that turns everything upside down."

The concept extends beyond individuals into the social, economic, and political realm. He even believes that America's difficulty in competing with Japanese companies is traceable in part to its abandonment of the ideal of servanthood:

"Eventually deterioration in the concept of service reached a point where car manufacturers decided that fully effective quality control at the factories was too expensive. Their surveys convinced them that they would be better off to repair mistakes at the dealership level.

"So the cars came off the line with little things untended. The buyers drove them a short while and something would malfunction. When they took them back, the dealers made the repairs and sent the bill to the manufacturer. Almost inevitably something else would happen to the same car, and the process would be repeated. It was terribly inconvenient for car buyers, but it was less expensive for the manufacturer."

He contrasts these deficiencies with the situation in Japan: "There, thoughts of service penetrated deeper into the industrial consciousness. The desire grew to end shoddiness and to give customers the best products on the road. The industry would serve the people.

"Secondly, management and labor began to work at the idea of becoming servants of one another. Companies took pains to instill in their managers the thought that they were servants of the workers. 'We're here to make their jobs better, to improve their environment, to solve their problems,' they repeated. Furthermore, they became like little children and listened to their workers. 'We want to learn from you,' management said, and before long workers were each submitting eighteen or nineteen suggestions a year for improving the work process, and management was adopting at least 80 percent."

The "law of unity": "Reject the dissension and negativism of the world. Choose harmony and unity at every level of life—unity centered on the will of God. Mankind flowing in unity will accomplish marvelous results in all endeavors.

"We need only think of those businesses that have fallen on hard times because they abandoned clear-cut unity of mission in favor of diversification. A great electronics company floundered because it tried to make large computers. A chemical company ran into trouble when it tried to be a land developer. Successful organizations, as well as successful individuals, are those unified around a relatively simple statement of goals and mission."

It is in the human rights area that the role of private faith in public policy becomes the most conspicuous, in that faith has historically been the well-spring of many reform leaders throughout American history. "The abolition of slavery," he claims, "was seen as a necessarily long, slow process until the second Great Awakening." He points out that to the nineteenth-century revivalists, slavery was perceived simply as a sin and therefore something to be eradicated as a stain on the soul of society, and something that should be eradicated promptly. This thinking was later applied successfully to the cause of women's suffrage.

The point here is that private religious convictions may reflect the ethical thinking of many people who are not as spiritual in their orientation, but historically the spiritually motivated people had the greatest impact. Their commitment was more thoroughgoing and absolute.

* * *

147

How does this radical and seemingly utopian ideal of mutual respect apply to human rights questions? When is government permitted or obliged to intervene? To answer this, one might survey his views on certain current controversies: defense of the unborn and the rights of Christians and secularists in the schools.

First, one should consider his view of the judicial branch of the federal government, a view that he first formed at Yale law school and became the basis of his disillusionment with law.

"I became disillusioned with law even as I studied it. Like the universities, the legal system of this nation had forgotten its history. The courts had drifted away from their historic moorings in the Constitution. And the great directions for law and government as outlined by the Declaration of Independence had been forgotten by a legal community dedicated not to the biblical principle that all men are created equal but to a manipulative, often cynical use of the law."

The most emotional of all the questions related to judicial review is that of abortion. On the one hand, his views of the abortion issue highlight his attitude that government at the federal level has become too strong, and yet his concurrent view that, in the area of abortion, government at the state level has become too weak:

"Roe vs. *Wade,* with its legalization of abortion, is just one example of the dangerous and destructive effects of this current notion of judicial review.

"First, with no constitutional authority, the Supreme Court struck down laws against abortion in almost every state. It was an inexcusable infringement upon the rights of the people in each state to decide that complex social issue for themselves. The state legislatures had decided against indiscriminate abortion. In one blow, the Supreme Court struck down all those decisions.

"Second, in place of all those state laws, the Supreme Court created another law legalizing abortion. Seven men decided that law against the will of the majority of the American people. In every Gallup poll taken since that 1973 decision, at least 75 percent of the citizens of this nation do not agree that abortion should be allowed under all circumstances, and a solid majority would eliminate the 95 percent of abortions that are performed for social convenience.

"Third, the Supreme Court established a moral precedent regarding the definition and value of human life that disregards the universal laws revealed in nature and in the Judeo-Christian Scriptures. Most abortions are performed between seven and thirteen weeks of pregnancy. Yet by the seventh week, the unborn child has fingers, toes, eyes, lungs, a beating heart, and brain waves. Nature is clear. Abortions kill babies. And the revealed laws of God about such killings in both the Old and New Testaments are easily understood.

"Mother Teresa of Calcutta said she fears for America because the women of America are killing their own babies. She believes society is doomed when women become so heartless that they will kill their own young. Abortion is not only unthinkable, it is also the height of pagan barbarity."

Despite his interest in history, Robertson was an outstanding student of human biology at Washington and Lee and, though not an expert on that subject, has developed some very well-defined opinions on the subject of evolution. He is convinced that scientific evolution must remain at the level of theory and that it is negated by one empirical fact: there has never been one observable case of any creature shifting (or evolving) from one biological class to another or from one phylum to another. There is no case where we have remains or fossils of an animal that died during the evolutionary process. The reason is clear. The Bible says that God made each animal "after its kind" through a special act of creation for each one of them:

"I think the greatest example of this truth is the mule. The mule is a cross between a donkey and a horse. Mules are born sterile. They are unable to reproduce themselves. In other words, the horse and the donkey were close enough in the biological ladder to interbreed with each other, but their offspring could not continue the breeding process. Even that close link could not reproduce. Certainly nobody has ever bred a bird with a snake or an ape with a man. There is no reproductive evidence to support evolution."

Nothing elicits the charge of "Fundamentalist!" more quickly than the refusal of many Christians to accept the Darwinian explanation of the origins of humanity. For Robertson, however, the issue is not so much a matter of rejecting Darwin as it is of affirming the right of significant numbers of people to fend off a view of things that, in the words of CBNU president Bob Slosser, "takes God out of the equation." The issue is the mirror image of the viewpoint that Robertson would try to ram his opinions down the throats of other people; he believes that some people are ramming their opinions down the throats of those who accept the Genesis description of the creation. "In many schools across the nation," he writes, "the Genesis story of creation has been replaced by a secular view of evolution that eliminates not just the biblical view of humanity's origins, but even Darwin's own view that God used evolution in the creation of mankind.

"The state is attempting to assert control over the thought life of children. For instance, the federal government published a course called 'MACOS: Man, a Course of Study,' that attempted to indoctrinate young children into the teachings of humanism. The federal and state governments also have been at the forefront of liberal experimentations with amoral sex education. Humanist values are being taught in the schools through such methods as 'values clarification.' All of these constitute an attempt to wean children away from biblical Christianity."

Related issues, pertaining to voluntary school prayer and other expressions of religion in the public schools, remain matters of human rights in Robertson's mind—the protection of the rights of what he believes to be not a minority but the majority—and he has established the National Legal Foundation to support selected court challenges to the relevant laws. An experienced trial attorney, Robert Skolrood, heads the foundation and is frequently quoted in the press on these issues.

A decision that particularly outraged Robertson came in 1986 in Los Angeles when the school board, at the behest of the American Civil Liberties Union, decreed that the graduation ceremonies at the schools throughout the system must not include any prayers or mention of God. Robertson's reaction: "The parent who brought the suit against prayer, the ACLU lawyers who supported and defended it, the courts, the school board, the students, and the general public who remained silent were all players in a historic tragedy.

"What happened to the rights of the majority in the issue of creation? In 1982 the results of a nationwide Gallup poll on the origins of humanity were reported in *The New York Times*. Forty-four percent of all Americans polled believed in the account of creation as found in the Old Testament book of Genesis. Another 38 percent believed that God was involved in the process of evolution, while 9 percent were undecided. Only the 9 percent remaining believed in a theory of evolution having no place for God. In case after case investigated, supported, and defended by Baldwin and the ACLU, however, the opinions of the majority have been set aside and a minority opinion has taken their place. The Bill of Rights of the United States Constitution guarantees the right to freedom of speech, freedom of the press, peaceful assembly, petitioning the government, bearing arms, security against unreasonable search and seizure, and speedy and public trial by jury. But nowhere in the Constitution is the minority given a right to silence the majority or to replace majority views with its minority opinions."

Pat Robertson, in sum, has created an entire system of thought based on the Bible as he believes it applies to every aspect of contemporary life. Far more than Sunday-morning inspiration to him, the Bible "is a practical book with a system of thought and conduct that will guarantee success, true happiness, true prosperity, not the fleeting, flashy, inconsistent success the world usually settles for."

The Bible for him is far more than the "laws of the kingdom" and other spiritual principles, and it is crucial to see this point to make sense of his idea of politics. The Bible is above all a book of history, not of truths explained so much as events narrated— invested by God with eternal significance and yet occurring within time and space. Again and again on the *700 Club,* Robertson would search out those mystical connections that make the everlasting quality of Scripture relevant to the transitory occurrences of each day.

It was in this spirit that he became the leader of a demonstration involving more than half a million people from throughout the country in 1980. A neighboring minister in Tidewater had come to him to ask for support: "John Gimenez heard the prophet's ancient call and began to dream of what might happen to America if her people, too, were called to return to righteousness. He pictured a mass of people assembling in the nation's capital to pray, to confess, and to call the nation back to her spiritual roots.

"In November 1978, John shared his dream with me over lunch at a motel restaurant in Virginia Beach. I suggested April 29 as the target day for his great march on Washington. On that same day in 1607 members of the first permanent English settlement in the New World planted a cross on the beach at Cape Henry, Virginia, and dropped to their knees in the sand to ask God's blessing on this new land. What better day could there be to remember the nation's spiritual heritage and to call the people to pray that God might renew his blessings upon us?

"John's dream captured me, and together we began to tell others about our emerging plan for an April 29, 1980, mass rally and march on Washington. Bill Bright, the founder and director of Campus Crusade, joined me as co-chairman of 'Washington for Jesus,' serving with our national chairman, John Gimenez.

"Many times during that incredible day I sat on the platform watching men and women of faith from all across the nation as they prayed. They were every color, every class, every denomination imaginable. They were chief executive officers of large corporations, and they were unemployed, blue-collar workers. They were old and young, rich and poor, well-dressed and shabby. But they were one, and their prayer for the nation was one prayer. And God was hearing and would answer their prayer. April 29, 1980, was the beginning of a spiritual revolution. And I joined with the 500,000 people in the mall and the millions watching on television in praying that one day this same spiritual revolution would sweep the nation."

It is only at our peril, in Robertson's eyes, that we attempt to construct political or ethical systems that are not soaked in the spirit and sometimes the letter of Scripture: ". . . We must ask ourselves again, can we endure if we forsake the God of our fathers and strip from our national consciousness the teachings of the Holy Bible? Can we endure if we continue such profligate waste in government, the accumulation of such an unsupportable debt, and the amassing of power in the central government with the resulting loss of freedom and individual initiative by the people? Can we endure as a free nation when over 50 percent of our people receive some payment or subsidy from the federal government? Can we endure if we lose the understanding that the source of our wealth is the individual initiative of our people rather than the largesse of various government bureaucracies? Can we endure if we refuse to declare acts of our citizens either right or wrong and if we accept as part of our life-style blatant immorality, adultery, drunkenness, and drug abuse?

"Remember our ancestors kneeling in the sands of Cape Henry seeking God's guidance and strength. Remember our forefathers meeting in Philadelphia to create a Declaration of Independence on behalf of life, liberty, and the pursuit of happiness. Remember George Washington leading an army of farm boys, traders, and immigrants against the crack troops of George III to win and secure those rights for each of us. And remember President Lincoln in the bloody ruins of Gettysburg asking if a nation 'conceived in liberty and dedicated to the proposition that all men are created equal' . . . can long endure."

History is not just what has happened in the past; it is what is going on before us at this moment, and Robertson sees the tenure of President Reagan as the beginning of the nation's becoming replanted in the spiritual soil that made it great:

"Through Ronald Reagan the nation has begun its return to those spiritual and political ideals upon which it had been founded. The legislators gathered beneath the dome of the Capitol and the tens of millions watching on television or listening on radio had high hopes that during the President's second term in office he would bring that goal of national renewal another step closer to fulfillment."

History for him also includes events that are still to occur, at least if the American people are adequately aware of these views and agree with them:

"America stands at the crossroads. A moral and spiritual

153

renewal of historic proportions is under way. People across the land are crying out for leadership by statesmen and stateswomen who care about future generations instead of politicians who care only about the next election.

"Either we will return to the moral integrity and original dreams of the founders of this nation, and from that renewal to a future filled with technological advance, increasing prosperity for all our people, and a new birth of freedom on the earth that will ensure our triumphant entry into the twenty-first century, or we will give ourselves over more and more to hedonism, to all forms of destructive antisocial behavior, to political apathy, and ultimately to the forces of anarchy and disintegration that have throughout history gripped great empires and nations in their tragic and declining years.

"With the irreligion, cultural relativism, and militant human-ism deeply entrenched in our nation's schools and universities, with the incredible strains on our nation's families produced by the Great Depression, a world war, a population explosion, and two smaller wars, with the pervasive influence of motion pictures, television programming, and periodicals that continually hammer at our long-established moral values, it is not difficult to under-stand what has happened to our culture. In truth, unless there is a profound religious revival to bring us back to our roots, the long-range future of our democratic institutions is clearly in doubt."

Just as the nation has a history, so does each individual, and in some persons the two are intertwined in a very obvious way. He believes himself to be one of those persons, and this synopsis of his thinking concludes with some of his own reflections on that history:

"My mother, Gladys Churchill Robertson, was typical of many keeping alive her own family's history. She was an heir to the heritage and traditions of the great English family that produced Sir Winston Churchill and generations of honorable, hardwork-ing Britons and Americans. Carefully she uncovered the roots of her family and of my father's forebears, the Robertsons and the Harrisons. Through the Jamestown Society we traced eleven gen-erations directly to the first permanent English settlement at

Jamestown; to Benjamin Harrison, a signer of the Declaration of Independence; to Captain A. Robertson, one of the officers in the Revolutionary War; and through the Harrison line to two American Presidents. My mother took great delight in our heritage deep in Virginia's colonial history, and she insisted that our family take seriously the responsibilities endowed to us by that heritage.

"It was after returning to civilian life that I entered Yale law school, determined to be a lawyer and eventually a statesman like my father. But at Yale my questions about the meaning and purpose of life remained unanswered. In my classes I began to experience personally what happens when history is rewritten and the spiritual dimension of man is ridiculed, caricatured, or ignored entirely. That great university, founded by ten Congregational clergymen 'to plant and propagate in this Wilderness, the blessed Reformed, Protestant Religion, in the purity of its Order, and Worship' had moved away from its original Christian charter and had virtually written God out of its curriculum. The academic standards were rigorous and admirable, but the real questions of life and death were seldom answered there.

"During law school I worked one summer as staff investigator for the Senate Appropriations Committee, of which my father was a member. When the committee sessions were over he and I would sit in his office sipping glasses of bourbon and branch water, discussing the issues troubling Congress and the nation. America's political system, like its universities and courts, seemed to be drifting, without any real direction. I found myself more and more discontented with becoming a lawyer or a politician and more and more determined to find answers to the questions that haunted me."

It's been said that we live a cut-flower civilization, that the material manifestations of our lives are pleasant to look upon but that, like cut flowers thriving for a day in a glass of water, our lives are threatened by the separation from our roots. Robertson is returning to his own roots as an individual and urges the country to do the same.

CHAPTER EIGHT

Beyond
Church Walls

During the late seventies Robertson sensed that he was being called to establish an educational institution. "It's possible when people get a little bit older that they begin to think about the next generation," he says. "When a person is just starting, survival is all that matters. The second phase is growth and all that matters is to fulfill the destiny of the thing at hand. Then there is a time to begin considering the next generation and wonder how we can pass on something of value to someone else."

Like most people, he had no idea how to establish a university, but unlike most people, he refused to dismiss the idea from his mind. Among the people he consulted was Dr. David Clark, a young communications professor and marketing consultant from Bowling Green University in Ohio. Clark recalls telling him, "Look, I don't think you really want to attempt this. There are a lot of real problems in higher education. It's a very expensive proposition. You have to go before state boards continually, you have to seek funds from other sources continually. You'd better look at this carefully."

Clark recalls that Robertson didn't respond directly to that observation and instead asked, "Tell me, what is left of the great leaders of this country from the past? What still remains, for example, from the ministry of D. L. Moody? The most important thing that anyone can do in life is set up an institution that will live after them."

"That is true," says Clark. "Long after Pat Robertson is gone, this university will be training young people. And it will be doing that with a Christian perspective." Clark mentioned that the charter of Harvard was the first of many to establish an institution where young men would be trainined for Christian service and ministry and secondarily as a school from which they could go out into the world and pursue a profession.

Clark recalls having lunch with a friend, Bob Jones, who is the mayor of Virginia Beach and practices law there. "The discussion came around to the question of where people should apply their efforts. Robertson said, 'We might consider what the most important social institutions are, the ones that make the biggest impact. I could mention four areas—religion, government, education, and business.' At that point he spoke about training people in those areas and thereby having an impact on society. 'If you look at those institutions in society, you can gain leverage. It's like the concept of controlling a company by owning a certain small percentage of stock or buying a company by borrowing a relatively small amount of money. In like manner, if we can influence those few institutions, then we can have an enormous impact on public attitudes and mores.' He's a global thinker and he likes to surround himself with people who are global thinkers. He doesn't want to listen to a lot of unrelated facts that have no bearing on the big picture."

Robertson says, "I didn't quite know for a year or two what kind of school it would be until I had a chance to write up the articles of incorporation and the mission statement of what we were going to do. I had no desire to get into education. It's very expensive and a tremendous burden, but it has been enormously blessed."

From the first, CBN University was not established with the vague goal of merely educating youth, laudable though that goal may be. The goal was gradually to infiltrate secular society with committed Christians who were at least as well prepared as their uncommitted colleagues and thereby to permeate the social fabric with biblical values.

The discussions regarding the type of university to be created explored a wide range of possibilities. Clark recalls, "The first concept of CBN was the idea of a senior college—just the junior and senior year. But then we thought we had to begin with freshman year, but there were problems with creating a whole new undergraduate school. The expenses were tremendous and there were quite a few Christian colleges already. But then he went on a trip to Kansas City and out there really had a sense that his destiny was to build a series of graduate schools. This was a unique idea. There were already a number of free-standing schools of medicine and theology, but not a whole university of graduate schools. This was to be a first."

Robertson wanted mature students who already had a vision for their lives. "What I wanted," he says "was older students who were already pretty much set in their life's pattern and who wanted to get the training needed to focus on a major career goal. I didn't want a bunch of kids who were still trying to have big parties and grope around in life in more than one way."

Bob G. Slosser, author and former assistant national editor at *The New York Times* and now president of the university, comments that CBNU will help reverse the academic trend toward removing faith from the educational process. Slosser believes that the original intention of separating religious conviction from academic pursuits was to make religion neutral, but the result has been to create a hostility toward religion in academia and in society in general. The educational process is seen as the ultimate cause—and hence the ultimate remedy—for this hostility.

"It was education that caused business, media, and law to abandon the Judeo-Christian values," Slosser says. "Charles Norton Eliot at Harvard began this process at the turn of the century, trying to take religion out of the scholastic life of the country. We've taken God out of the equation, removing from consideration the Lord, who understands what it's all about. Pat Robertson saw education, therefore, as more fundamental than broadcasting. He believes that the university will be seen as the most important thing he has ever done because it will affect broadcasting and other aspects of society."

The task of establishing the university was one that Robertson largely delegated to Clark and a close circle of others with academic experience. "It really was an audacious plan, but it never occurred to us that we'd fail," Clark says. "Pat had a clear idea and he left us alone to get the university begun and accredited. Pat had the vision and he expected it to be carried out right. He's like that. If he has a mandate, he's going to get it done one way or another."

The reactions from educators ranged from incredulity pure and simple to incredulity mixed with amusement. When Clark and fellow CBN administrator David Geyertson visited the state Council on Higher Education, the state administrator said, "You're going to do *what?*" Says Clark, "It was funny when you really think about it. A couple of guys in their early thirties—working out of office space that we rented—and here we were telling them that we were starting a university! But eventually they became supportive and very rapidly we had full accreditation."

The early days of establishing a new university had an *Alice in Wonderland* quality about them, with the original administrators wondering why they would leave conventional academic situations to embark on this kind of adventure. They hired faculty with no certainty that their salaries would be paid.

Clark had a prosperous consulting business going on in addition to a tenured position in communications at Bowling Green State University in Ohio. "We had no buildings, no library, nothing. All we had were students who were coming and we were interviewing faculty members. We had leased some office space on Virginia Beach Boulevard.

"Some of the faculty were leaving tenured positions, and we were just hoping that this was all for real. We rented a building in Chesapeake and established a library, although the standing joke was that our library was closed because three students had checked out all three books. Now we have one of the finest communications libraries in the country, especially in radio, television, and film, since we hired one of the really well-known communications scholars in the country, Chris Sterling."

In 1977, Robertson drew up the corporate charter and officially opened classes for the CBN University. It was the first and is still the only free-standing set of graduate schools in America.

A crucial test was faced by the university staff when the infant university uttered its first demand: a library. Without a library, accreditation was impossible, studying was difficult, and the future growth of the school would be sharply curtailed. The university's board debated about whether to build a small library with classrooms or a large library with a lot of classroom space. The decision was made to build a library with classrooms that could gradually be squeezed out as more library space was needed.

The newly formed board of regents, however, was riddled with uncertainty and dissension about building a major library. Recalls one board member, "I remember a meeting here during the summer when money was tight. We had been planning to build the library but there were a lot of folks saying we couldn't afford to do it. Pat came in and said, 'We've got to build a library. The university's future depends on it. If you don't agree, do two things. First, be quiet and don't spread your disagreement. Second, don't give a nickel to the library. If God wants it built, He will build it.' Pat honestly believes that if God is in something, the money will be there. He doesn't demand things from God, but he dreams big things for God."

As Robertson recalls, "It was a united effort and it was the kind of unity we needed within. It was only after the board put their affirmative stamp on it that I began to raise the funds. I think that to run ahead of the governing group is a mistake. I don't ever try to run over people. I try to have their concurrence. But I had an urgent feeling about the library. If we hadn't done it, the university would have died."

In the face of opposition by the board and others, the library was completed in 1981 at a cost of over $13 million. By the time it was furnished everyone who had contributed saw that Robertson's risk had been carefully calculated. "Some people were very generous and some weren't all that generous, but it was a question of committing ourselves to do this," says Robertson.

Some were counseling him to go borrow money, Robertson

recalls. "But I just didn't feel that was the wise way to go. It's easy to get a loan in the beginning, but it is hard to pay it off in the end. Not only do you pay a lot of principal, but you pay huge amounts of interest that can amount to two or three times the principal."

The library was built debt-free. "The money wasn't there when we began," says Clark, "but God provided. We learned that in God's economy there is limitless wealth. If I sat down and tried to plan a way to supply the money, I couldn't do it. But man's extremity is God's opportunity. If you're going to do something for God, do something so big that God has to intervene. Just be sure that God is in it. If the money isn't there, it probably wasn't God's will, just man's invention."

Says Lee Buck, a board member, "When the university signed the contract to spend $13 million to build a new library and the money did not materialize, Robertson remained absolutely unflappable. 'When the time comes,' he said, 'the money will be there.' He was not shaken by the apparent recession that hit the ministry, nor did he push a panic button. In the end, he was right. The money was there."

Like the library, the university overall was built from out of the ministry's cash flow, without support from stock or loans. "I don't want to knock bankers," Robertson said, "but huge buildings for organizations that depend on contributions are not too attractive to banks."

The state of Virginia very quickly gave CBN the approval for the school and after only a few years of existence the school was formally accredited by the Southern Association of Colleges and Graduate Schools. "It was an extraordinary thing," recalls Robertson, "because they were not familiar with any other school that was organized quite the way CBN is.

"We believe in integrating all the disciplines. There are Scriptures that pertain to every aspect of your life. If you take the profession of journalism, for example, when it is built according to biblical principle, it differs in important ways from the usual model of journalistic behavior."

Today CBN University's budget is over $10 million a year. There are few universities more prominent.

CBN University's School of Communication is a graduate program emphasizing professionalism in television production. "We don't 'play' television here, we produce the real thing," says Dr. Robert Schihl. The school, only nine years old, began a doctoral program in communication during the fall term of 1987—the first Ph.D. program for the university. Students in the School of Communication may concentrate their course work in areas such as radio, television, drama, film, public relations and advertising, media management, and journalism and communication studies. Television majors, for example, use state-of-the-art facilities—including CBN Cable News Network equipment—to produce *Newsight*, a weekly summary of religious news aired nationwide via CBN Cable, as well as spots for local stations and music videos for Word Records. Radio majors may audition for WXRI-FM, the CBN radio station in Norfolk, Virginia.

As chancellor of CBN University, Robertson has assembled an accomplished and dedicated faculty who bring not only years of valuable experience to their students but also distinction to the university within the broader academic community. For example:

In 1984, Robert Combs, then an associate professor of photojournalism at CBN University, was presented the Photographer of the Year Award by the Council for the Advancement and Support of Education, a national association comprising most major colleges and universities in the United States. Professor Combs earned the award for his photography in CBN University publications.

Speaking at the eighth graduation ceremonies of CBN University in May 1987, David Aikman, foreign correspondent for *Time* magazine, stressed the need for Christian excellence in the professional world. Aikman's address wasn't falling on "deaf ears":

A CBN University film, *Bird in a Cage,* won the student Oscar given by the Academy of Motion Picture Arts and Sciences in 1987 for best dramatic film of the year. The hour-long drama was written and directed by Antonio Zarro, a CBN University student.

Robertson's educational initiatives, in addition to being at the level of graduate education, are also at the opposite end of the spectrum—literacy. Responding to questions at a forum held at Yale in 1987, he voiced his alarm concerning this important contributor to America's industrial decline:

"We have 27 million functional illiterates in America. You might not know that 73 percent of all the kids in New York's public schools read below their grade level. So whatever they're reading is gibberish to them. And they have a 43 percent dropout rate, and so only, say, 60 percent of the people actually finish high school in New York City. This ties in with crime. Sixty percent of all the people in the prisons are functionally illiterate. So they have no hope, and because they have no hope, they will either commit crimes or become welfare cases, and in either case, it doesn't do the society any justice."

On June 17, 1985, he and his co-host at CBN, Ben Kinchlow, appeared in Watts, a black section of Los Angeles, to commence a massive new literacy-through-phonics program, called Heads Up, by introducing the program to local pastors. Also targeted for the program during the ensuing weeks were New York, Houston, Chicago, and Detroit. The centerpiece of each meeting was the pastors' presentation, and in each city Heads Up was hosted by local churches, with local pastors, educators, and interested members of the public also attending. The program has been particularly well received in black areas, such as those in Detroit, where Mayor Coleman Young presented Robertson with a key to the city.

To its advocates learning to read through phonics has become a cause worthy of passionate efforts. They claim that the "look-say" method, which replaced phonics in the thirties and now predominates, results in the high levels of illiteracy the country is currently experiencing and that only a return to pure phonics will reverse that trend.

The program used by Heads Up, called Sing, Spell, Read and Write, attempts to make the process entertaining as well as fruitful. "Children love it," says one education researcher, "and what they love, they pay attention to, and what they pay attention to, they learn." Devised by a New Jersey grade school teacher named Sue Dickson, it was brought to the attention of CBN University by Bob Sweet of the White House Office of Policy

Development. Through Sweet's efforts the program has won the support of President Reagan, who wrote Robertson that the program deserved the "closest cooperation from government and the private sector, community service organizations and individual members of the public." Reagan added, "I am confident that Sing, Spell, Read and Write can significantly reduce illiteracy and thus enrich many thousands of lives."

Despite such commendations at high levels, most of the support for the program has come from individual teachers rather than school systems as a whole. CBN offers literacy workshops that had been open to the public, and individual teachers have sometimes taken it upon themselves to drum up support. "I want you to know," a Virginia teacher told Robertson, "that I called thirty-one people to come hear this."

Specialists in teaching immigrant children to read and speak English have been particularly enthusiastic, as have teachers of children who are aphasic or autistic. According to one researcher, it works even with teachers who are simply bad: "One of the primary advantages of Sing, Spell, Read and Write in comparison to other phonics programs is that it is virtually teacher-proof. It can be taught with very little preparation and even by those with little education background."

The program has also taken hold in a number of school districts. At the Selma Unified School District in California, it was instituted as a pilot program in several schools, at a cost of about $350 per classroom, with striking results. For example, even though half the first-grade students in one school using the program had little or no speaking knowledge of English, 83 percent of them rose above the fiftieth percentile ranking on the California Achievement Test for reading.

Linked in Robertson's mind with general literacy is the issue of what he calls "biblical literacy." He feels that the moral and spiritual tone of society would be enhanced dramatically by the simple awareness of what that one book contains and that otherwise educated people are disturbingly ignorant of it. To combat this trend he initiated the publication of *The Book,* a modern-language Bible with a new cover and "user-friendly" reading features that would sell in department stores and other retail outlets. *The Book* has been a runaway best-seller in the United States and several other countries, including Japan. Other materials for children, including videotapes known as "Superbook," have also been major revenue producers for CBN.

With all of his economic and social programs that feed, clothe, and educate all of the disadvantaged, Robertson appears to apply the same moral imperative as a liberal New Dealer. The distinct difference lies in his view of the sources of funding, which he believes should be local. He believes that government should never be more than merely a framework and a means of protection for the family and local religious organizations such as the church or synagogue.

While Robertson was still struggling to raise the funds for the library, he recognized a direct challenge out of Isaiah 58.

"I had never read Isaiah 58 the way I read it that day, and I realized that feeding the poor and clothing the needy and taking care of the homeless was not something in the Old Testament, it was a clear command to everybody—reaching out in compassion to those less fortunate is something that will please the Lord."

Robertson took his initiative from Scripture and announced a new program on the air. "Look," he told the television audience, "we want to find everyone in this audience who has a need and then find those who have ability and we'll match the needs with the abilities and call it Operation Blessing because it will be a blessing for everyone."

So in 1978, Operation Blessing was born. Since that time over 26 million people have been fed, clothed, housed, or otherwise assisted. Operation Blessing's efforts result each year in contributions of about $50 million, some of which flows through CBN itself but most of which comes from local churches who are made aware of the need by CBN.

One project of Operation Blessing is the planting of one million trees in Kenya. On a visit to the arid Sahara, Robertson said of one of the major problems of the people, the desert, "Maybe if we could get trees planted, we could restore the topsoil. After all, years ago there were trees all the way up to the Mediterranean. The desert was formed because people cut the trees down, the topsoil went, and all that was left was hot, burning sand."

So Robertson and others began planting trees. They contacted a European who had also worked in the tree-planting effort and had a beautiful oasis with jungle creatures. Now there are 350,-000 trees in the ground and 450,000 in a nursery waiting to be planted. The trees will change the ecology of the land and bring moisture back. Moisture—and trees—will bring life back to the Sahara.

Operation Blessing has participated in other work in that region. Robertson and television crews carried over $3.5 million in medicine to Sudan during the drought. Robertson worked in the refugee camps in Guatemala. He has traveled to refugee camps in Honduras and resettlement camps in El Salvador, bringing food, medicine, or simple toys for children—all as a part of Operation Blessing.

His travels to hurting and oppressed people have not always taken him out of the United States. Robertson has seen the faces of despair and pain in Watts, the South Side of Chicago, the Inner City of Detroit, Philadelphia, and in the poor sections of Birmingham.

Operation Blessing is designed to help people, not produce overhead or bureaucracy. Unlike government programs, less than 1 percent of the contributions to Operation Blessing go toward operating costs. The cost of his Sing, Spell, Read and Write program, which has taught over 123,000 people to read and write, is $8.00 per person. A similar government program would cost over $400 per person, says Robertson. "We use volunteers and people who love these kids without taking any salary. Volunteers would work in a government situation if they would just do it the way we do. I think that the government can work with partnership if the church is a private, nonprofit group. The churches can give spiritual hope and the feeling of family that no government agency could ever give. The government is always known as 'the man' and most people who need help either take the help for granted or resent it. But private help is given where needed and without restriction, and with a lot more help. We don't try to get someone's life history to give them a bag of beans. They get the beans, and that's it."

Ben Kinchlow, now an executive vice president at CBN, recalls that his first experiences working for Robertson weren't always comfortable. "I think everybody, when they first meet him, is a little afraid of him because of his ability and the obvious call of God on his life," says Kinchlow. "I was kind of walking on eggshells when I first joined the staff, but at our first telethon in California, at the conclusion of the meeting, he called all of us together at a Howard Johnson's motel and said, 'I just want to tell all of you how much I appreciate all you've done.' He said how much he loved and appreciated us, so, being emboldened by what had happened, I went up and said, 'I've got to tell you, I'm afraid of you.' He just said, 'Brother, don't be afraid of me, let's pray.' So we prayed together and he threw a big bear hug around me.

"Pat's always been concerned about people. There are things he would do that he didn't want to talk about, but one day at home he was reading Isaiah 58 and he called us together and said, 'Ben, I've got something for you today.' I said, 'Wonderful, what is it?'

"He said, 'Take the provisions of Isaiah 58 and start helping people. CBN will put some money in the pot, so go do it.' So we went out and came up with a name for the program—Operation Blessing—and it has now become one of the most important things we do at CBN.

"Pat believes in the dignity, the value, and the worth of every individual. One of his favorite sayings is 'Sin is forgivable, but stupid is forever.' He always believes that an individual has the God-given responsibility to utilize and maximize the talents that God has given him. He recognizes that there is a natural progression in maturity that people who have been given opportunities, responsibilities, and resources have as their responsibility, the right to help those people who have not been given the necessary resources.

"So in Operation Blessing, if we know a dentist we try to get him to share his skills with people who perhaps cannot afford them. That doesn't mean the dentist is to become poverty-stricken, but simply that he takes a portion of his time to help those people who cannot help themselves. At the same time, it is the responsibility of those who receive help to look around and see what they can do to help someone else. Perhaps they don't have money, but they could clean house for a shut-in, baby-sit, or something. It's a concept of people who have something—any-thing—helping those who do not have something."

Apart from Pat Robertson himself, Kinchlow is the most signifi-cant face on television and the *700 Club*. As recounted in his book called *Plain Bread*, Kinchlow is a classic story of a man who sought everything that the world had to offer by way of pleasure, ex-perienced much of its depravity and degradation, and then finally converted to Christianity.

He married and had children, but the marriage soon broke up; he began seething with hatred against people in general, and against whites in particular.

After thirteen years in the Air Force, he earned a business degree and became a salesman and a driver of test cars. Upon his conversion, he became an ordained minister in the African Meth-odist Episcopal Church and opened a ministry to teenage runa-ways before moving to a farm for drug addicts in nearby Kileen, Texas.

"My job is not to communicate to blacks or whites but to people that in Christ there is hope for peace, worth, dignity. Once I found acceptance, approval, equality in Christ, I became a full-orbed person, capable of thinking in broader terms than simply the black or white community, broader than just thinking as a male or an American."

The big change came for Kinchlow while he was driving a test car around the track and an old spiritual, "My Heavenly Father Watches Over Me," kept pressing in on his mind. It reminded him of key moments in his life when he felt the message of that title had some point: one, when he was spared in an automobile accident that killed another man; once during his Air Force stint, when he set out to kill another man himself and an odd set of

circumstances prevented it, and third, when someone set
kill him and failed. As many Christians before him, Kir
asked God if he really existed and he sensed with a simpl
certainty that God really did exist. Important confirmatior
later when he involved himself with the healing ministry
farm. "I watched God take addicts off drugs with no witl
symptoms. That's not humanly possible. It's not even wi
realm of the possible, but I saw it."

Kinchlow's rise to become one of Robertson's close
dants was meteoric—in fact, almost immediate after t
encounter. In late 1976, while he had been running th
Texas as a halfway house for recovering drug abusers
supporting himself and family at the facility, known as
Farms, by earning $100 a month as a bus driver and
teacher in the local schools.

One day he received a telephone call from the Dal
that carried the *700 Club,* inviting him to appear. I
happened to be in Dallas, so he personally interviewed
who shared his experiences at the farm with the view

Kinchlow assumed at this point that his association wi
son was over, but he soon received another call, this
CBN headquarters in Virginia. He was asked if he
available to be flown to Portsmouth to "help out wi
Club" the following week. He assumed they needed
to help with the telephone calls coming into the sho

On arriving, Kinchlow found a place off camer
telephones, a few minutes before airtime. "The sta
looked my way. 'Sir, please take your place,' he said.
then gravitated to the stage and sat in the guest's ch
that the planned show would be a retake of his D
ance.

"Sir, we're ready to start the show," the stage
peated. "Please take your place."

Kinchlow answered, "Well, exactly where am I
be?"

"You mean—nobody told you?"

"Told me what?"

"Pat's in Israel. You're the host!"

He says, "Before I had time to get scared, I was saying, 'Welcome to the *700 Club.*'"

When Ben Kinchlow joined the *700 Club* he was not only a guest host, he was also a chauffeur who would pick up guests for the show at the airport, check them into their hotel rooms, meet them for lunch, and then interview them on the show.

The camera crew was always short-handed, he recalls. "When we had only two cameras, one for the guest and one for the host," he recalls, "once I was looking at the host camera and I noticed that it began to rise slowly in the air. I glanced at the monitor and saw that my head was slowly sinking toward the bottom of the screen. The guy who manned the camera had fainted, and it took some time before the director caught the camera. What could I do? We just kept on going."

At the time of Kinchlow's arrival the show was much simpler. "We would have long, long interviews, sometimes twenty-eight minutes, and sometimes we would just sit and read prayer requests about bunions, callouses, cancer, etc. We had music by people who really didn't sing all that well, but 'they really loved the Lord.' We talked about things that interested only a narrow group of people, people of the charismatic or pentecostal persuasion.

"But Pat's goal was to make it a program to show what God was doing today," continues Kinchlow. "In the late seventies the show moved up in sophistication and experimented with new ideas. Once we even copied the *Tonight Show*—Pat even came out and did a monologue. That lasted for about three shows. But we tightened up interviews and started sending camera crews out to talk to people. We cut back on music somewhat and our sets became a little more sophisticated. We also added dramatizations of testimonies, minor recreations, and Pat felt strongly that we needed to move into the area of pressing issues that were significant for all of America. We began to address significant issues outside the realm of Christian television—the economy, world news and how it related to prophecy.

"Pat saw that we had to fish or cut bait. We had to either stay

as a Christian talk show that appealed to a small group of people or we were going to have to take a bold stand and address the issues that are important to a majority of people in America. That's when Pat got together with a group of people and we went off on a retreat and prayed and did some studies to find out what people were really interested in and"—he snaps his fingers—"the concept of journalism with a different spirit was then introduced. We began to specifically address the economy, politics, and international areas, and we started to develop a news organization."

He believes that the private sector should be more involved in social service. "If we had five hundred Operation Blessings in this country, we wouldn't need a welfare program." He thinks the government is too big and ought to get out of some of these activities, but that the private sector must get involved first.

"Pat will speak to God in his prayers: 'Lord we've continued to practice Isaiah 58 about feeding the poor and you know our hearts and I believe that you're going to take care of this. This is all we can do.' It's the principle of reciprocity again."

"It surprised many that Robertson took a black man like Kinchlow on as a co-equal as a host and also on the business side," says Bob Slosser. "He recognized talent in Kinchlow right away and he recognized him as a spiritual brother, too, and he did it because of Kinchlow's obvious talent. Pat has an instinct for these things. Kinchlow was the first black man on national television in a role like that."

"Pat, being Scottish, is very tight with a dollar," Kinchlow says. "He always wants a dollar and eighty-nine cents' worth for every dollar he spends. When Operation Blessing was started, we both wanted to help the poor, but neither of us wanted to simply pour money out the window.

" 'How can we magnify our results?' we wondered. We came up with the idea of matching—not hatching, matching, and dispatching—but if a church needed $100, we'd hold up $50 and ask them to put up $50.

"One lady in Spearfish, North Dakota, heard on the *700 Club* about the unemployed auto workers in Detroit. She went to her farming neighbors, who agreed to donate wheat. She called Operation Blessing, they contacted a railway that agreed to ship it, and then we contacted Pillsbury, who agreed to grind the raw wheat and bake it into bread. So thanks to a woman and the folks at Operation Blessing who put everything together, the auto workers in Detroit had bread.

"One thing I've always appreciated about Pat is that he feels the most practical thing in existence is the Kingdom of God, which will manifest itself in real ways. You can't sit in a beautiful building like the one here at CBN where right up the street people are still using wood stoves for heat. Once we had a severe snowstorm and the very next day Pat was concerned about those people on our street not having wood to burn. He sent people from Operation Blessing to make sure those people had wood.

"He's a very liberal individual when it comes to helping others, but he has a very conservative sense of fiscal responsibility. 'Don't waste my dollar,' he'd say, 'but give it to the person who needs some wood.' "

Operation Blessing has distributed about $50 million in aid working through almost 15,000 churches at the local level. The central principle of Operation Blessing is to leverage financial support and commitment at the local level rather than to create an aid bureaucracy from any one point. Of the approximately $50 million, about 60 percent of that figure has come from matching gifts plus in-kind services and products, whereas the remainder has come directly from financial contributions by CBN itself.

The Crisis Counseling Segment probably goes closer to the heart of the entire CBN network than any other single element because it embodies that quality of interaction that made CBN successful as a broadcast program in the first place. It also embodies that element of participation and commitment that no other element of CBN can emulate. More than 100,000 calls pour into the center every week, with about 20 percent of those referring to family problems. Last year 14,000 people were rescued from suicide through this particular form of outreach.

Terry Heaton, the show's producer, notes that people with incredible testimonies often stir Robertson deeply. "He was always blown away by Soviet defectors or people who could tell him incredible pieces of information unavailable anywhere else. People who had life-after-death experiences, people from behind the Iron Curtain, stories of struggles with persecuted Christians in the Third World really touched him. He really cares about hungry, hurting, homeless people.

"In 1985 we did a story on the homeless and after the show we gathered silently in Pat's dressing room. He said something about how most conservatives don't even acknowledge the problem or just don't care."

Tim Robertson remembers telling his father perhaps he'd fare better as a Democrat than a Republican candidate. " 'The thing you've got that appeals to people is an extraordinary heart for people and the need and desire to care for human need wherever you find it,' " Tim told his father. " 'You may hold to capitalism as a system for human economics, but you have such a strong belief in individual responsibility to care for those less fortunate than yourself.'

"But from a foreign-policy and fiscal standpoint he is a strong conservative," says Tim. "But when you talk about the poor and suffering, his heart is so full of compassion for these people, it's an entirely different thing."

"Pat is not one to walk around on cloud nine all the time," says Kinchlow. "I feel comfortable here—there are no people who are so heavenly minded that they are no earthly good. Decisions made here are predicated on sound business principles rooted firmly in unwavering faith in a real and present God. When a decision to build something is made, the cash flow, current excess of revenues, costs, future projections—everything is examined and we try to do as much as possible on a pay-as-we-go basis. Pat is not one of those people who has a wild vision to go to a mountain without knowing how we are going to get there. He always has a clear idea of where the pieces will fit to get the job done, yet there is enough challenge involved that there is never a sense of complacency."

"Operation Blessing reflects a lot of what Pat feels," according to CBNU President Bob Slosser. "He doesn't fawn over people to show that he's a compassionate man. I remember going to Bogotá and the street kids, and I'd watch his eyes as he talked to these kids, and he was overcome by the sadness of that whole situation. One doesn't see Pat ever faking compassion.

"On the board of directors, someone might say, 'We're tight on such-and-such, so why don't we cut Operation Blessing.' But Pat will say absolutely no. 'We're where we are because we give.'"

CHAPTER NINE

The Body Politic

"**E**ach generation has someone it loves to hate," says a Republican party official in Maryland. "Blacks, Jews, Catholics, Eastern Europeans, and any number of other minorities. Toward each, bigotry was at one time in vogue.

"I guess it was inevitable," says the official. "As long as fundamentalists stayed 'nice' Christians who knew their place, everything was fine. But once we started leaving the pews and walking the precincts, all hell broke loose—if you'll pardon the expression. It is now fashionable to ridicule our beliefs. If we run for office or speak out on the issues of the day, our religion becomes the issue."

This is one of the chief problems facing Pat Robertson as he embarks on a new political effort. In an effort to foil these negative expectations, he has taken the major step of resigning his ordination in the Southern Baptist Church. He also resigned his leadership of the Christian Broadcasting Network, and according to his son, Tim, will not resume his role there whatever happens during the 1988 election year.

But Robertson's attempts to undermine what some appear to think is a politically "second-class" status for conservative Christians are much more positive than merely resigning ordinations

Instead, he has sought to make his political judgments widely known. He wants them to be judged on their own merits. Thus he has taken public stands on a variety of important and controversial issues.

Much of Pat Robertson's political outlook comes from his perception of this "second-class" status in regard to conservative Christians' social and political views. Those in the media, he feels, believe that the Christian viewpoint is not as important as anyone else's.

"The humanistic point of view is that everything has to have balance," says Robertson. "If the President makes a speech, then some leader of a cult of fifty members has to be given equal time to attack the President. . . . We give equal time to the devil."

Someone Robertson has always admired is the late Christian philosopher Francis Schaeffer. It was he who described the 1960s–1980s as the "post-Christian society," meaning that the prevalent world view was humanistic rather than Judeo-Christian. Among the many works authored by Schaeffer is *A Christian Manifesto*, an essay on Christian attitudes and apologetics, the application of Christian ethics toward government, and various civil and social issues.

Robertson respects Schaeffer as a contrast to many of the bad stereotypes associated with Christians, such as emotionalism and a general idea that they are living in the past. Schaeffer has been considered by many outside Christian circles to be one of the great philosophers of his time.

One of the reasons why he and other Christian thinkers are not better known, Robertson feels, is the mainstream media treatment of Christians. It has been an important factor in motivating him politically. Robertson fumes at the denigration suffered by Christians who try to be taken seriously, either in the realm of politics or philosophy, only to be told, either by insult or omission, that theirs is not a credible view.

Speaking of the media treatment of Schaeffer, Robertson says, "There's no question about it. They know very well if they can identify somebody as a 'right-wing fundamentalist,' they have effectively neutralized his intelligence and what he says. A case in point," he continues, "*Newsweek*, in its capsule pages at the

beginning of the magazine, describes Francis Schaeffer as a 'fundamentalist propagandist,' or words to that effect. Francis Schaeffer was a profound philosopher," says Robertson. "But the minute they identified him as a 'fundamentalist' they had automatically trivialized him and rendered him impotent.

"They do it deliberately," says Robertson, "there's no question about it. If they had said 'moderate thinker' or 'profound intellectual,' they would have given him status. Instead, by calling him 'a fundamentalist,' they took that away from him." Indeed, Schaeffer's 1977 best-seller, *How Shall We Then Live,* was never even reviewed by *The New York Times.* A $16,000 full-page ad in the *Times,* paid for by Schaeffer and his publisher, asked why.

Journalist Cal Thomas, a contemporary of Pat Robertson, has reported that the "so-called best-seller lists of *Time, Newsweek, New York Times,* and *Washington Post* and others are nearly inpenetrable mysteries."

Thomas has likened big media's attitude toward Christians in the arts and literary world to the exclusion of blacks from major-league baseball in the 1930s and 1940s. The Christian market is treated as the 'Negro League' of publishing," says Thomas, "in that Christian books, or merely books by or about Christians, are considered 'specialty' publications." Robertson is concerned that not only do the powers-that-be in a liberal secular world effectively treat Christians in a derogatory manner, they freely admit doing so.

In 1982, Schaeffer's *A Christian Manifesto,* one of Pat Robertson's favorites, sold twice as many copies as one of Jane Fonda's exercise books, yet the Fonda book appeared in May of that year as number one on *The New York Times* best-seller list; remarkably, *Here Comes Garfield,* about the cartoon cat, appeared on the same list, while Schaeffer's book was absent. This demoralization of one of his heroes helped to forge some of the activist edge to Robertson.

Says Thomas about *A Christian Manifesto,* "A serious book about civil disobedience on the basis of religious principle is a 'specialty' item and *Here Comes Garfield* is not?"

Thomas relates a similar story about one of Pat Robertson's best-sellers, *The Secret Kingdom:* "A rare breakthrough in the best-seller-list fortress occurred as the result of a battering ram by the name of Sam Moore." Moore was president of Robertson's publisher, Nelson Publishers of Nashville. "Moore raised a huge stink with *Time* magazine, which then took a look at the large sales of one of the company's books, *The Secret Kingdom,* by Pat Robertson. As a result of Moore's persistence," says Thomas, *"Time* put Robertson's book on its best-seller list in one of its February issues. It was an honest-to-goodness best-seller, but that usually is not enough to make one of these lists." *Time* has since abandoned best-seller lists.

Some have suggested that the idea of Christians in the public arena is a cause for discontent in the church-going ranks. Robertson, instead, sees the mistreatment as a unifying force, in spite of what appears to be infighting. He says, "I think the statement that the 'religious right' or the evangelical movement is factionalized is simply wishful thinking on the part of those who would like to see us go back into our churches and be quiet."

Robertson's seemingly easy political recruitment and mobilization reflect a growing discontent among committed Christians, many of whom are tired of the bad stereotypes and exclusionary, patronizing treatment. Many of them see it as a form of persecution. Robertson saves his Christian political apologetics to America's historic heritage rather than the current issues of agenda of the New Right.

He, and people like him, he reasons, are not trying to make America a religious nation. Instead, it has been that religious nation all along. Like the restoration of the decrepit Mount Vernon church, and one of his favorite biblical stories, that of Nehemiah restoring a crumbling, weed-filled Jerusalem, Robertson's main vision is that toward America.

At one time, he insists, just about everyone had close to the same values as Pat Robertson. And America was a better place because of it. Significantly, the concept of the separation of church and state is grossly misunderstood, and miserably applied, according to Robertson. "I'm a student of history, and I go back to the roots of this nation," he says. "I live here in sort of the cradle of American democracy in this part of Virginia. And in those days the leaders of our country were profoundly religious people.

George Washington, John Adams, Madison. These men were deeply spiritual people."

Robertson will admit that early America was not entirely populated with committed Christians. The same generation that spawned the republic was also influenced by the Age of Enlightenment back on the Continent.

The late eighteenth century saw the writings of Hobbes, Locke, and Rousseau coin the modern application of secular humanism, the basis of which demoted God and promoted man as the center. Of the Founding Fathers who were not the twentieth-century equivalent of committed Christians, Robertson feels that for the most part they were a deeply religious segment who may have peripherally believed in God or merely attended church out of obligation or political expedience.

That is just fine with Robertson. The remaining non-churchgoers were still by and large a pretty moral crowd. The straggling few that he might refer to as secular humanists, such as Thomas Paine, Benjamin Franklin, and to some extent Thomas Jefferson, were by far the exception rather than the rule. Still, they fully recognized and bowed to traditional religious standards. It was the sometimes agnostic Jefferson, Robertson likes to say, who mentioned "Creator" in the Declaration and not "primeval slime," as well as "the laws of Nature, and Nature's God." He reasons that, if today's America is philosophically a secular humanist society where Christian people are expected to take a back seat, early America was just the opposite. The renegade humanists were the ones who were expected to know their place.

Robertson's conviction hinges on the idea that America was founded on religious grounds by religious people, even if they all did not conform to his precise brand of born-again Christianity. He is fond of pointing out that the words "separation of church and state" appear nowhere in either the U.S. Constitution, Declaration of Independence, or Bill of Rights.

"I don't think our forefathers intended religion to be separated from the government," he says. "But they just didn't want some big church trying to dominate them. They didn't want a federal church. And I totally agree with that."

If Robertson disagrees with a functional separation of church and state, he recognizes the assertion of a practical one. He believes that his views on the First Amendment can be embraced by most Americans, Christian, secular, and even atheist, if only they would hear him out: "I don't think that the institutional church, as such, should be trying to manipulate the government. The government should be . . . neutral in matters of religion, and they should ensure freedom for all people."

"Government," says Robertson, "should encourage the right values instead of the wrong ones. Should we uphold the traditional family? I think the answer is yes. Should we try to limit gross pornography? I think the answer is yes. Should we do something to curb the invasion of drugs? I think the answer is yes. Should we pay for babies that are begotten out of wedlock by fathers who have no desire whatsoever to care for them and who laugh at the system? I think the answer is no. We should force men to take care of their own children."

Robertson is often asked if he believes that America is a Christian nation. "It used to be, but it's not anymore. I don't think anybody realistically expects it to become one anytime soon."

American Christians have long been involved in politics, and throughout history have embraced various issues, ranging from abolition to temperance to William Jennings Bryan's "Cross of Gold" speech in 1896. After a few generations of relative isolation, a definite watershed that initiated the present cycle can be identified in the rise and fall of Jimmy Carter. After the nightmare of Watergate, Carter's appearance on the national scene like a breath of fresh air was the conservative Christian's spiritual reawakening. He would also prove to baptize them in fire. The disappointment of Carter as an unabashed liberal served to forge the conservative Republican Christian alliance of which Robertson rides the crest.

The first true Deep South President in over a century, he is a direct descendent of "King" Carter, once the largest landowner in colonial Virginia. Ironically, Carter's and Robertson's ancestors had known each other since before the Revolution.

In 1976, Carter was a no-holds-barred, Southern Baptist, born-again Christian who taught Sunday school in his home church. The term "born-again" was still a bit foreign to mainstream

America, and for several years publications such as the *Washington Post* chose to leave it in quotes. Well over half of all born-again Christians voted for Carter in 1976.

But four years later, 56 percent of those who called themselves "born-again" abandoned Carter, and even another born-again candidate, Independent John Anderson, for the man least definite on the issue, Ronald Reagan. "Born-again" meant less to the born-again voter, and there was a separation of the sheep from the goats, so to speak. By 1984 almost 80 percent of born-again Christians voted for Ronald Reagan.

A decade later many Christians agreed that Jimmy Carter's presidency just may have been God's will all along—only that Carter began to look less like God's blessing and more like God's judgment. Robertson supported Carter in some of the primaries, but as they developed a personal relationship—including an exclusive election-day interview with the new President-elect—he ended up voting for President Gerald Ford in 1976. "I interviewed him for my television program several days before the election," recalls Robertson, "and after I had had that experience, I voted for Gerald Ford."

James Wooten, an ABC Network newsman who had been assigned to the Carter campaign, and who later became a White House correspondent during the Carter years, remarked, "Having spent so much time with Carter, I find the comparison between him and Robertson personally unavoidable. Carter, it seems to me, was essentially a religious man who committed himself to politics; Robertson strikes me as a secular man who went into religion. Each brought with him the accouterments of his original bent. For Carter, that meant a presidency that conveyed the continuing hopelessness of a sinful world and the dour Christian duty of dealing with it as it was, without much promise of a better day."

Beginning in the eighties, Robertson began to take an increasing interest in the various political races and started endorsing candidates. Although remaining a Democrat, he supported President Reagan in 1980 and changed his party registration in 1984. "I was a Democrat for about fifty-five years," he comments. "I think they moved so far to the left in 1984 that I just couldn't go along. And I have been more at home for a number of years with the national platform of the Republican party, so I finally made it official."

One consultant to Republican candidates says of Robertson that he "can definitely have an impact in the [Republican] convention due to his organization skills." Referring to Robertson victories in Michigan, South Carolina, and, later, Iowa, she says that Robertson supporters know how to be at the right place, get there early, and bring visibility to their cause. "The biggest problem he faces," says the Republican consultant, "is the continued unfavorable image that he has. Many pollsters . . . ask the question 'Who would you least like to see President?' Robertson always scores the highest."

Others discount Pat Robertson as a credible candidate due to his lack of political experience. Robertson discounts the potential liability: "The people are looking for a person of integrity and for a decisive leader. Merely having been in politics doesn't guarantee either one of those. . . . As a matter of fact, being a politician may be a drawback, because most politicians have had to buy into compromises."

He is quick to discuss Dwight Eisenhower as an example of someone with skill in leadership who surrounded himself with talented people. "Many times a citizen such as General Eisenhower, who was no politician, turned out to be a wonderful President because he didn't come to the office with the baggage of twenty to thirty years of political deals." As for his experience, he will not belittle himself: "My father went to Congress when I was two, and I've been brought up in politics all my life."

Robertson had always been drawn to things political, like an appearance at Yale by Democratic presidential candidate Adlai Stevenson in 1952. "I remember hearing him speak at law school in New Haven, up on the Green there. It was in the fall of '52, when he was campaigning the first time and lost. I thought, 'This guy is telling too many jokes. . . . Joke after joke. He wasn't serious. The American people are not going to elect a comedian. No matter how witty and everything else he was he had a fault. We want a serious President, one with humor sure, but not somebody who was trying to be a clown. That didn't keep me from coming out in his favor four years later." A few months earlier Robertson attended the Democratic National Convention, which selected Stevenson. At that time he was impressed with his speaking ability.

He was even more impressed with Alben Barkley, then Vice President under Harry Truman, who made an impassioned speech at the convention for the nominee. "I remember struggling with the governor of Virginia in a polite way to get the Virginians' banner up on the floor for Stevenson. They had a procedural matter where they had not been appropriately seated and so the governor said that it was innappropriate for them to join the parade for Barkley. I said, 'Let's go and demonstrate for the "grand old man," and he said, 'I can't do that because of procedure.' "

Later, in 1956, when Robertson lived on Staten Island, he attended a luncheon at the residence of a prominent Stevenson supporter. There he met Margaret Truman Daniels, Harry Winston, and a few former members of the Truman Cabinet. "We talked politics and we talked Stevenson and I was somewhat decided about the candidate because I was still a Democrat and believed in my own man. So after Staten Island I attended the meeting of the group of volunteers supporting him and they elected me the head of it. I remember the great thrill of going into one of the downtown hotels, the Astor or something like that, and there was the great man and I shook his hand and he thanked me for the work that I had done on Staten Island, as he did hundreds of others."

Robertson actually downplays his political importance at this time, as well as any close association with Stevenson. "After the convention, of course, the regular Democratic party sort of took over the action and the volunteers were on the side. I had a rally for him, and on Staten Island did some work. It was an introduction, it wasn't all that big. But if I had known then in a sense how vacillating and indecisive he was I don't think that I would have been that enthusiastic for him."

Neither was Robertson enthusiastic for Richard Nixon. He incurred the wrath of President Nixon in July of 1974 by calling on him to repent. "Because I was so shocked," he told his supporters, "by the profanity and the seeming lack of regard for the common good that the Watergate tapes showed, I went on the *700 Club* with fear and trembling and called upon our President to do what I had just done—namely to confess his sins before the Lord and to call upon the gracious forgiveness of our Savior despite the personal cost."

Politics aside, Robertson views himself as extremely qualified for the Oval Office: "I have run one of the largest nonprofit organizations in the country, and the government, regretfully, is another nonprofit organization. I have had the experience of making enormous business decisions involving tens of millions of dollars. I started a university. [In 1985] we helped about eight and a half million needy Americans in the major inner cities of our country. So I have experience in dealing with the welfare problems and the family problems, the educational problems and the social problems of this country."

Barry Hon is a highly successful California land developer, as well as chairman of CBN University's Board of Regents. Hon says of Robertson, "He's able to construct a consensus, which is very important in any large organization that is not dictatorial. He's able to lead to a consensus so that everyone feels a part of the decision and enthusiastic to get behind the project."

"I have seen him move," says Lee Buck, a retired senior vice president of marketing for New York Life, also a regent. "He's a mover. He *is* a mover. Plus the fact that I think he'll know how to deal with the Congress. Because when he's with you, he wins you. And he'll win those people."

Regarding foreign affairs, Robertson feels that he is as qualified as anyone running: "I have talked to the heads of state of many nations, and I've done business in many countries." One analyst remarked, "A political boss would probably kill for a candidate with the following credentials—high name recognition, probably known by more than half of America; a solid base of support among 20 or 30 million Americans, most of whom would vote for him if he was running; founder and head of a major television network that reaches more than 30 million people daily; good-looking, highly telegenic, and charismatic personality."

While Ronald Reagan has not endorsed Robertson, he has

stuck up for him more than once, citing his own background as a nonpolitician. "You shouldn't judge someone by how he makes his living," he said. "I just have to go back to a time when there were people that felt that there was something wrong with an actor seeking public office. And my answer then and now is that I don't think that any legitimate trades or professions should be barred from participation in public life. That's the meaning of democracy."

After the victory in Michigan in 1986, Reagan also denied that he thought that conservative Christians were trying to take over the Republican party. "I haven't seen any efforts they've tried to dominate our party," Reagan said. On the issue of a candidate's faith, the President has also pointed out that John F. Kennedy, the first Roman Catholic in the White House, "took his case directly to the other religions and spoke to them in their meetings . . . and he was elected President."

Also in 1986, New York Congressman Jack Kemp, another self-professed born-again Christian, was asked by reporters about his feelings toward Robertson as a credible candidate. "Robertson is broadening the base of the Republican party, and that's good. He is as welcome to our party as Jesse Jackson is to the Democratic party." While the reporters laughed at this statement, Kemp quickly countered that the remark was not intended as an insult.

Former Delaware Governor and Republican presidential candidate Pierre S. "Pete" duPont disagrees with the Jackson-Robertson parallel, to Robertson's discredit. He sees Jackson less as just the black candidate rather than just another liberal, whereas he views Robertson as just a televangelist. "I don't think religion is to the Republican party what left-wing liberalism, Jesse Jackson, is to the Democratic party," says duPont.

Most of the Republicans, though, are not quick to count out Robertson. No doubt he is reshaping the GOP, and his presidential run will have changed that party in years to come. In Michigan a majority of Robertson people have taken control of the state Republican party. His strength was determined when 1,750 out of a possible 1,870 delegates who attended the state convention were asked to sign petition cards to indicate their support for

Robertson. The outcome was that Robertson's majority proceeded to elect 63 out of 101 members of Michigan's Republican State Committee. Robertson supporters now control the group that will select Michigan's at-large delegates to the GOP National Convention in August 1988. "We are clearly in the driver's seat," said Robertson's Michigan director.

The swing to Robertson was particularly evident as the chairman of the Michigan convention, who was also president of the Michigan Conservative Union, wore a button on his lapel stating "I Switched to Pat" during press conferences after the convention. Oddly enough, heavily urban, unionized Michigan has not had the reputation of such potent conservatism. Said Robertson's Florida state chairman, "[He] is the first truly conservative Republican to win in Michigan in a Republican party convention."

A political analyst with the Brookings Institute suggests that Robertson has the power to "threaten or take over local and state Republican party organizations." According to the analyst, even if Robertson does not a thing more, he may serve as the impetus for the new agenda of the party, much like the candidacy of Barry Goldwater in 1964 paved the way to a Reagan victory in 1980. One former member of the Lyndon Johnson administration feels that while the bigger primary states like New York and California will not be of much help to Robertson, the caucus states, with their traditionally abysmal voter turnout, will be of the greatest benefit. "Robertson's support comes from pockets of conservative, religious voters . . . and a mere 20,000 to 30,000 votes can be decisive."

Robertson's campaign staff numbers seventy-five, in contrast to thirty-five or forty for George Bush. It is by far the largest of any Republican presidential candidate. There are seventeen field offices in sixteen states. His campaign manager, R. Marc Nuttle, is an expert on campaign spending laws and has worked on GOP campaigns in every state except Hawaii.

When asked which of the most pressing issues a Robertson White House will tackle first, he will usually reply with two items that often catch news reporters off guard because he doesn't mention a religious or traditional New Right theme. The issues are the trade imbalance and the federal budget deficit.

"He didn't mention religion," said one astonished reporter.

"In fact, the evidence suggests that he has a larger political agenda." The reporter recalled a Republican political consultant who said, "Pat Robertson is a politician whose profession happens to be religion."

Regarding tax reform, Robertson feels that the ideal thing to do would be to institute a new tax structure based on a flat tax on personal income. "Our tax code is too complicated, and it should be simplified drastically. A flat tax would free the creative energies of our people for increased economic productivity instead of tax avoidance."

One of the items on the tax agenda, he adds, is the necessity to pass the Tax Reform Bill of 1987 "to give industry back some of the privileges it took away from them in the Tax Reform Bill of 1986."

As a committed Christian, Robertson admits that while he is unyielding to various universal principles, compromise is essential in the progress of any successful leader. "I think that the only way people can accomplish anything politically in a pluralistic society as large as the United States of America is through coalitions and some degree of compromise." Robertson applies the principle of compromise almost exclusively to the area of the federal budget and the determination of where and how much fat should be pared.

Regarding the prospect that, as President, Robertson will have to cut deals, he replies, "I'm not in some ivory tower. . . . I have been in business for many years, and I deal with the real world every day. . . . There are certain principles you cannot violate. They are the core decency, morality, honor, and integrity. And you just can't compromise on them. But they are very few in relation to the many decisions that any person must make in politics. For example, the allocations of funds in a budget. How much goes to the care of the elderly? How much goes to defense? How much goes to building highways? Well, these are not absolutes."

Instead, Robertson feels that they are "pragmatic decisions that should be made through compromise. A major function of government has to do with the taxing and spending powers, and these things are negotiable.

"The government and its officials must never lie to the people,

187

or steal or cheat—in short, they must conduct themselves morally. But in terms of procedures, of various initiatives and the allocation of funds—these things are all matters of political compromise which I'm perfectly able and willing to do."

"The government," he says, "does not use taxes to accomplish or should not use taxes to accomplish social purposes. Taxes should be used to raise revenue. End of story." He believes we have written into the tax code a bewildering array of exemptions and preferences to favor special-interest groups that successfully lobbied Congress for a handout.

His strongest views on fiscal matters, however, are reserved for the federal budget deficit, which he believes must be rectified on the spending side rather than on the revenue-raising side. President Reagan, he says, hasn't cut the budget, he's only reduced the rate of budget increase in the past four years. The deficit problem strikes close to the heart of his most deeply held financial conviction, which is that people should not contract debt. This had been so much a mark of his business dealings over the years that at least one other prominent businessman has adopted that policy for his own secular purposes. "The federal deficit is a symptom of a deeper moral problem which says I want it now . . . instead of deferring gratification until funds are available to pay for it. In times of extraordinary prosperity, we have become the first generation ever to plunder the patrimony of its children and grandchildren. We have robbed them to pay for our wasteful excesses. . . . We did it because we have a Congress controlled by politicians who lack the will to say no to the clamor of special interest groups."

On a related issue, he believes that social security funds should be invested properly with insurance companies, banks, and private business. "This investment would be the biggest economic shot in the arm this country could have, an incredible opportunity to rebuild America." He points out that whereas seventy workers supported every retiree when social security began, now about three workers support every retiree. And before long each retiree will be supported by just two workers. He says he favors a constitutional amendment to balance the budget. "But that is an external restraint to force the Congress to do what they should do voluntarily. It's symptomatic of the fact that the Congress of the United States lacks the guts to make the hard decisions needed to bring runaway spending under control." Robertson feels there's an attitude of unwillingness to take personal responsibility that's got to be changed. We have relied on the government to do things for us.

Robertson appears liberal on the issue of equal opportunity, though he is generally opposed to any rigid institution of quotas. Rather, he feels, integration should be voluntary. "We must include women in our highest councils," he says. "We must include black people, Hispanics, Chinese, American Indians, and all other minorities in our midst. Gone are the days when exclusive clubs could determine how the world was going to be run and let the 'masses' take it."

Recalling the days of Southern resistance to integration, he says, "I spoke and debated as a matter of fact to colleagues that the filibuster was a means of maintaining freedom for minorities. And my father was a filibusterer. I gave the rationale of why it was necessary to have a filibuster, but I just was uncomfortable with the massive resistance that went on, the unwillingness to allow black people into the school, and segregation in general that put one class of people down. I just didn't feel that myself."

Robertson feels that the looming federal deficit can be reduced substantially merely by instituting the changes suggested by the Grace Commission Report. "Peter Grace says we can probably save $430 billion immediately and up to $2 trillion in the next ten years if we put certain savings—reforms and spending cuts— in place.

"Lack of restraint in government spending has pushed inflation to historic highs. Lack of restraint in personal spending has resulted in the highest load of personal debt in our nation's history. The two together have given our nation the lowest savings rate and the lowest gain in productivity per worker of virtually any of the major nations of the world. . . . Since 1940 our population has grown about 70 percent and government expenditures have grown about 4,600 percent. Obviously, things are out of balance. . . . The government is just out of hand, and it's running up these incredible deficits."

His thinking harps back frequently to principles enunciated in his book *The Secret Kingdom,* especially the law of reciprocity, "Do unto others as you would have them do unto you," or the Golden Rule. "The President deals with people; if he's gracious to people, if he's kind to people, they'll be gracious and kind back. If he's harsh and unyielding, if he's contentious and controversial, they'll be contentious and controversial back. The principles I've learned in the Bible underlie my own personal life and my ability to deal with people. That is more important perhaps than to say, well, this policy or that policy will have to be from the Bible." The question of being a strong Christian or a minister is one that he also interprets with respect to values—what people's values are, and to what extent they want a leader who represents those values in a strong and articulate way. He says ultimately the choice will be between two people, "then the question will be, will these people choose somebody who represents their points of view, who stands for their values, or will they go with somebody who doesn't."

The principal issue-related conviction that emerged from his experience in the ghetto is that the solution to poverty, particularly among the blacks, must affirm the integrity of the family. "Self-confidence is replaced by economic uncertainty. Men who leave their homes in the morning to look for work come home at night knowing only one thing for sure—that their benefits will be reduced. The indignity lies in the fact that they really know in advance when it will happen or by how much. They may lose one dollar of assistance for every dollar of gross earnings or a fraction of that amount."

Robertson believes that the services now supplied by government could be more effectively supplied by a competitive free-enterprise system. Citizens would receive vouchers for specific services, especially education vouchers. This would enable the recipients to choose the suppliers of social services that benefit them the most. He further advocates the abandonment of legal barriers that keep the disabled, mothers with children, the elderly, and others from working in their homes. And above all he favors policies that will keep families together. "What part will a black father play," Robertson asks, "where the rules of aid for dependent children make a mother choose between him and a welfare check? When assistance is paid directly to young mothers, bypassing the father of her children, the incentive for fathers to take responsibility for their own children evaporates." He quotes his old boss Peter Grace as having told him that "if we wrote a check to everybody in America who is under the poverty line and sent it to him every month in an amount to adequately bring his income above the poverty line, the cost to the federal government would be a tenth of what it now spends on poverty programs. Now what does that mean? It means that 90 percent of the poverty program money is currently going to bureaucrats and 10 percent is getting to the recipients." Also, he believes in the privatization of social problems. "It is the churches that could take the lead. It is not something that government can get involved in." Steeped as he was in a tradition that combined frugality and pervasive concern with military matters, Robertson seized early upon the evidence that military procurement was being mismanaged. "Our government does not need to purchase $700 stepladders and $25 screws." He feels, however, that the government should not stint on spending that is not only necessary for the defense of the United States but also necessary to lift the "yoke of oppression," which he believes the Prophet Isaiah commands us to do. "I think whether it is economic oppression, civil rights oppression of minorities, oppression against women, or oppression against billions of people under Communist domination, there is a positive duty to at least assist people in their struggle for freedom."

On the issue of education Robertson feels strongly that "you cannot educate children in a moral vacuum." He complains that public school textbooks have "expunged references to religious experience, denigrated capitalism, and pushed the educational agenda toward a socialistic and internationalist model. That was done with taxpayers' money, and it was a value judgment that someone made," says Robertson.

"There is no way that you can teach without teaching some system of moral values. If you do not teach the Judeo-Christian or some other religiously based morality in schools, you will ultimately teach humanism or atheism."

Issues pertaining to children have become the most commonly cited area used for examples. Biblical Christianity, in his view, upholds marriage as the context for sexual activity. Therefore any form of sex education that fails to inculcate biblical morality will tend to undermine that morality by creating the impression that pragmatic considerations are the only restraints worth mentioning. Likewise, attempts to teach ethics—known popularly as "values clarification"—may offer a rationalistic or practical set of considerations that leave the impression that the will of God is little more than an afterthought or an irrelevancy. The court system, moreover, is subject to his scrutiny regarding child-related cases:

"We have a severe problem with child abuse in this country, and the state obviously has a role in protecting children from unfit parents. However, state social welfare agencies have been known to prohibit Christian parents from disciplining their children in accordance with biblical precepts. But loving discipline is a fundamental part of child-parent relationships. Children need it and parents must give it if they love their children. To characterize normal parenting as abusive is itself an abuse of state power. In one instance a state attempted to take a daughter away from a divorced woman because she made her daughter attend church and forbade the girl to smoke marijuana or attend rock music concerts. A state social worker termed this conduct mental abuse. When things like this happen, the state is exceeding its proper bounds."

Regarding judicial reform, Robertson says, "Replacing retiring justices is probably the greatest opportunity to refocus judicial policy in our lifetime. Also in need of change are decisions regarding school prayer, forced busing, criminal jurisdiction, the exclusionary role, and others."

Robertson has a great desire to appoint judges to fill vacancies on the U.S. Supreme Court. Hopefully, a new high court would be able to "reverse the incredible interpretation of the establishment-of-religion clause in our Constitution." Naturally, Robertson sees abortion, too, as one of the priorities on the judicial agenda.

Being a lawyer, he has strong views about judicial policy. "In one of the more liberal law schools, the concept is taught that social change cannot be brought about through the political process but it can be brought about by the small minority working through the courts. These schools teach that liberal judges frame issues in their way, select their jurisdiction, and begin a body of law that would ultimately change our society without the changes ever being approved by the voters."

Though Robertson's foes chide him for the idea that he will "impose his morality on others," most recognize that the moral issues are the ones that seem to take precedence with an America that grows more skeptical as the years go by.

"Last year [1986], everyone thought that the farm crisis was the great issue here in Iowa," says a staff member of one Democrat stumping for the presidency. "But actually, and even more so this year, the overwhelming issues the rural folk are concerned with are crime and drugs."

"These big city problems are starting to appear in their towns," says another. "They're scared."

Under the headline "The 'Scandalous' Mr. Robertson," a Dallas *Morning News* editorial that was clearly hostile to Robertson did admit that it was indeed the moral issues that piqued the interest of plain-folks America: "This [is] a time when the principal public health worry is a disease communicated by once-taboo forms of sexual activity; when Bill Moyers reports gloomily on rampant teenage pregnancy in the black community; when Americans cynically sell military secrets to the Soviet Union; when drugs infiltrate the elementary schools." The editorial goes on to suggest, however, that morality should not be the main business of any government.

Robertson is diametrically opposed to such a political philosophy. For example, he would support a certain speed limit not because a plurality of the people feels there should be one, but rather because it is moral in that it saves lives. While some say that it is impossible to legislate morality, Robertson sees the two as inseparable, that legislation is in fact morality.

"A value system is inextricable from the type of government and the type of laws that people will have," says Robertson. "No government is neutral. All law ultimately represents somebody's values."

When asked outright, by *U.S. News & World Report* in July

1986, "Wouldn't [you] try to impose your religious values on people?" Robertson replied, "I believe in freedom for all people, and I would never see the power of the sword being used to enforce spiritual values on people."

Rather than quench other faiths at the expense of Christianity, Robertson is of the school that would provide for them all so that they could flourish in a free marketplace of ideas. He is also confident enough to believe that Christianity is desirable enough that it would rise to the top without special privileges from the government.

Again alluding to the "myth" of the separation of church and state doctrine, Robertson says, "Religious people who have religious views—whether they're Jewish, Christian, or whatever—owe it to the country to be involved at every level in political life, and I think the nation would be much healthier for it. We have in this country freedom of religion. But nobody ever intended freedom *from* religion."

He believes that the most attractive strength in both his politics and religion is the commitment to the traditional family unit. Robertson believes that "the family is the fundamental organizing principle in society. . . . Unfortunately, many forces, including our morality crises, high taxation, and certain government programs are tearing the family apart."

Robertson supports mandatory sentencing for those convicted of selling narcotics to children under eighteen. "I think that the government can do more. . . . The drug trade is a $100 billion-plus-a-year industry run by organized crime and warlords from the Far East, Middle East, and Central America."

He describes pornography as being "destructive to the concept of the dignity of women. . . . Laws already on the books," he says, "could be enforced by the Justice Department. But in the past, they've just chosen to ignore them."

Robertson believes that much of the crime in the street is committed by a reasonably small number of repeat offenders. The best way to combat crime, he feels, is to severely limit parole, and possibly eliminate plea bargaining entirely. "They should know that if they commit a crime, they're going to prison, or they are going to have to pay for what they do."

On the certain issues that disturb liberals most, he is frank. On the Cable News Network's *Larry King Live* program in 1987, he answered a call-in viewer from New York City who inquired of his stand on homosexuals in regard to gay rights:

"I think that, frankly, homosexuality, if you want to use a biblical term, is an abomination. I think it's wrong . . . it's a type of sexual perversion that a society should not give preferred treatment to. In the state of Virginia, homosexuality is called sodomy and it's against the law. It's a felony. The Supreme Court has upheld that. And I don't believe that people who practice homosexuality should have special privileges. The Gay Rights people want this life-style to be taught in the schools as an alternative life-style. I don't think it's an acceptable life-style."

Oddly enough, Robertson has made efforts to reach out to homosexuals. One *700 Club* commercial featured a narrative by a man with AIDS who described how the CBN telephone counselor listened to his plight and even prayed for him over the phone. The man described how he had been abandoned by friends and family after he was diagnosed, but did not mention if he had forsaken his homosexuality for Christianity.

In April 1987, Robertson said, "In the last few months our numbers of calls from homosexuals and lesbians at CBN has almost doubled over last year because these people know that we care about them. We love them. But we don't love their life-style. I don't approve of it."

The other controversial issue, abortion, is perhaps even more repugnant to Pat Robertson. "I don't see why we can't, in the name of civil rights, in the name of humanity, protect an unborn baby, by law, against being murdered in his or her mother's womb." Says Robertson, "I consider abortion murder because this is a human being whose life is being terminated violently. We protect other minorities by law. We certainly protect live adults against being raped or murdered."

On the legislative front, Robertson supports President Reagan's Pro-Life Bill, which would permanently prohibit federal funding of abortion, as well as opposing the controversial "Grove City" legislation, which would require all private and religious hospitals to provide abortions for Medicare/Medicaid patients.

He also supports constitutional language stating that life begins at conception. Through abortion, feels Robertson, "what we are doing is committing racial suicide."

Robertson is against farm subsidies, but his solution is not as drastic as to call for an immediate end to them. He would, however, wean the farmers away from them, eventually phase the programs out "over a reasonable period."

Robertson would extend opportunities for farm exports, while ending U.S. taxpayer support of foreign farm businesses that, he feels, put American farmers out of work.

Instead of farm foreclosures, Robertson favors restructuring. This would be a threefold process that would leave a producing farmer in possession of the farm, provide protection for the lender, and finally provide for a third-party mediator who would determine whether restructuring would be more favorable than foreclosure. The current system, Robertson feels, leaves both the farm family out of their land and livelihood and leaves the Federal Land Bank with thousands of dollars in foreclosure expenses.

Robertson believes that multiple factors are responsible for the trade imbalance, including uneven economic growth around the world, unpredictable currency exchange rates, and unneeded government involvement in economic policy.

He dismisses tariffs to protect American industry as a "quick fix" that fails to recognize long-term problems. His objectives are to make U.S. goods the best in the world and available at a competitive price. He would accomplish this by removing "the encumbrances that keep our workplaces from producing the success they are capable of."

By no means does he place the blame entirely on Americans, though. Robertson told the Economic Club of Detroit, considered one of the foremost economic organizations, that "where foreign policy is concerned, we must insist on fair trade. In fact, I think we should send a strong message to our trading partners in this new round of negotiations which is just beginning—especially to the Japanese—we demand free and fair trade. Either open up your markets to American goods, or we're going to shut the door of American markets to your goods."

Robertson supports a rollback of the bureaucratic barriers that hinder entry into small business, which he sees as the mainstay of

American economics. "Growth has come from the strength of new technology and the inventive genius of the American people," says Robertson, "the same genius that formed 700,000 new businesses [in 1985]. . . . Eighty-five percent of all the jobs in America are now found in businesses with less than two hundred employees. So, a lot of the nation's business vitality comes about through the creative impetus, which, of course, creates markets that didn't exist."

Robertson believes in big business, and that it, rather than the service sector, will carry the major load of the American economy. The idea of service industries now, or in the future, leading the nation is an illusion, according to Robertson. "Currently, we are being told by the writers and experts that because we are moving from an industrial to a service and information economy, we don't have to worry. . . . But you know, I do worry, because I know in order to survive an economy must produce tangible goods. No economy can survive that buys its goods from overseas and sells services and information on computer screens to itself."

What seems to be a strong bridge to the nonreligious vote is Robertson's steadfast anti-Communist stance. When working the crowds, religious or secular, Robertson finds his most popular issue and loudest applause in his hard-line stance toward the Soviet Union and Communist expansion in the western hemisphere.

Robertson is thoroughly committed against Communist expansionism. He would strive to stamp out existing Soviet-backed puppet governments, as well as attempts to export totalitarian governments. "If the Soviet Union is going to enlarge its sphere of influence and expand hegemony into places like Afghanistan, then we have every right to support groups fighting for freedom, which would bring countries out of Soviet hegemony."

Robertson accepts a confrontational rather than a conciliatory stance toward the Soviets. "As I look back in history, I find that Lenin indicated that lying was, to a Socialist, the key implement of policy. I don't believe that there has been a single treaty that the Soviets have kept in the past where it served their interest to break it."

Robertson does not seem to trust them for a moment. "They've broken the Helsinki Accords. They've violated the earlier SALT treaties. They've violated the other treaties we've signed with them over the years. They're performing absolutely unspeakable acts against the people of Afghanistan at this moment."

Unlike many conservative Republicans, Robertson does not seem to accept some totalitarian governments at the expense of others, particularly ones sympathetic to the United States. He often quotes Alexis de Tocqueville, the nineteenth-century student of America who felt that "the wielding power in foreign relations has been the province of empires, tyrants, and despots. The keepers of such empires enjoy the freedom to pursue their goals, unbridled by democratic processes."

"Citizens do not fare so well," says Robertson, "for their lives and their labors are often confiscated and laid waste as though they were somehow lesser humans than the despots they serve."

In view of this anti-Communist posture, critics have accused Robertson of using Operation Blessing funds to support the Contra forces attempting to overthrow the Communist government of Nicaragua. Some of the unfounded accusations include CBN dollars being used to train troops. Robertson denies these allegations, none of which have stuck, nor have they caused any falloff in contributions. He makes no secret of his distaste for the Sandinistas and the hesitance of Congress to appropriate the necessary money to aid the Contras. "I favor the Contras," says Robertson, "and I favor the cause of freedom any place in the world against Communist oppression."

Robertson does view Nicaraguan leader Daniel Ortega in the same class as Muammar el-Qaddafi, Ayatollah Khomeini, and Fidel Castro: modern-day despots. "I think that Daniel Ortega has fastened a repressive Communist regime on the people of Nicaragua. There have been atrocities against the Mesquito Indians. There have been atrocities against the civilian population and there has been a systematic persecution of the churches.

"However, my alleged activity [in Central America] is grossly misrepresented. I'm accused by some leftist groups or liberal evangelical groups of giving $3 million to the Contras for arms. They say I am starting an army. What we have done is facilitate the shipment of medicine and food to needy refugees in Honduras, Costa Rica, and Guatemala." In 1986, Operation Blessing spent $2 million for the transport of $20 million worth of goods for distribution to Guatemalan refugees. "Its all humanitarian aid," says Robertson. "I'm very proud of it. It's very worthwhile and obviously it's endorsed by the supporters of CBN."

Robertson has flown with his camera crews down to the border of Nicaragua and has had extensive discussions with refugees from the Sandanista regime. As he stated in his speech in Constitution Hall on September 17, 1986, "One year ago this spring, I visited a refugee camp in Honduras near the Nicaraguan border. I took my camera crew inside a dark tent with a dirt floor. Sitting on a rough cot was a Nicaraguan woman less than five feet tall. She told a tale of horror at the hands of the Sandanistas. Her husband had been a bus driver. The Sandanistas accused him of being sympathetic to the Contras. Without a trial, they seized him, and before her eyes they dismembered his body. Then they raped her and lowered her into a well half-dead with shock and fear. She regained consciousness, struggled out of her confinement, and made her way across the border to freedom. As I think about this little woman, I realized that she is just one victim of the Communist tyranny that since 1917 has claimed through war, starvation, murder, and torture an estimated 250 million lives."

He believes that Soviet Russia is "destined to fall" but says he doesn't believe the United States will have to go to war with them to see it happen. His antipathy also extends to the continuing domination of the People's Republic of China by communism. He questions that China is becoming less Communistic. "For human rights purposes," he says, "China operates under the old guidelines of Mao. Criticism of the government is still an offense that is punishable by imprisonment. Amnesty International reports that most Chinese prisons contain political prisoners, many of them still untried."

He rejects, however, the criticism sometimes leveled against him that he might seek to manipulate events to bring about the final Armageddon, which he believes will ultimately and inevitably come. "The Bible also says as much as life is in you live at peace with all men. No one in his right mind wants to go to war or begin a war, certainly a nuclear war. The charge that evangelicals are somehow trying to help God by bringing about Armageddon shows a total misunderstanding of biblical truth."

Pat Robertson believes that the single most crucial issue facing the nation for 1988 is "an attitude of unwillingness to take personal responsibility—that's got to be changed. We have relied on government to do things for us. I believe there needs to be a sense of self-reliance and freedom, and a reliance on God as opposed to government. That is central."

For example, Robertson believes that the suggestion that government is even marginally responsible for the deeds of the individual is scandalous, particularly on the issue of children. If elected President, Robertson would place high on the agenda legislation that would hold parents solely responsible for the welfare of their offspring, and would even garnishee pay and belongings to meet any need.

"The second problem flows out of it, which is the huge federal budget and the huge federal budget deficit," says Robertson.

Following the lead of many Republicans, however, the prospect of tax increases is definitely out. Like Ronald Reagan, Robertson feels, in his own words, that "a combination of tax cuts and budget cuts is the way to go. One would stimulate the economy and bring about growth. The other would limit the enormous impact that the government makes. We can cut $100 billion out of our government spending without hurting any current programs. A number of programs, such as the Legal Services Corporation, should be abandoned altogether."

Another place where the ax is poised is the Department of Education. "At $10 billion a year, [it] probably could be eliminated without a great deal of strain."

He believes that the Grace Commission estimate of $430 billion in savings over three years is attainable, and that it can be done without changing major federal programs.

Robertson feels that some agencies should be dismantled entirely—"not just improved business management but whole departments." Among them are Amtrak, Conrail, and the Department of Energy.

Robertson believes in the Gramm-Rudman deficit-reduction package, including the plan to slash $36 billion a year in order to achieve a zero deficit by fiscal year 1991. He also advocates across-the-board cuts of nonexempt programs by a uniform percentage to reach those targets. By privatizing, or applying free-market principles to many familiar government institutions, Robertson feels that incentive and profit motive can be restored, thereby stimulating a more effective government program.

On the family front he would raise the dependent exemption, which he feels still translates into pre–World War II dollars. Robertson would also eliminate any marriage penalties, such as those that would prohibit spouses from working at home.

Robertson cites a myriad of tax policies that the government has been encouraging so that people would have fewer children. "We essentially are dying out. We are depopulating America."

He also strongly supports "freedom of choice" in education through tuition tax vouchers.

Robertson's remedy for governmental patronage would drastically change the face, as well as the size, of the public service pool.

Regarding the formation of his administration, "The first thing a President must do is discharge all the discretionary officers in the government. There are as many as 100,000 who come in that category." It would be possible to reappoint certain ones, Robertson believes, but "it's absolutely necessary for a President to have people in the administration who share his philosophy."

"Secondly, I think the civil service laws must be overhauled. They go back over a hundred years. They're antiquated. I think we need to recognize that whenever you have an organ that is spending a trillion dollars a year, that has 2.6 or 2.7 million employees, that is giving checks to over 50 percent of the American people, that organ is enormously powerful and it is obviously [responsible for] certain types of behavior."

On September 17, 1986, the 199th anniversary of the Constitution, he made a fiery speech to supporters in Constitution Hall, calling attention to the decadence he perceives in contemporary society. He said:

"Illegal drugs are being sold to fourth-grade schoolchildren. Half of our high school children have tried marijuana. High school children use drugs estimated to have a value of $120 billion annually.

"There are a million illegitimate pregnancies to unwed teenagers every year in the country. Of these, 400,000 babies are aborted, yet 600,000 are born each year to youngsters hardly old enough to be away from their parents. In the black community, according to a CBS report, 60 percent of all births are to women without a man in residence.

"On the darker side of society, an estimated one quarter of all our children are sexually assaulted while they are growing up. And each year between 1.2 and 1.5 million teenagers are either runaways or throwaways, and to match our new sexual freedom this year, there will be an estimated 8.6 million new cases of venereal disease in our country, and the dread, incurable killer AIDS may already have infected one million Americans.

"Our schools, with what is called progressive education, have become progressively worse. We have in our society 27 million functional illiterates. Each year we add 2.3 million to their number. Instead of being the most literate nation on earth, we rank number 14 among the developed nations in literacy and we are falling fast."

At the conclusion of the speech he announced that he would run for the presidency if he received three million signatures on forms requesting him to do that. Robertson's presidential aspirations received their first major boost when his organization took control of Michigan's Republican State Committee at the district caucuses held in February 1987.

Shortly after this victory, however, a cloud passed over television ministries with revelations of sexual and financial improprieties by Tammy and Jim Bakker of the PTL operation.

In 1972 the boyish Jim Bakker resigned as co-host of the *700 Club* and traveled to California to work with the fledgling Trinity Broadcasting Systems. After only six months of working with Paul and Jan Crouch, Bakker resigned that position and vowed never to work with or for anyone else again. PTL, for People that Love or Praise the Lord, was established in Charlotte, North Carolina, and later moved to Fort Mill, South Carolina.

Robertson's Christian Broadcasting Network was first to enter the religious airtime market, PTL followed soon afterward, then the Trinity Broadcasting Network arrived. Bakker's PTL ministry flourished, opening a theme park, a home for unwed mothers, condominiums, a time-sharing resort, a water park, a home for homeless men, and a pricey shopping mall.

But March 1987 brought events that shook all of contemporary

American Christianity and particularly the realm of television evangelists. On March 6, Jim Bakker announced that his wife, Tammy, was being treated for drug dependency and would not appear on PTL's *Jim and Tammy* television show.

On March 19, Jim Bakker resigned as chairman of PTL, saying that he had been blackmailed by "treacherous former friends" who knew of a sexual encounter he had had with Jessica Hahn, then a church secretary, seven years earlier. Jerry Falwell, another leading television evangelist, agreed to step in as chairman of PTL indefinitely.

On March 22, Richard Dortch took over Bakker's pulpit and sent out appeals for donations to let them know "this ministry is going to stay strong." The next day, Bakker says he resigned to head off a hostile takeover of PTL. Jimmy Swaggert was accused, and denied, the takeover attempt.

In the weeks that followed, Bakker accused Falwell of "stealing" PTL, and the Charlotte *Observer* discovered that Hahn was paid $265,000 for remaining silent about Bakker's affair. Jim Bakker was accused by his own denomination of prostitution, homosexuality, and of "fleecing" his television flock to the tune of millions of dollars.

The news made every national newspaper and magazine, and the principals involved adorned the covers and pages of *Time, Newsweek, Playboy,* and *People.* The eyes of America focused with fascination on the life-styles of those who professed religiosity and lived a life-style that, to most Americans, seemed wanton and hedonistic. Suddenly other evangelists adopted an attitude of accountability and fiscal openness. Falwell published a report that illustrated the fullness of his ministry's outreach, and Robertson and others made their salaries a matter of public record.

Though Robertson had not been involved with Bakker in business or the ministry for years, and though he did manage to stay above the scrabbling "Holy Wars" that began after the Bakker incidents became public, he felt tremors from the Bakkers' downfall. A survey for Robertson in April 1987 noted a slight dip in his standing as a potential candidate. Experts noted that the hoopla was likely to hurt Robertson simply by his association with televangelism.

Jeffrey Hadden, a sociology professor at the University of Virginia, told *People* magazine the scandal wouldn't hurt Robertson to any great extent. "I think he has got to be feeling, 'Lord, why does this have to happen now?' " Hadden said. "But I don't see it as a major setback. If anything, it may help draw a distinction between Robertson and the other TV preachers. Robertson is an intellectual, a scholar. He's better read than all the others, who tend to fly by the seat of their pants."

But the scandal hurt deeply. While all religious organizations felt a decrease in financial contributions, in June CBN reported $12 million in lost revenues for the three-month period between April and June, and it projected a $28 million loss for 1987. About 80 percent of the network's revenue is from donations.

Though Robertson's organization had done all it could to maintain credibility and openness, the American public had become skeptical and suspicious of all television evangelists. Robertson was forced to tell 500 faithful employees to break out their résumés—they would have to look for other jobs. Lost jobs meant a curtailed program of ministry, and Robertson was keenly disappointed that one minister's blunder had brought so much damage to so many people. The 500 employees were about one third of the CBN staff.

Aside from the financial difficulties involved, Robertson is distressed over the effect the Bakkers' downfall has had on other, highly reputable ministries: "Years ago I was working with the forest service in Montana. A guy took me out to a log-cutting detail where we were to trim the trees that had fallen on a telephone line. It was July or August, and we walked that hot morning, working, climbing poles, cutting cross cuts. I had a saw and an ax on my shoulder plus a pack.

"We had been up there for about an hour or so and I asked him if he had any water. He said, 'I didn't bring any water, and neither did you.' So we kept on working until noon, then we came off the ridge and headed down to a valley where there was a creek. I was so glad to see it that I just threw myself in and started drinking. But when I looked up—there about two hundred yards *up* stream was a herd of cattle in the water.

"Well, this is sort of Jim and Tammy in the very clear, beautiful pool. I wasn't having any problem and the people in America were excited and it was a new thing. It was a sense of purity and excitement and it was high integrity and there was great trust—just like the people were drinking from a pure stream. Although as long as he was working with me it was okay, because I was making sure that all of the dealings were high level. Then suddenly the thing down there in Charlotte, it was like cattle stamping in the stream with their feet muddying it up. What had been pure and very blessed, it was suddenly in the last year made a word of derision and the object of scorn and ridicule; in our case it was pretty much undeserved, but in his case it wasn't. It was that somebody would go into something that was just a great benefit and begin to tear it up. But that's what happened."

A Gallup poll taken in the spring of 1987 indicated that since 1980 there had been a sharp decline in approval for four of America's most prominent TV preachers: Oral Roberts' approval rating dropped from 66 percent to 28; Jimmy Swaggert's dropped from 76 percent to 44; Robert Schuller's dropped from 78 percent to 61, and Pat Robertson's dropped from 65 percent to 50 percent.

Three quarters of the CBN's annual income is derived from its millions of contributors. Another one fifth is derived from cable revenues, while the remainder is from miscellaneous categories. Of its expenses, which in 1987 totalled $177 million, the largest category went to broadcast purposes, and those totaled about 30 percent, administration 13 percent, Operation Blessing 11 percent, Crisis Counseling and Prayer 8 percent, cable programming 18 percent, with the remainder in other categories.

The mission statement of CBN spells out the overall guidelines with respect to the money question. "We believe that God's work, done according to the principles of His kingdom, will prosper financially. We cannot serve God and money, so service to God and His call always takes precedence over conflicting considerations of money. Nevertheless, we recognize that only those activities that are economically viable can continue in our present society, so planning must take into account economic viability. We also categorically state that the payment of accounts when due is a key ingredient of integrity. We seek to finance our activities by all lawful and morally correct means, including but not limited to contributions, sales, and investment income. In planning we will endeavor to project adequate income for current activities, plus generous surpluses from which we can build and expand."

"Some ministers who have a large cash flow coming to them can really get off base," says Dick Simmons, Robertson's colleague from Brooklyn days. "That happened, of course, with Jimmy and Tammy Bakker, but I don't fear for Pat simply because there's no way he can walk away from what he experienced down there in the slums. Jim and Tammy were victims of the prosperity mentality. I'm excited about what has happened with them. I was sick with what was going on and I think God put the knife in."

On October 1, 1987, Pat Robertson stood in front of the tall brownstone where he and Dede had lived in 1959. The house, now painted a grayish purple, still stands in the midst of Bedford-Stuyvesant's poorest district. Local residents watched their street become transformed by a maze of cameras, television reporters, police, and campaigners. An elementary school choir of black children dressed in plaid jumpers sang the national anthem. "Rabbis Support Robertson for Family Values," read one placard in the Brooklyn audience as Pat Robertson formally announced his candidacy for President of the United States.

Other placards in the crowd said, "Greenwich Village for Robertson" and "Robertson for God and Country." Yosef Friedman, an Orthodox rabbi who carried the "Family Values" sign, came with a group called "Jews for Morality." A young man screamed at Friedman, "You're the kind of rabbi who supported the Nazis!" But the rabbi maintained his support of Robertson and suggested that other Jews should support him as well, since "on many issues we agree with him," he said.

The Gay Rights protesters, with banners likening Robertson to the Ayatollah Khomeini, shouted, "Go home, Pat!" Robertson supporters countered with "We want Pat!" With all the shouting of protesters and supporters, the singing of the choir, and the music from a jazz band playing for the assembled crowd, Pat and Dede were hardly noticed when they stepped out of the brownstone that had been their home.

When Robertson stood to make his prepared address, a wave of chanting protests drowned out his attempts. He asked for—but did not receive—a "right to be heard." The protesters, calling out for causes ranging from gay rights to black pride, caused Robertson to shelve his prepared text and speak extemporaneously.

The New York Times reported on the "ferocity" of the hecklers, including one group called "Act Up." One of the members described "Act Up" as "a coalition of militant gays" and shouted, "Bigot!" and "Extremist!" at Robertson during the speech. "Is it possible," Robertson shouted above the din, "to restore fundamental moral values? Is it possible to restore the industrial might of America through moral strength? Yes, it is!"

Throughout his life Robertson has come to be known as a risk-taker. But political campaign-watchers have wagered that launching his presidential bid in such an uproarious setting would work against him. The "angry, disorderly scene may convey the image of a gutsy candidate," suggested the *Washington Post,* "but it may also strengthen the fears of some Republicans that Robertson and his largely religious following will be a polarizing force."

Some Republican party activists do indeed fear the Robertson campaign. Among a group of thirty activists in Washington, the *Post* reported, Robertson lacked a single supporter. Many see his strong grass-roots support as a threat to the GOP they have known in the past. As one highway department employee told the *Washington Post,* "There's a very great underground swell, and I think a lot of people are going to be very surprised at the amount of strength he can come up with among the Christians."

But the disturbing scene in Brooklyn that October day was far from the final event in Robertson's plans for announcing his candidacy. As *Time* magazine reported, "A New Hampshire rally that evening showed Robertson's ability to generate revival-meeting rapture. His announcement speech, finally given in its entirety, was interrupted by ten standing ovations. The crowd of 1,200 roared with delight as he talked of returning prayer to the schools."

New Hampshire, the location of the first state primary election in the presidential selection process, is a long way from Lexington, Virginia. The route Pat Robertson followed to get there is an unlikely one. As much as anything else, his appearance in a campaign rally in New Hampshire illustrates Robertson's capacity for the unexpected. He could never be accused of a failure of imagination. If there are no precedents for his campaign for the presidency, neither were there any precedents for a Christian Broadcasting Network, a *700 Club,* or a family-oriented cable TV network.

Moreover, none of this happened in a vacuum. Robertson has long enjoyed the support of a sizable national audience. His early, startling political victories in South Carolina, Michigan, and Iowa demonstrate both the fervor of his support and its considerable strength. He has clearly touched the heartfelt needs and desires of millions of Americans, and they are responding with a conviction often absent in other more pragmatic political arenas. Thus Pat Robertson's own convictions are not private dreams but widely shared beliefs. In the final analysis, Robertson's lifelong habit of perseverance reveals not the lone defender of narrow values, but the advocate of the moral society for which so many yearn.

Index

Abraham Lincoln: Theologian of American Anguish (Trueblood), 124
Act-Up, 207
Adams, John, 179
Aikman, David, 162
Allen, Steve, 104
American Civil Liberties Union (ACLU), 150–51
America's Dates with Destiny (Robertson), 125, 139
Anderson, John, 181
Annenberg School of Communications, study by, 103
Answers to 200 of Life's Most Probing Questions (Robertson), 125
Arlan, Jay, 70
Armistead, John, 5
Armstrong, Dr. Ben, 121–22; on Robertson as broadcaster, 121–22
Arnon, Michael, 88

Bakker, Jim, 64, 70, 79, 105–08, 202–06; conflicts with CBN, 105–07; quits and is rehired (1966), 79; resigns CBN to create own ministry, 107–08; PTL ministry scandal and, 202–06

Bakker, Tammy, 64, 70, 79, 105–08, 202–06
Barkley, Alben, 183
Beasley, Fred, 66, 68–69; donates country house, 68–69; donates money and home to CBN, 66
Beyond Reason (Robertson), 125
Bird in a Cage (film), 162–63
Book, The, 164–65
Book of Proverbs, 133
Boone, Pat, 104
Bredesen, Gen, 36
Bredesen, Harald, 1–3, 36, 37, 47, 52, 57; on Robertson as assistant pastor, 2–3
Bright, Bill, 151
Bright, Tim, 46, 48, 50–51, 54; sells TV station to Robertson, 50–51
Broadcasting, 118
Bryan, William Jennings, 180
Buck, Lee, 161, 184
Bush, George, 104, 186
Buthelezi, Gatsha, 104
Byrd, Harry S., 11, 12

Cable television, 119–21
Campus Crusade, 152
Carter, Jimmy, 180–81; as born-again Christian, 180–81
Carter, "King," 180

209

Cash, Johnny, 104, 115
Castro, Fidel, 198
CBN (Christian Broadcasting
  Network), 50–55, 57–60;
  advertising on, 81; cable
  television and, 119–21; CBN
  Northeast, 83–84; divine
  guidance and, 118; early
  morning market and, 102; early
  telethon successes of, 69–72;
  explosive growth in 1970s,
  99–104; as family-oriented
  station, 114; first daily overseas
  program, 116–17; first telethon,
  69–70; international expansion
  of, 85–86; *It's Time to Pray,
  America,* 115; as journalistic
  organization, 104; new
  equipment negotiations with
  RCA, 86–87; Portsmouth
  studios, 110–11; Radio and
  Television Broadcasting Center,
  80; radio broadcasts, 82–84;
  recession of 1974 and, 101;
  regional telethons, 102; satellite
  network and, 115–17; Scott
  Ross and, 82; syndication and,
  99–100; teenagers and, 81–82;
  "testimony" on, 103, 104;
  Tidewater station purchase and,
  50–55, 57–60; "value
  exchange" concept and, 103–04.
  See also 700 Club; WYAH-TV
CBN Cable Network, 120
CBN Northeast, 83–84
CBN University, 156–63;
  accomplishments of, 162;
  accreditation for, 159, 161; early
  days of, 159–60; establishment
  of, 156–65; goal of, 157–58;
  Judeo-Christian values at,
  158–59; library for, 160–61;
  School of Communication,
  161–62; as university of
  graduate schools, 158
Chiang Kai-shek, 143
Christian Manifesto, A (Schaeffer),
  176, 177
Churchill, Winston, 5, 16, 154
Clark, David, 103–04, 156–58,
  159–60, 161; on CBN
  University, 156–58
Coates, Jim, 59
Colson, Chuck, 115

Combs, Robert, 162
Continental Telephone Company,
  83–84
Crisis Counseling Segment, 172–73
Crouch, Jan, 202
Crouch, Paul, 109, 202
Curry Sound Company, 31, 33

Daniels, Margaret Truman, 183
"Deaf Hear, The," 62
Dickson, Sue, 164
Ditchfield, Stan, 100, 101, 102, 109,
  112, 117
"Dominion, law of," 136–37
Donahue, Phil, 81, 119
Dorch, Richard, 203
Doubleday and Co., 111–12
duPont, Pierre ("Pete") S., 185

Edgar Cayce Foundation, 78
Einstein, Albert, 146
Eisenhower, Dwight D., 182
Eliot, Charles Norton, 158
Eliot, T. S., 20
Elmer, Ralph (brother-in-law), 26
Eskelin, Neil, 58, 63, 84

Faith at Work, 34
Falwell, Jerry, 203
Finney, Charles, 126
Fonda, Jane, 177
Ford, Gerald R., 144, 181
Franklin, Benjamin, 133, 134, 179
Full Gospel Businessmen's
  Fellowship International, 57

Garthwaite, Bill, 106
Gay rights, 194–95
Gearhart, Lt. John, 23
Geyertson, David, 159
Gilman, John, 64
Gimenez, John, 152
Goldenson, Leonard, 118
Goldwater, Barry, 186
Grace, Peter, 28, 189, 191
"Greatness, law of," 145–46
Greenlaw, Doug, 120–21; on CBN
  cable success, 120–21
Gregory, Bill, 70, 86
Grubb, Norman, 37

Hadden, Jeffrey, 203–04
Hahn, Jessica, 203
Hanks, Nancy, 6

Harrison, Benjamin, 5, 155
Harrison, William Henry, 5
Heads Up, 163–64
Heaton, Terry, 136, 172–73
Here Comes Garfield, 177
Hill, Napoleon, 131
Hiss, Alger, 142
Hobbes, Thomas, 179
Homosexuality, 194–95
Hon, Barry, 184
Horstman, Jerry, 105–08; Jim and
    Tammy Bakker and, 105–08
How Shall We Then Live (Schaeffer),
    177
Hunt, Bunker, 95, 96, 97
Hunt, H. L. ("Hap"), 89–98;
    involvement in Lucy Greathope
    "donation," 89–98
Hunt, Hassie, 91, 95
Hunt, Herb, 95, 96, 97
Hunt, Mrs. H. L., 89
Hurricane Gloria, 136

"It's Time to Pray, America," 115

Jackson, Jesse, 185
Jackson, Gen. Stonewall, 3, 4
Jacobs, Andrew, Jr., 21, 23
Jefferson, Thomas, 179
John XXIII (pope), 85
Johnson, Lyndon B., 140
Jones, Bob, 157
Jones, Shirley, 58

Kemp, Jack, 185
Kennedy, John F., 185
Keynes, John Maynard, 140
Khomeini, Ayatollah, 198
Kinchlow, Benjamin, 116, 137, 165,
    167–68, 168–72, 173;
    biographical sketch of, 168–69;
    on Operation Blessing, 167–68;
    on Robertson, 171–72; as *700
    Club* host, 170–71
Kissinger, Henry, 144
Kotler, Philip, 103
Krulak, Gen. Victor, 22
Kunkel, John, 86–87

Laffer, Arthur, 104
Latture, Dr. Rupert, 6
Lauderdale, George, 45, 47, 48, 52
Lawrence, D. H., 20
League of Nations, 16

Lee, Gen. Robert E., 15, 17
Lenin, V. I., 142, 197
Lincoln, Abraham, 6, 124, 128
Lindsey, Lt. Christopher, 23
Literacy-through-phonics program
    (Heads Up), 163–64
Locke, John, 179
Lopez, Sixto, 85
LTV Electrosystems, 92
Lumpkin, Dr. William L., 59
Lumpkin, Mrs. William L., 56

McCloskey, Paul, Jr., 21–23;
    accusations concerning
    Robertson's military service,
    21–23
McDowell, Charlie, 14, 17, 19
Madison, James, 179
Mao Tse-tung, 143, 199
Marcos, Ferdinand, 104
Marketing for Nonprofit Organizations
    (Kotler), 103
Metternich, Prince Klemens von,
    16
Moody, D. L., 157
Moore, Sam, 178
Morris, Paul, 52–53, 90
Mother Teresa, 146, 149
Moyers, Bill, 193
Mubarak, Hosni, 104
My God Will Supply (Robertson), 35,
    43
My Prayer for You (Robertson), 118

National Legal Foundation, 150
National Religious Broadcasters, 121
Nixon, Richard M., 183–84
Novak, Robert, 104
Nuevo Continente, 85–86
Nuttle, R. Marc, 186

Operation Blessing, 165–68, 172,
    174
Oral Roberts University, 91
Ortega, Daniel, 145, 198

Paine, Thomas, 179
Panorama, 81
Peale, Norman Vincent, 104
"Perseverance, law of," 75, 98, 128,
    134–35
Phillips, Conoly, 113, 114
Plain Bread (Kinchlow), 168
Poor Richard's Almanac, 133, 134

Pro-Life Bill, 195
PTL Network, 109, 203

Qaddafi, Muammar el-, 198

Reagan, Ronald, 104, 153, 164,
181, 184–85, 186, 188, 195,
200; on Robertson's candidacy,
184–85
"Reciprocity, law of," 128–30,
131–32, 189
Roberts, Oral, 99, 205
Robertson, A. Willis, Jr. (brother), 5
Robertson, Adelia ("Dede") Elmer
(wife), 2, 26, 29, 30–31, 34–36,
41, 43–44, 45–49, 52, 53, 56,
59, 65, 66–68, 90, 92, 98, 105,
206; courtship and marriage of,
26–27; initial reaction to
husband's religious commitment,
34–36; spiritual changes in,
43–44; Tidewater "slum house"
and, 66–68
Robertson, Ann (daughter), 67
Robertson, Elizabeth (daughter), 34,
67, 68
Robertson, Gladys Churchill
(mother), 5–6, 18, 32–33, 41,
154; influence upon son of, 6,
8–9; reaction to son's entering
ministry, 32–33
Robertson, Gordon (son), 37, 67
Robertson, Marion ("Pat") Gordon:
on abortion, 148–49, 195–96;
accused of avoiding military
combat service, 21–23;
admiration for Francis Schaeffer,
176–77; on alcohol and drugs,
132, 194; on American hostages
in Iran, 145; announces
candidacy for president, 206–08;
anti-Communist stance of, 197;
arrival in Tidewater, 45–49; as
assistant pastor in Mount
Vernon, 1–3; on "bamboo
curtain," 143; based in
Bedford-Stuyvesant
neighborhood, 37–43; "biblical
literacy" and, 164; birth of, 4–5;
birth of daughter Ann, 67; birth
of daughter Elizabeth, 34; birth
of son Gordon, 37; birth of son
Tim, 27; blacks and 2–3, 19,
189; as businessman, 80–81;
cable television and, 119–21; on

capitalism, 142–43; on capital
punishment, 141; on Jimmy
Carter, 180–81; CBN Northeast
purchase by, 83–84; CBN
University and, 156–63;
childhood of, 6–14; on China,
143, 199; on Christians
embarrassed by own faith,
136–37; on Christians'
involvement in social issues,
126; on civil service laws, 201;
college life-style of, 19–21; as
conservative, 173; Contra
support by, 198–99; Curry
Sound Company and, 31, 33;
gets Dallas station from
Doubleday, 111–12; decision to
buy Tidewater TV station,
45–49; decision to enter
ministry, 31–33; as
decisionmaker, 114–15;
dependence upon God and, 135;
Depression years and, 11–12; on
disciplining children, 192;
disillusionment with law, 24–25,
148–49; distinguished maternal
lineage of, 5–6; divine guidance
and, 118, 135; early telethon
successes of, 69–72; on
economics, 133–34, 187, 188,
189, 200; "entire system of
thought" based on Bible, 151;
on evolution, 149–50; on farm
at thirteen, 9; on farm problems,
195–96; father's defeat in Senate
race (1966) and, 78–79; on
federal budget deficit, 188, 189,
200; first telethon of, 69–70;
foreign policy and, 184;
"frugality" and, 134; Full
Gospel Businessmen's
Fellowship International and, 57;
on gay rights, 194–95; gives
away Bogotà station, 111; as
global thinker, 157; government
and Christian ethic, 152–55; on
government's role, 137–39; on
Gramm-Rudman, 200; on
"Great Society" programs, 140;
on human rights, 145, 148;
human suffering and, 130;
Hurricane Gloria and, 136; on
integration, 189, 201; on
intellectual appeal of
communism, 19, 142; on "iron

curtain," 143–44; as "iron ruler," 113–14; on Japanese competition, 146–47, 196–97; job with W. R. Grace Company, 28–31; on judicial reform, 192–93; Ben Kinchlow and, 169–70; on the Korean War, 23–24, 143; lack of political experience of, 182; on law enforcement, 141–42, 194; on League of Nations, 16; Robert E. Lee as hero of, 15; Lexington (Virginia) as birthplace of, 3–4; at Lexington High School, 14; library for CBN University and, 160–61; on Lincoln, 128; literacy programs and, 163–64; Lucy Greathope as potential benefactor, 89–98; on lying, 137; at the McCallie School, 15; at the McDonough School, 13–14; joins Marine Corps, 21; marriage to Adelia ("Dede") Elmer, 26–27; Michigan's Republican Party and, 185–86; military service of, 21–24; "miraculous interventions" and, 136; morality as main business of government, 193–94; on "most pressing political issues," 186; mother's standards for, 8–9; new-equipment negotiations with RCA, 86–87; at New York Theological Seminary, 34; on Nicaragua, 198–99; on Richard Nixon, 183–84; Nuevo Continente and, 85–86; Operation Blessing and, 165–68; organization skills of, 182; at Park View Baptist Church, 65–66; personal ethic and discipline, 127; on personal responsibility, 199–200; on "political compromise," 187–88; political heritage of, 10; political views of, 125–26, 176–202; as "politically suspect fundamentalist," 175–76; politicians on qualifications of, 184–85; on poverty, 189–90; Providence and vocation and, 123–24; PTL ministry scandal and, 202–06; purchase of Tidewater station, 50–55, 57–60; radio broadcasts and,

82–84; "ratings games" and, 114; RCA debt by Tidewater station and, 53–54; on Ronald Reagan, 153; religiously based morality in schools, 191–92; joins Republican Party in 1984, 181–82; on Franklin D. Roosevelt, 30, 139–40; satellite network and, 115–17; on school prayer, 150–51; sells property according to Luke 12:33, 38–39; on separation of church and state, 178–80, 194; as serious thinker, 123–26; 700 Club initiated by, 69; on social security, 188–89; on social services, 190–91; on Soviet sphere of influence, 144–45; "soybean nutrition" and, 48–49; on Adlai Stevenson, 182–83; on Supreme Court, 24–25; syndication of programming and, 99–100; on taxes, 187; teenage years of, 14–15; on trade imbalance, 196–97; on tuition tax vouchers, 201; on United Nations, 16; on Vietnam, 144; as "visionary planner" for CBN, 109; at Washington and Lee University, 15–17, 18–21; on Washington, D. C., 138–39; "Washington for Jesus" and, 151; at Yale Law School, 24–28

Robertson, Sen. A. Willis (father), 3, 9–13, 18–19, 46–47, 78–79; character and life of, 9–13; defeat in 1966, 78–79; as "distant presence" to son, 13; frugality and, 9; influence on politics of son, 18–19; role as senator, 11, 12–13

Robertson, Tim (son), 27, 29, 35, 41, 43–44, 49, 68, 75–76, 106, 111, 112, 113, 173, 175; on determination of father, 112; on early Tidewater days, 49; on father in childhood years, 75–76

Rolloff, Lester, 91

Roosevelt, Franklin D., 11, 30, 139–40; Robertson on, 30, 139–40

Ross, Scott, 82, 83–84

Rothschild, Baron, 133

Ruby (brothel madam), 39

Rummel, Beardsley, 12

Ryder, Gene, 88–98; Lucy Greathope "donation" and, 88–98

Sadat, Jihan, 104
Sawyer, Major, 22
Schaeffer, Francis, 176–77
Schihl, Robert, 162
Schuller, Robert, 205
Scientific-Atlanta, 116
Secret Kingdom, The (Robertson), 75, 124, 125, 127, 128, 145, 177–78, 190
700 Club, 69, 72–74, 99–100, 103, 104, 127–28, 170–71; as breaking new ground, 99–100; changes in format of, 170–71; four basic goals of, 103; Kinchlow as host of, 170–71; original format of, 72–73; prayer and, 73–74; telephone counselors and, 73
Shamir, Yitzak, 104
Sharon, Ariel, 104
Shepherd, General, 22
Simmons, Barbara, 38, 39, 41
Simmons, Dick, 37–39, 40, 42–43, 131, 206; on Robertson's work in Brooklyn, 42
Sing, Spell, Read and Write, 163–64
Skolrood, Robert, 150
Slosser, Bob, 124–25, 128, 158–59, 174; on education, 158–59; on The Secret Kingdom, 124–25
Somoza, Anastasio, 145
Stalin, Joseph, 142
Stallings, Rev. John, 62, 84; on Robertson, 84
Sterling, Chris, 159
Stevenson, Adlai, 182–83
"Superbook," 165
Swaggert, Jimmy, 203, 205
Sweet, Bob, 163

Teach-In, 64–65
Think and Grow Rich (Hill), 131
Thomas, Cal, 177–78

Tocqueville, Alexis de, 198
Tolbert, Sam, 116
Tracy, Ed, 86–87
Trueblood, Elton, 124
Truman, Harry S., 143, 183
Turner, Ted, 101, 107, 108–09, 119
Twain, Mark, 120
Twohig, Sam, 53

UHF stations, 78
United Nations, 16
"Use, law of," 127, 128

Vanderbreggen, Cornelius, 33
"Value exchange" concept, 103
Vatican Council II, 85
Vinson, Fred, 17
Virginia Military Institute, 3, 4

Waff, Harvey, 58, 59, 62
Walker, Bob, 52, 57
Warner, Sen. John, 23
Washington, George, 153, 179
"Washington for Jesus," 151
Wheeler, Martha, 107, 108
Wheeler, Sandy, 107, 108
White, Harry Dexter, 142
Winfrey, Oprah, 81
Winston, Harry, 183
Wooten, James, 181
Word of Life Inn, 36
Worldwide Evangelization Crusade, 37
Worldwide Gospel Foundation, 91
WXRI-FM, 83
WYAH-TV, 45–49, 50–60, 61–63, 64, 65, 74–75, 77; advisory council idea for, 65; decision to buy, 45–49; early mishaps at, 61–63, 64; programming at, 62–65; transmitter for, 74–75, 77

Yeats, W. B., 20

Zarro, Antonio, 162